The Sculpture of
William Edmondson

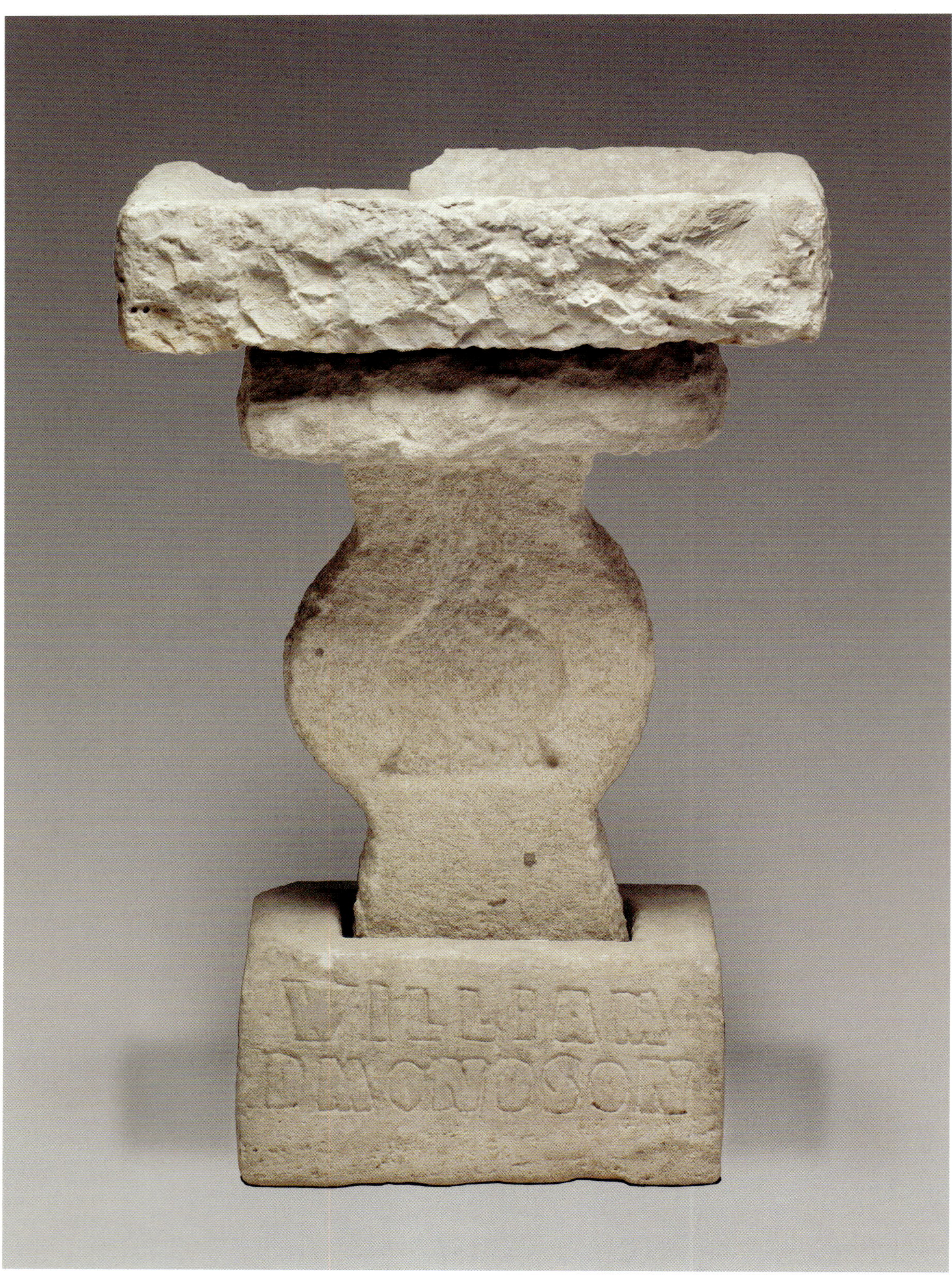

Cat. 1. William Edmondson, *Birdbath*, 1938

The Sculpture of William Edmondson

Tombstones, Garden Ornaments, and Stonework

Cheekwood Estate & Gardens and Fisk University Galleries Nashville, Tennessee

Marin R. Sullivan

Vanderbilt University Press
Nashville

Published by Vanderbilt University Press.

First printing 2021
Printed in Canada

Cheekwood Estate & Gardens, Nashville, Tennessee,
August 12–October 31, 2021
Fisk University Galleries, Fisk University, Nashville, Tennessee,
August 12–October 31, 2021

The publication of this catalogue is generously supported by The Wyeth Foundation for American Art.

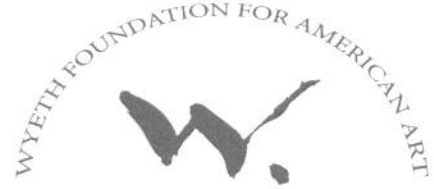

The Sculpture of William Edmondson: Tombstones, Garden Ornaments, and Stonework is generously supported by the Henry Luce Foundation. The Henry Luce Foundation seeks to enrich public discourse by promoting innovative scholarship, cultivating new leaders, and fostering international understanding. Established in 1936 by Henry R. Luce, the co-founder and editor-in-chief of Time, Inc., the Luce Foundation advances its mission through grantmaking and leadership programs in the fields of Asia, higher education, religion and theology, art, and public policy. A leader in arts funding in the United States, the Luce Foundation's American Art Program was established in 1982 to support museums, universities, and arts organizations in their efforts to advance the understanding and experience of American and Native American visual arts through research, exhibitions, publications, and collection projects.

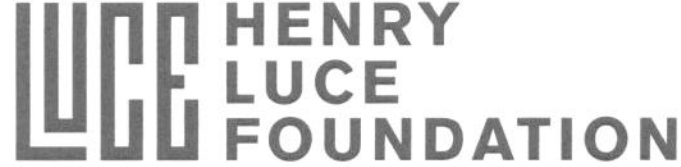

The Sculpture of William Edmondson: Tombstones, Garden Ornaments, and Stonework made possible by the Terra Foundation for American Art.

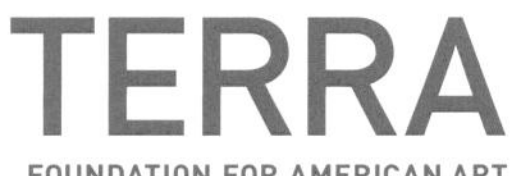

Cover image: *William Edmondson, Sculptor, Nashville, Tennessee*, 1933–37. Cheekwood, Nashville. Gift of the Artist (1964.3.11). © 2021 Center for Creative Photography, Arizona Board of Regents / Artists Rights Society (ARS), New York, Center for Creative Photography, University of Arizona: Louise Dahl-Wolfe, Archive/Gift of the Louise Dahl-Wolfe Trust

Library of Congress Cataloging-in-Publication Data
Names: Sullivan, Marin R. Tombstones, garden ornaments, and stonework. | Cheekwood Museum of Art, organizer, host institution. | Fisk University. University Galleries, organizer, host institution.
Title: The sculpture of William Edmondson : tombstones, garden ornaments, and stonework / Marin R. Sullivan ; contributions by Renée Ater, Kéla Jackson, Ellen Macfarlane, Anne Monahan, Betsy Phillips, Learotha Williams.
Description: Nashville : Vanderbilt University Press, [2021] | "Cheekwood Estate & Gardens and Fisk University Galleries, Nashville, TN." | Includes bibliographical references.
Identifiers: LCCN 2021009793 | ISBN 9780826502360 (paperback)
Subjects: LCSH: Edmondson, William, 1882?-1951—Exhibitions.
Classification: LCC NB237.E35 A4 2021 | DDC 730.92—dc23
LC record available at https://lccn.loc.gov/2021009793

Contents

Foreword and Acknowledgments

Here, for the first time in over twenty years, is an encyclopedic examination of the work of William Edmondson. The core of this exhibition is drawn from the Cheekwood collections, which hold the greatest breadth of this artist's work, along with material exploring this native son of Nashville. As such, it is not surprising that Jane MacLeod, Cheekwood's president and CEO, championed the idea of embarking on the quest to examine the work of Edmondson through a twenty-first-century lens. Those visitors who are taken with the range and quality of these objects are reminded that this show includes only a part of Edmondson's output. Marin R. Sullivan, Cheekwood's curator-at-large, embraced MacLeod's charge and chose the works in this exhibition to reflect the keenness of Edmondson's approach and the diversity of his work, visible among his most significant pieces. That, above all, is what this project celebrates with enthusiasm and conviction.

We are particularly pleased that by hosting *The Sculpture of William Edmondson: Tombstones, Garden Ornaments, and Stonework*, our museum continues the tradition of recognizing the public importance of his work. Sullivan organized this exhibit and completed the scholarly editing of the exhibition catalogue, also contributing one of the essays, along with supplemental documentation in the book. Her exploration drew from an earlier Cheekwood exhibition, *The Art of William Edmondson* (2000), to which she is deeply indebted for the archival materials generated and retained in the Cheekwood archives. We are grateful to her, but also to the many individuals, including the contributors of the catalogue who worked with such efficiency and grace to make this exhibition a reality: Renée Ater, Kéla B. Jackson, Ellen Macfarlane, Anne Monahan, and Learotha Williams Jr.

This exhibition and catalogue would not have been possible without the support and cooperation of numerous individuals. Warm thanks are due to Betsy Phillips, our tireless editor and sincere Edmondson enthusiast, catalogue editor Joell Smith-Borne, and all our partners at Vanderbilt University Press. Additional thanks to Eric Wheeler, who produced the stellar photographs of works from the Cheekwood collection, assisted by Veronica Davids.

The organization and development of an exhibition requires a commitment from participants across an institution. At Cheekwood, particular thanks are due to Julie Choma, registrar, for her careful compilation of vital statistics related to the Edmondson works, her handling of a myriad of factors with the appearance of ease and meticulous attention to detail; Kody Cassady for his dedication to preserving and digitizing Cheekwood's Edmondson archive; Dan Derwelis, chief preparator and mount fabricator, and his team for the careful and thoughtful installation of exhibition, ensuring a beautiful presentation and safety of the works; Elizabeth Epley Sheets, chief advancement officer, along with her team, especially Abigail Sanderson, former senior manager of institutional relations, for their support and dedication to this exhibition; Chanel McDaniel, vice president of marketing, for her constant enthusiasm in sharing her excitement for this exhibition with audiences throughout Nashville and beyond; and, Nathalie Lavine, vice president of education and outreach, and her fellow educators for the stalwart support of this exhibition.

Beyond the gardens of Cheekwood numerous individuals lent support through encouragement, information, and contacts to realize this exhibition including Anne Monahan as well as Jennifer Jane Marshall, associate professor of art history at the University of Minnesota. At Vanderbilt University in the Department of Art and Architectural History, we appreciate Kevin D. Murphy and Rebecca VanDiver, who so generously agreed to co-organize a symposium in conjunction with the exhibition. Special thanks go to Teresa Gray, curator of special collections at Vanderbilt University, for helping access archival images, and Celia Walker and Emily Weiner from the Fine Arts Gallery at Vanderbilt University. At Fisk University, DeLisa Minor Harris, assistant director of library services, and Jamaal Sheats, who was so incredibly supportive and collaborative of the exhibition from inception as well as agreeing to co-present part of the exhibition. To Katherine Jentleson, the Merrie and Dan Boone Curator of Folk and Self-Taught Art at the High Museum, and Leslie Umberger, curator of Folk and Self-Taught Art at the Smithsonian American Art Museum, both of whom offered expertise and guidance early in the exhibition planning process. Also, deepest thanks to Elizabeth Elkins, president of Historic Nashville; Mark Schlicher, Edmondson documentarian and co-chairman of the Save the Edmondson Homesite Park & Gardens Coalition; John Ollman, Fleisher/Ollman Gallery; Frank Maresca of Maresca/ Ricco Gallery; and Halley K. Harrisburg, Michael Rosenfeld Gallery.

An exhibition is not possible without the immense generosity and sacrifice from those institutions and individuals who so graciously lent their works to this endeavor, sharing with others their joy in, and respect for, Edmondson and his work. Their names and contributions are detailed in the included checklist of the exhibition.

We recognize the Henry Luce Foundation, the Terra Foundation for American Art, and the Wyeth Foundation for American Art for their tremendous generosity and support of this exhibition and accompanying catalogue. Special thanks also to Teresa A. Carbone. We acknowledge AllianceBernstein and Case Antiques, especially Sarah Campbell Drury, for their enthusiasm and support of the exhibition.

Above all, of course, our deepest and ultimate debt of gratitude is reserved for William Edmondson, for without his creative spirit and timeless work this exhibition would not be possible.

James W. Tottis
Vice President of Museum Affairs
Cheekwood Estate & Gardens

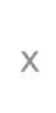

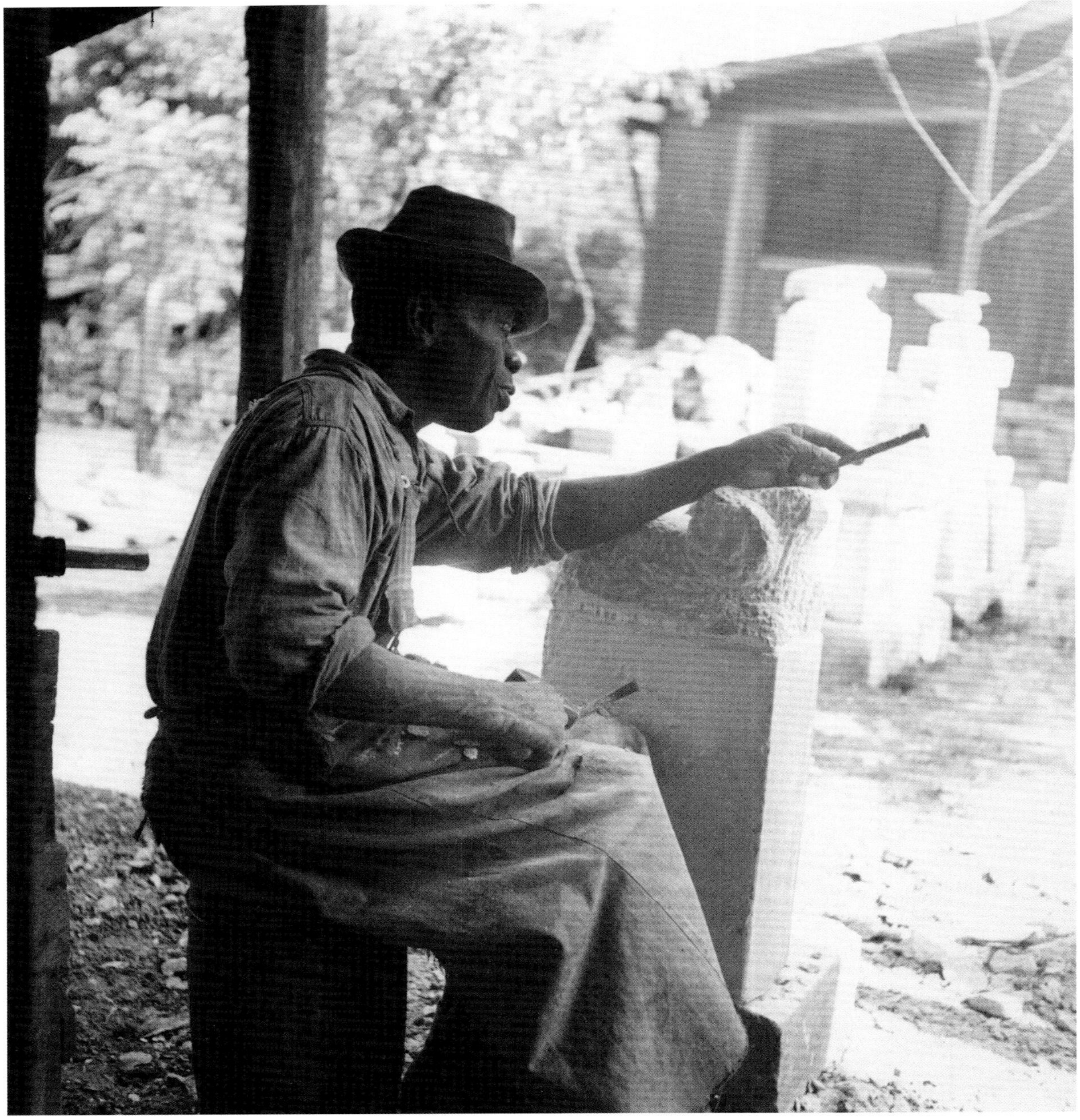

Cat. 2. Louise Dahl-Wolfe, *William Edmondson*, 1937

Tombstones, Garden Ornaments, and Stonework

Marin R. Sullivan

The author would like to thank Dr. Anne Monahan for her invaluable feedback during the drafting of this essay.

William Edmondson was and remains Nashville's most renowned sculptor. He was born in 1874 in Davidson County, Tennessee, to Jane Brown and Orange Edmondson, who had been enslaved at the Edmondson and Compton plantations and at the time of their son's birth still worked that land as fieldhands. In 1890, following the death of his father, Edmondson moved to Nashville with his mother and siblings, where he would remain the rest of his life. He held a number of jobs, working for the Nashville, Chattanooga and St. Louis Railway, for example, before a leg injury led him to seek employment as an orderly and janitor at the Woman's Hospital. He purchased property on Fourteenth Avenue South in Nashville's Edgehill neighborhood. His sister Sarah lived with him and he remained close to his family, though he himself never married. In 1931, in the midst of the Great Depression, he lost his job at the hospital, worked briefly as a stonemason's assistant, and then turned his attention to stonework fulltime. Within a few years, his yard would be full of sculptures and sculptural objects, with a sign hanging above the porch he often carved on that read:

Fig. 1. Edward Weston, *Stone Sculpture, Wm. Edmondson*, 1941. Gelatin silver print, $9 \frac{9}{16} \times 7 \frac{9}{16}$ in. Center for Creative Photography, University of Arizona: Edward Weston Archive.

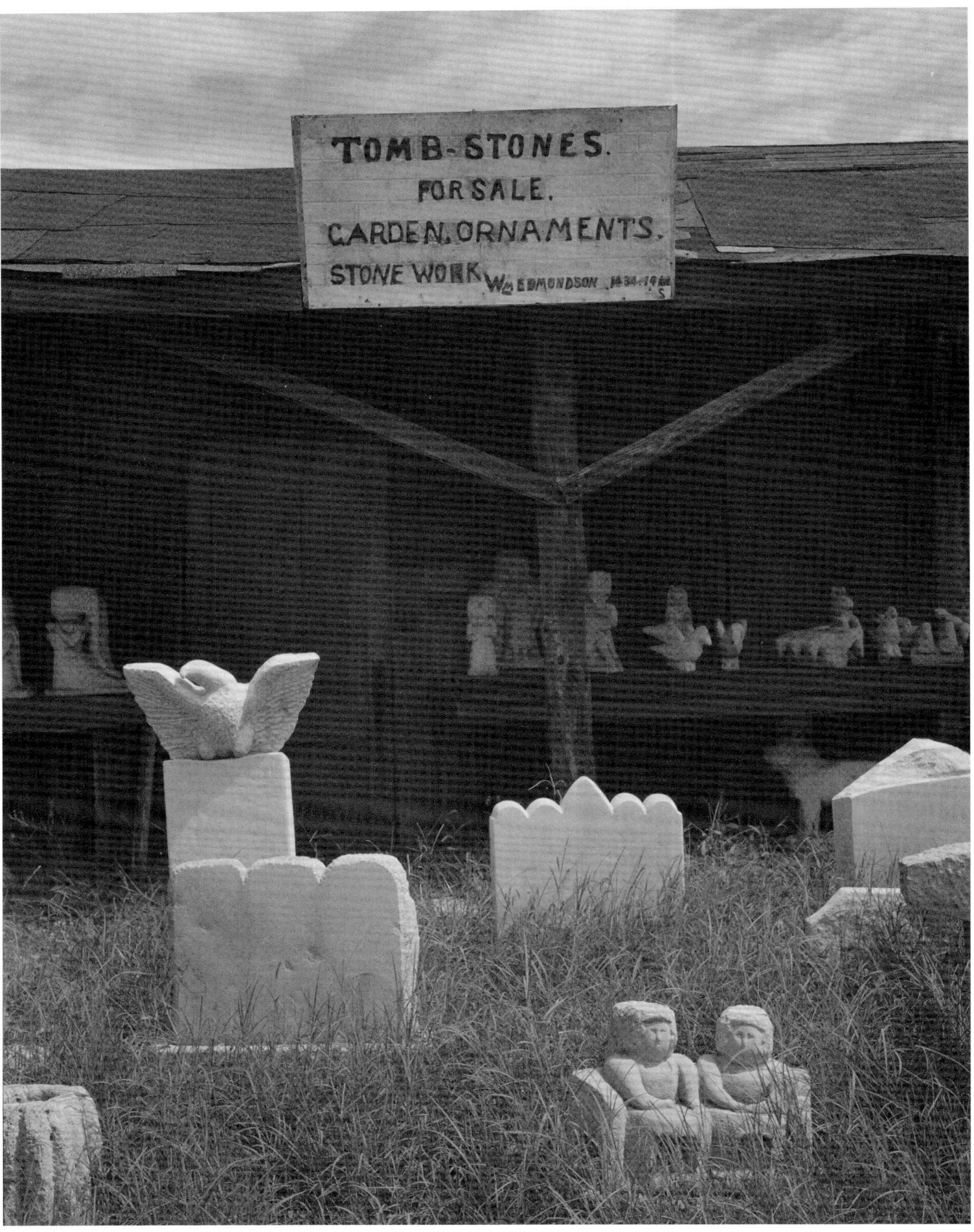

Fig. 2. Photograph of a Young Sidney Hirsch. Courtesy of Special Collections Library, Vanderbilt University.

Fig. 3. Reunion of The Fugitives at Vanderbilt University, 1956. Courtesy of Special Collections Library, Vanderbilt University.

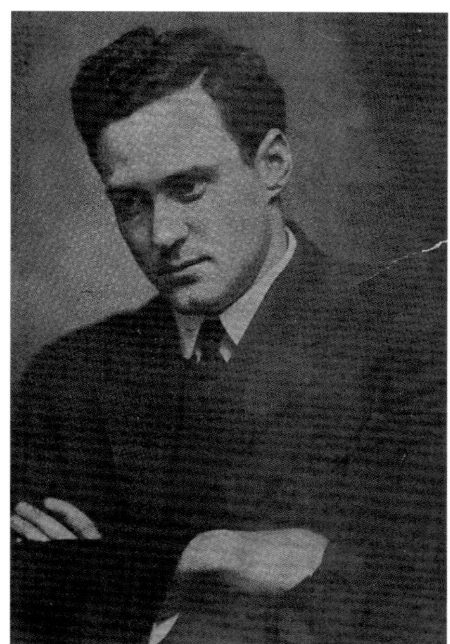

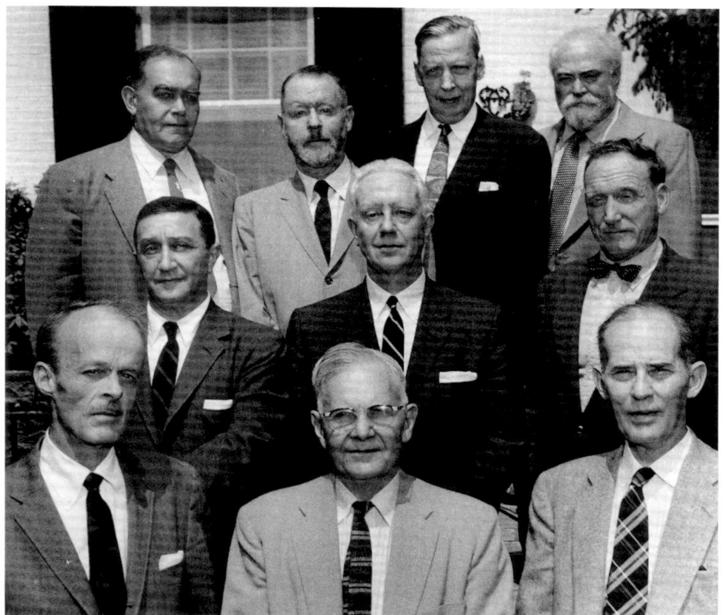

TOMB-STONES.
FOR SALE.
GARDEN. ORNAMENTS.
STONEWORK Wm Edmondson 1434 14th S

One of Edmondson's neighbors in Edgehill was Sidney Mttron Hirsch, who would often walk by the sculptor's property on his way to teach at the nearby George Peabody College for Teachers. Hirsch had been a member of the Fugitives, a group of writers and intellectuals active in the 1920s at Vanderbilt University that also included John Crowe Ransome, Robert Penn Warren, and Alfred Starr. The latter was the owner of the Bijou Theatre in downtown Nashville, one of the South's leading African American entertainment venues at the time, and was childhood friends with Meyer Wolfe, who like Starr had grown up in the small Jewish community in Nashville. In the mid-1930s Hirsch brought his friends, including Starr, Wolfe, and their wives—Elizabeth Lyle Starr and noted fashion photographer Louise Dahl-Wolfe—to meet Edmondson and see his work. These individuals would set off a chain of events that led to Edmondson being the first Black artist to have a solo exhibition at the Museum of Modern Art

Fig. 4. Louise Dahl-Wolfe, *At Alfred Starr's Theater, The Bijou, Nashville, Tennessee*, 1932. Gelatin silver print, 13½ × 10½ in. Center for Creative Photography, University of Arizona: Louise Dahl-Wolfe Archive / Gift of the Louise Dahl-Wolfe Trust.

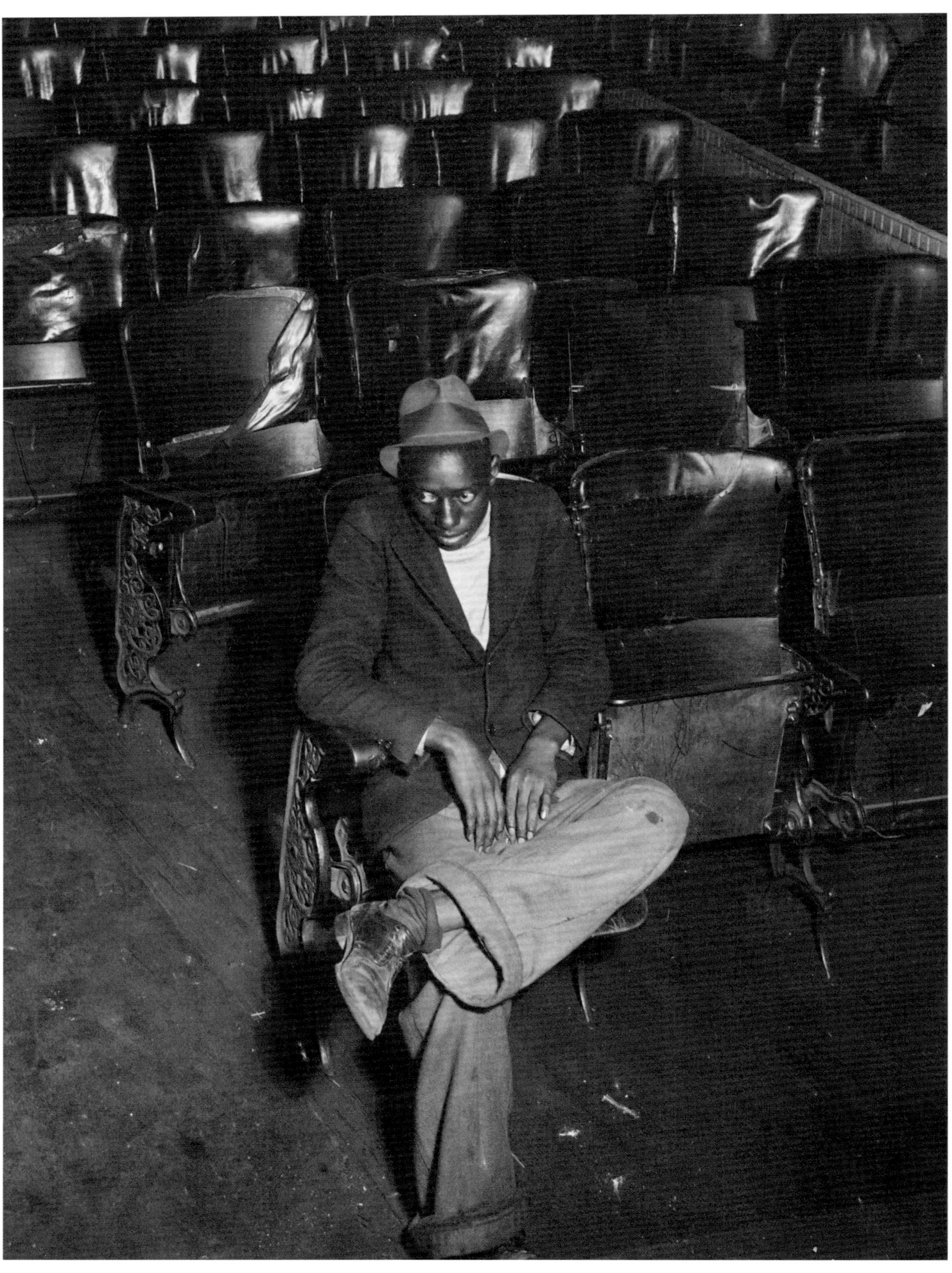

Fig. 5. Press release for the exhibition *Sculpture by William Edmondson*, October 20–December 1, 1937. The Museum of Modern Art, New York.

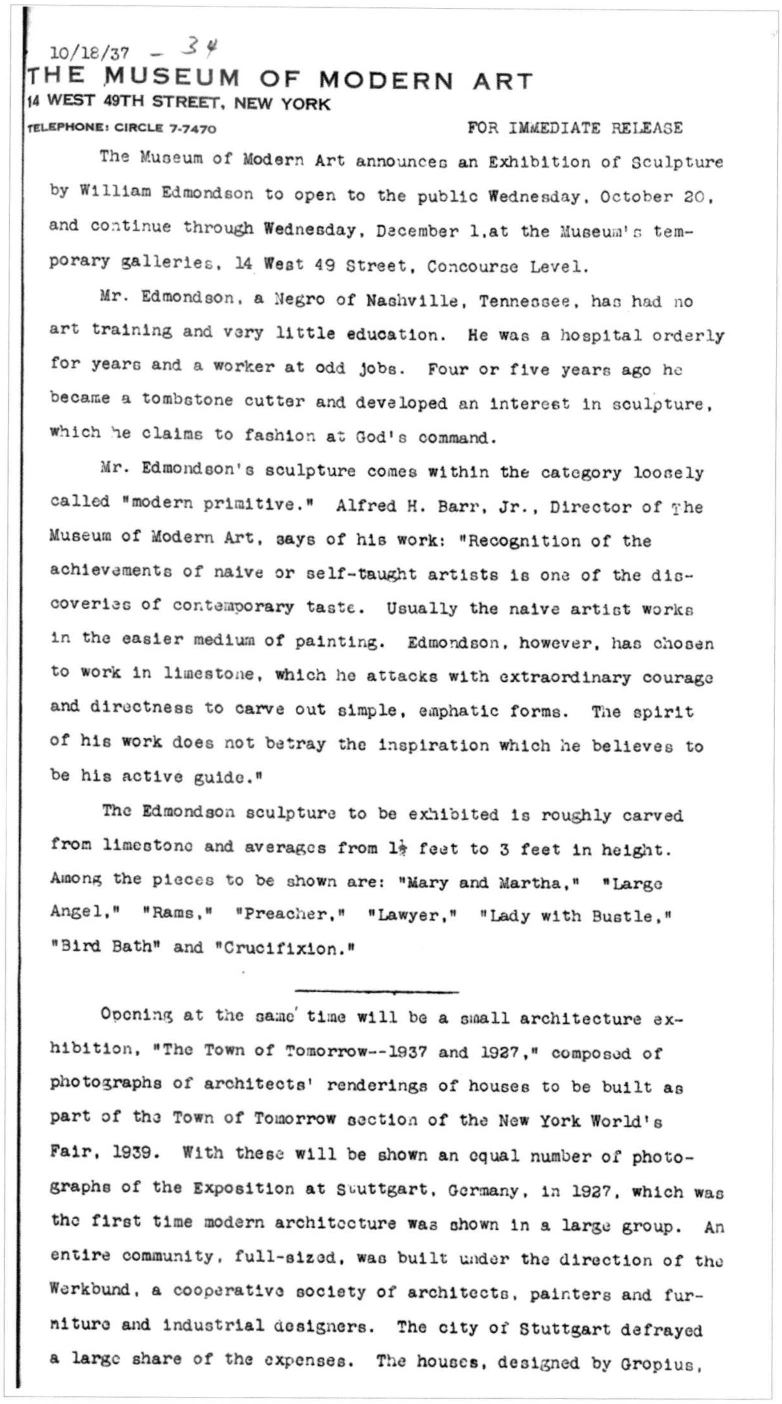

10/18/37 – 34

THE MUSEUM OF MODERN ART
14 WEST 49TH STREET, NEW YORK
TELEPHONE: CIRCLE 7-7470

FOR IMMEDIATE RELEASE

The Museum of Modern Art announces an Exhibition of Sculpture by William Edmondson to open to the public Wednesday, October 20, and continue through Wednesday, December 1, at the Museum's temporary galleries, 14 West 49 Street, Concourse Level.

Mr. Edmondson, a Negro of Nashville, Tennessee, has had no art training and very little education. He was a hospital orderly for years and a worker at odd jobs. Four or five years ago he became a tombstone cutter and developed an interest in sculpture, which he claims to fashion at God's command.

Mr. Edmondson's sculpture comes within the category loosely called "modern primitive." Alfred H. Barr, Jr., Director of The Museum of Modern Art, says of his work: "Recognition of the achievements of naive or self-taught artists is one of the discoveries of contemporary taste. Usually the naive artist works in the easier medium of painting. Edmondson, however, has chosen to work in limestone, which he attacks with extraordinary courage and directness to carve out simple, emphatic forms. The spirit of his work does not betray the inspiration which he believes to be his active guide."

The Edmondson sculpture to be exhibited is roughly carved from limestone and averages from 1½ feet to 3 feet in height. Among the pieces to be shown are: "Mary and Martha," "Large Angel," "Rams," "Preacher," "Lawyer," "Lady with Bustle," "Bird Bath" and "Crucifixion."

Opening at the same time will be a small architecture exhibition, "The Town of Tomorrow--1937 and 1927," composed of photographs of architects' renderings of houses to be built as part of the Town of Tomorrow section of the New York World's Fair, 1939. With these will be shown an equal number of photographs of the Exposition at Stuttgart, Germany, in 1927, which was the first time modern architecture was shown in a large group. An entire community, full-sized, was built under the direction of the Werkbund, a cooperative society of architects, painters and furniture and industrial designers. The city of Stuttgart defrayed a large share of the expenses. The houses, designed by Gropius,

Cat. 3. William Edmondson, *Martha and Mary*, c. 1930–39

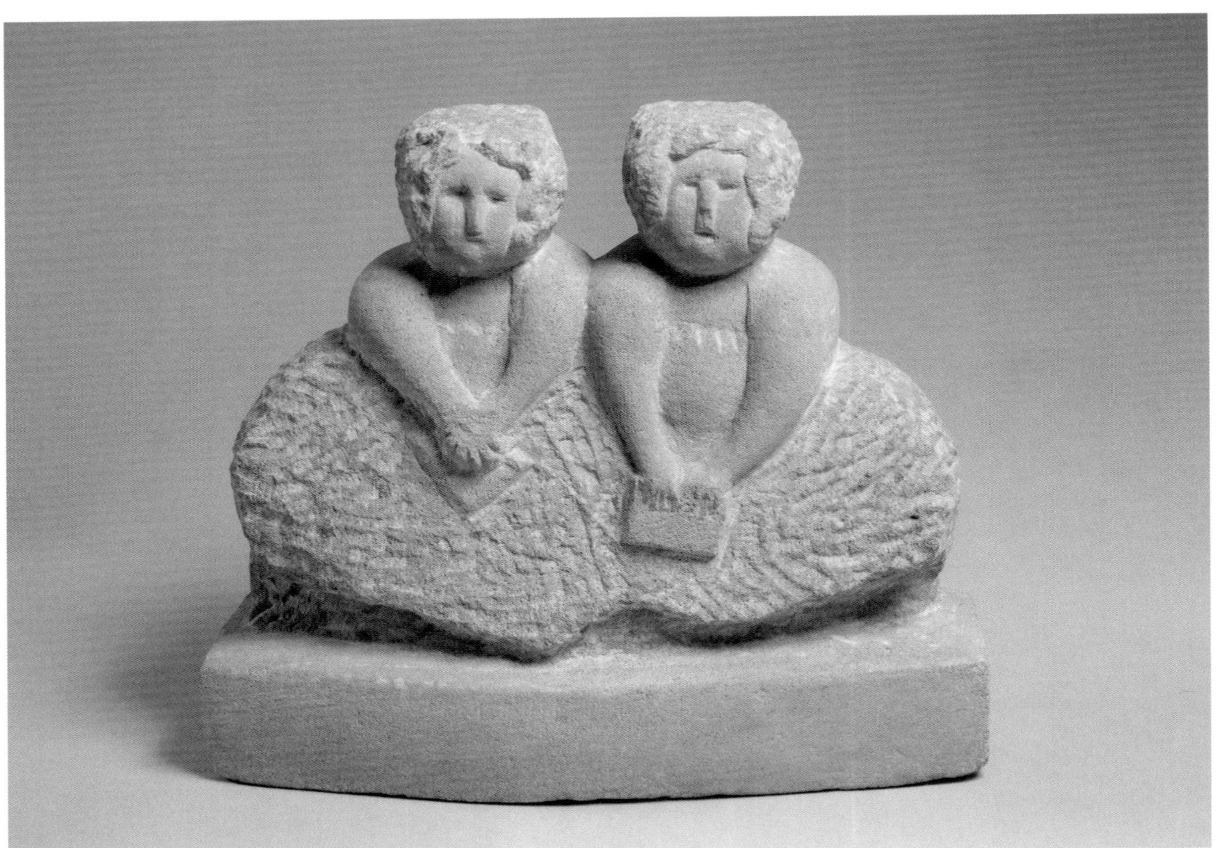

(MoMA) in New York and firmly established his significance within the history of American art.

Dahl-Wolfe returned to Edmondson's yard shop on several occasions to photograph the sculptor at work. She was unable to persuade her primary employer, *Harper's Bazaar*, to publish the resulting images, owing to the racism of its owner William Randolph Hearst. Dahl-Wolfe, however, also showed her photographs of Edmondson to MoMA's interim director Thomas Mabry, a Nashville native who was already aware of the sculptor, and founding director Alfred Barr Jr. who, along with curator Dorothy C. Miller, decided to organize an exhibition of the sculptor's work at the museum in the autumn of 1937. This exhibition would catapult Edmondson to national and international fame. Major publications including the *New York Times*, the *New Yorker, Time*, and *Life* reviewed the exhibition. Pathé filmed the opening for one of its newsreels. When MoMA organized its major exhibition *Trois Siècles d'Art aux États-Unis (Three Centuries of Art of the United States)* at the Musée du Jeu de Paume in Paris in 1938, they included

Fig. 6. Edward Weston, *William Edmondson, Tennessee*, 1941. Gelatin silver print, 9 9⁄16 × 7 5⁄8 in. Center for Creative Photography, University of Arizona: Edward Weston Archive.

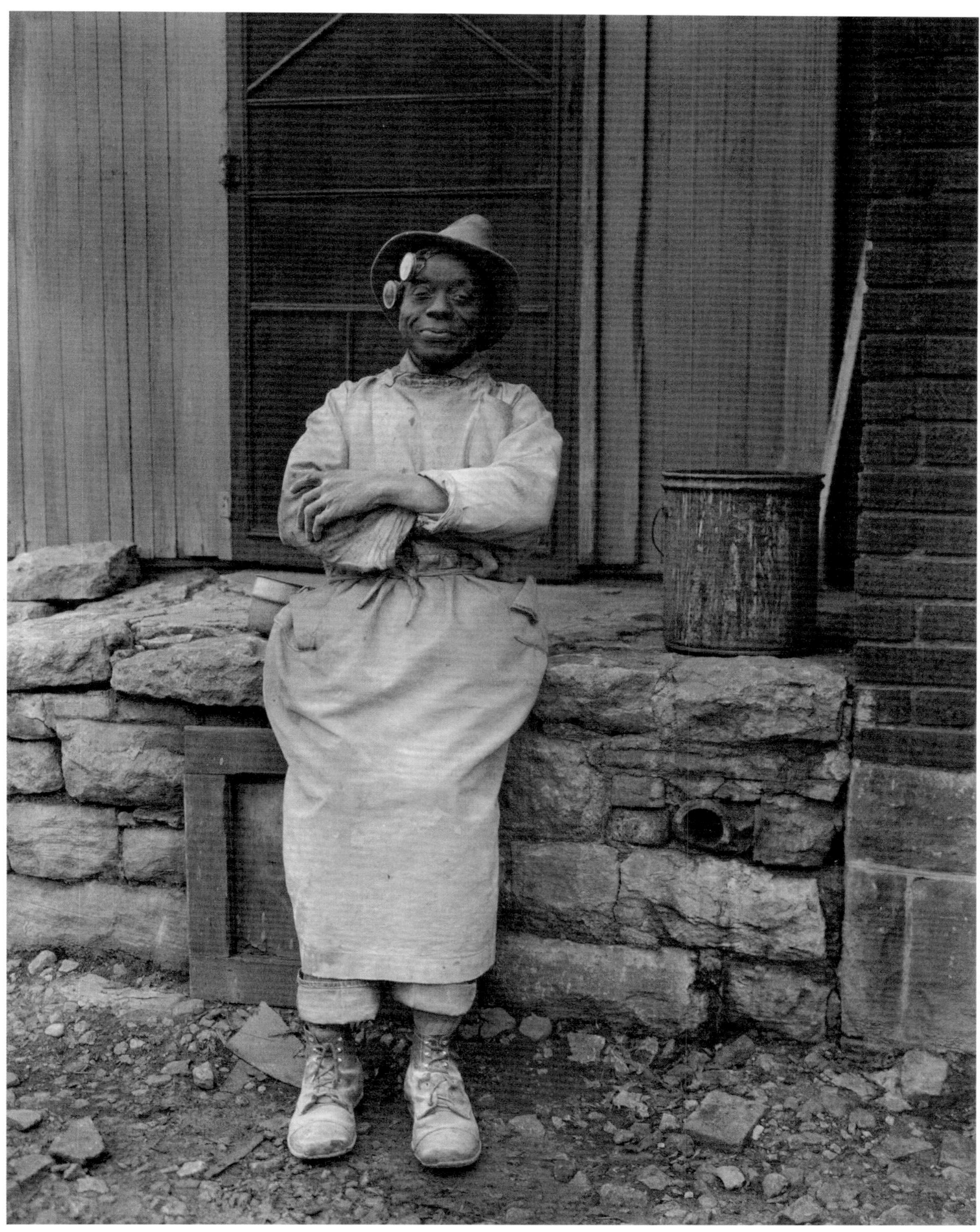

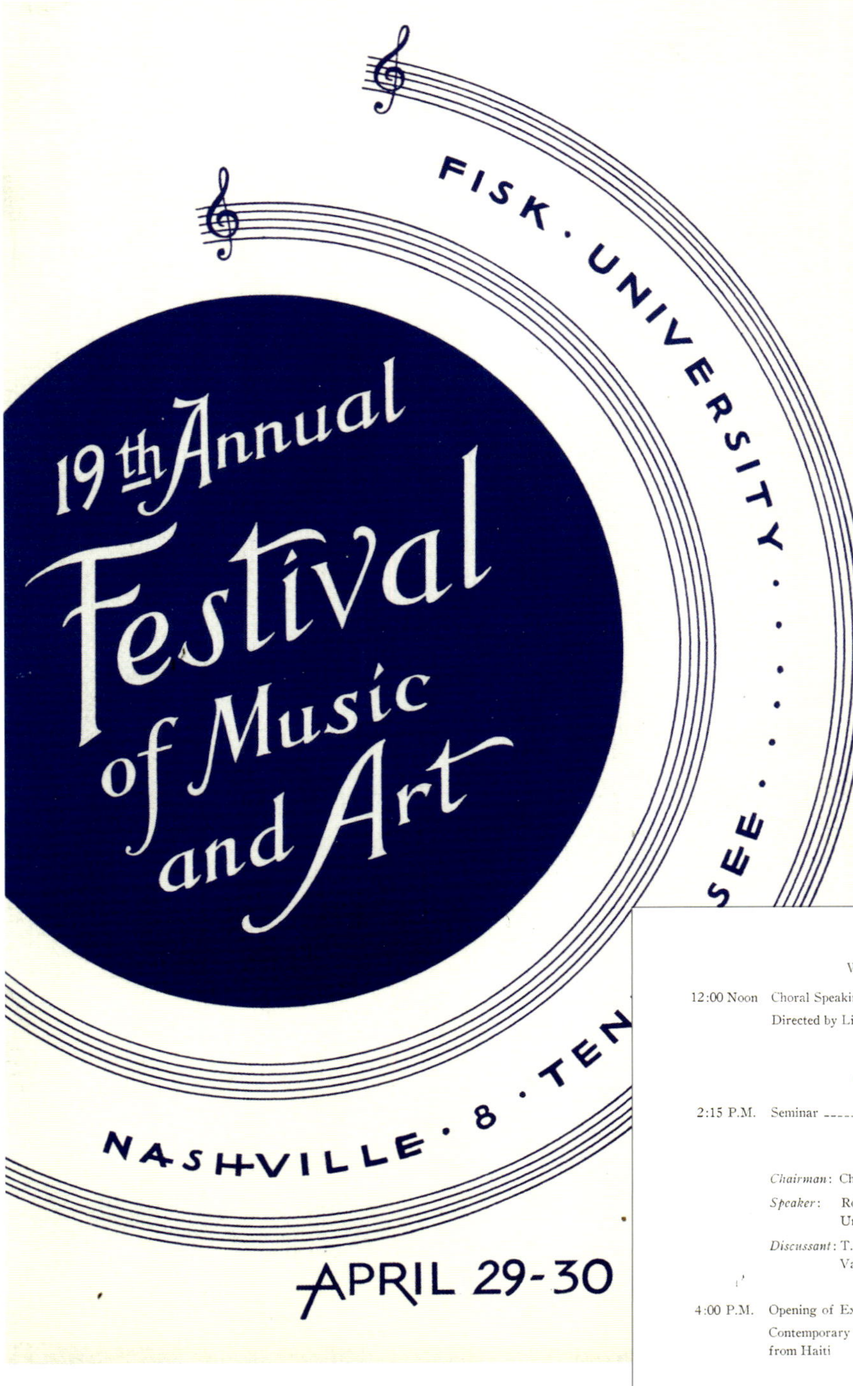

WEDNESDAY, APRIL 28

12:00 Noon Choral Speaking Program ---------- Fisk Memorial Chapel
Directed by Lillian W. Voorhees

THURSDAY, APRIL 29

2:15 P.M. Seminar ---------- Livingstone Auditorium

Folk Society

Chairman: Charles S. Johnson, President, Fisk University

Speaker: Robert Redfield, Chairman, Department of Anthropology, University of Chicago

Discussant: T. Lynn Smith, Chairman, Department of Sociology, Vanderbilt University

4:00 P.M. Opening of Exhibition ---------- International Student Center
Contemporary Paintings from Haiti — Stone Carving by William Edmondson

4:15 P.M. Tea ---------- International Student Center

Hostesses:

Mrs. Isaiah T. Creswell, Chairman	Mrs. Henderson A. Johnson
Mrs. William J. Faulkner	Mrs. George St. John, Jr.
Mrs. Mayme U. Foster	Mrs. Harold F. Smith
Mrs. Helen Y. Howard	Mrs. A. A. Taylor
Mrs. Charles S. Johnson	Miss Lois Towles

8:15 P.M. Concert ---------- Fisk Memorial Chapel
Edward Matthews, Baritone

Fig. 7. (Above) Cover of the pamphlet for the Fisk University Spring Arts Festival, 1948. Courtesy of Fisk University, John Hope and Aurelia E. Franklin Library, Special Collections and Archives.

Fig. 8. (Right) Interior page of the pamphlet for the Fisk University Spring Arts Festival, 1948. Courtesy of Fisk University, John Hope and Aurelia E. Franklin Library, Special Collections and Archives.

one of the pieces they had shown in New York the year prior, Edmondson's *Martha and Mary* (Cat. 3). The work was illustrated in the accompanying catalogue in the "Art Populaire et Artisanal (Popular and Folk Art)" section, with Edmondson's brief biographical notation simply reading, "Black tombstone sculptor."[1]

Further magazine and newspaper features followed over the next decade, in both Nashville and national publications. Edmondson was briefly employed for two six-month periods by the Works Progress Administration (WPA) between 1939 and 1941. Other notable modern artists and photographers, including Edward Weston and Consuelo Kanaga, came to see Edmondson working at his shop. His work was included in the exhibition *American Negro Art: Nineteenth and Twentieth Centuries* held at the Downtown Gallery, New York in 1941 and organized by the noted intellectual and "Dean" of the Harlem Renaissance Alain Locke. Later that same year, Edmondson's work was also featured in a solo exhibition at the Nashville Art Gallery. Fisk University exhibited his sculptures as part of a folk-art-themed iteration of their annual Spring Arts Festival in 1948. By the end of the 1940s, however, Edmondson was in bad health and unable to undertake the demanding physical work of carving stone. He died at home in 1951, at the age of seventy-seven, a mere twenty years after he started working in stone. While he was buried at Mount Ararat Cemetery in Nashville, the exact location of his grave is unknown and unmarked today.[2]

Over the past seventy years, the appreciation and value of Edmondson's work has grown, but the myths that took root during his lifetime, born of a Jim Crow South and a racist art world, have remained all-too entrenched. Though with some minor variations of exactly who and when, the same stories, particularly those that emerged from the press coverage of the MoMA exhibition, have become well-trodden lore. Such tales, ostensibly based in Edmondson's biography, framed him as a simple, isolated, illiterate individual who was "discovered" by white patrons, and by none of his own doing, "crashed" New York's most "exclusive museum of modern art."[3]

1. Alfred Barr, ed., *Trois Siècles d'Art aux Etats-Unis (Three Centuries of Art of the United States)* (Paris and New York: Musée du Jeu de Paume and Museum of Modern Art, 1938), 53.
2. For a more comprehensive record of Edmondson's biography and the history of his exhibition at the Museum of Modern Art, see *The Art of William Edmondson* (Nashville, TN: Cheekwood Museum of Art, 1999); Romare Bearden and Harry Henderson, *A History of African-American Artists: From 1792 to the Present* (New York: Pantheon, 1993); and Darby English and Charlotte Barat, *Among Others: Blackness at MoMA* (New York: Museum of Modern Art, 2019). "Negro Sculptor with God-Given Genius to Have Work Displayed in New York," *Nashville Banner*, October 9, 1937.
3. "Negro Sculptor with God-Given Genius to Have Work Displayed in New York," *Nashville Banner*, October 9, 1937. Untitled review of Edmondson exhibition at MoMA, *New Yorker*, November 6, 1937.

Cat. 4. Louise Dahl-Wolfe, *William Edmondson, Sculptor, Nashville, Tennessee*, 1933–37

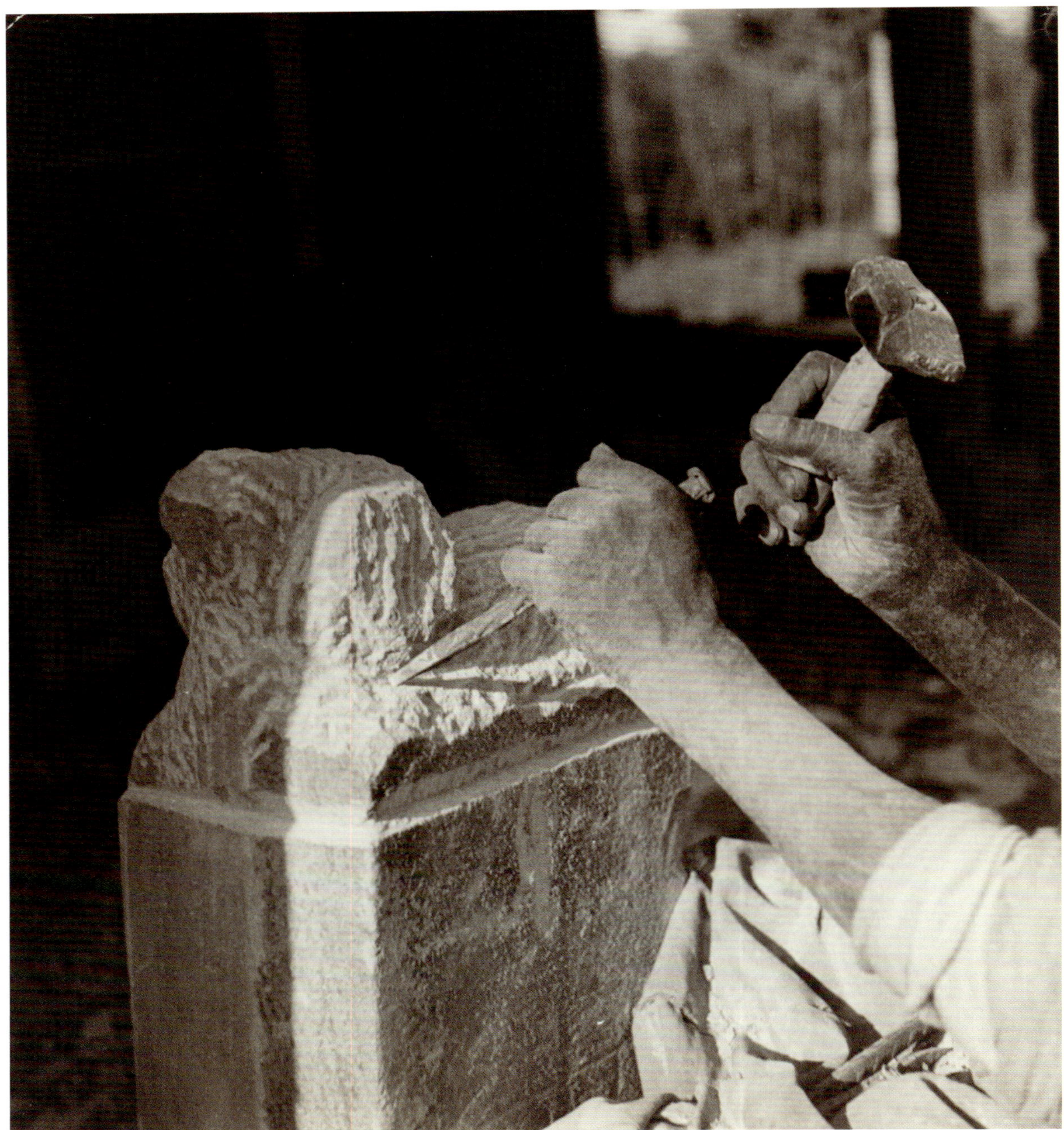

In one of the reviews of the MoMA exhibition, for example, the *New York Times* effectively questioned Edmondson's legitimacy as an artist and his technical proficiency, stating, "The question isn't whether this work of his should be considered, per se, 'important.' It is a question of spontaneous aspiration, achieving form by means of a craftsmanship unskilled yet oddly,

Fig. 9. Franklin D. Roosevelt and Eleanor Roosevelt with two unidentified men in car during visit to the campus of Vanderbilt University, Nashville, November 17, 1934. Courtesy of Special Collections Library, Vanderbilt University.

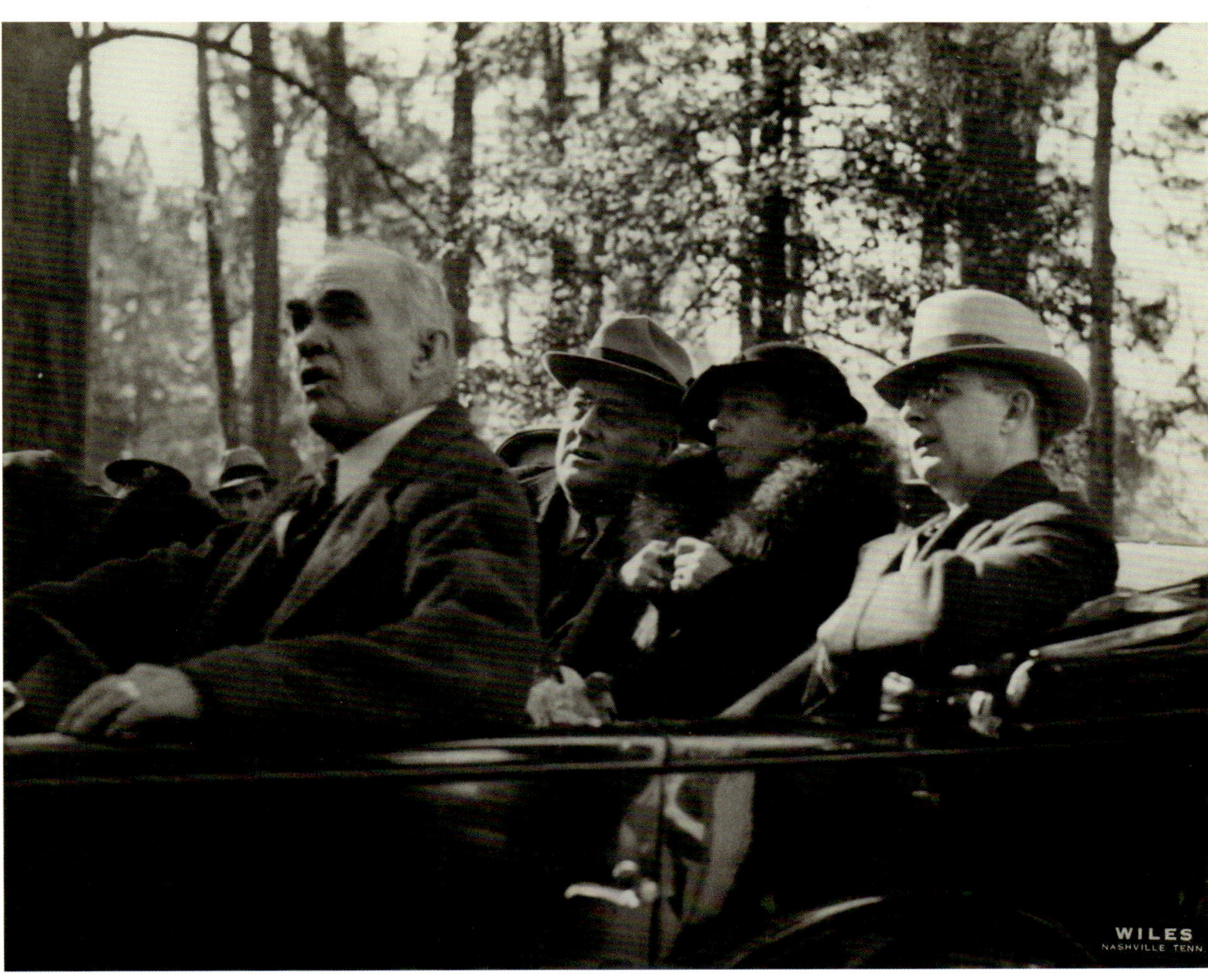

sometimes enchantingly, eloquent."[4] The *New Yorker* similarly expressed surprise over the charming naiveté and substantive form of Edmondson's sculpture but heaped praise instead on MoMA for its "find" of this unknown "Nashville negro." The magazine concluded of his work, "The figures are not decorative enough to be attractive to many, nor have they really enough emotion or intellectual content to be of lasting interest."[5]

One of the most oft-repeated stories about Edmondson originated with the sculptor himself. He frequently told friends, visitors, and reporters that his decision to take up stone carving was the result of divine intervention and a manifestation of the Lord's work. Edmondson's religiosity was genuine, but when his recollections of God telling him to carve tombstones and figures were published, they were taken at face value and

4. Edward Alden Jewell, "Tennessee Negro Shows Sculpture," *New York Times*, October 20, 1937.
5. Untitled review of Edmondson exhibition at MoMA, *New Yorker*, November 6, 1937.

used to underscore his racial, class, and regional identities. *Time* magazine, for example, quoted Edmondson directly but made sure to do so in a manner that emphasized his dialect, using, as critic Robert Storr suggests, a heavy dose of "Uncle Remus imitations" intended to make the sculptor fit "the bill of a self-effacing folk hero":[6]

> Dis here stone n'all those out there in de yard—come from God. It's de work in Jesus speakin' his mind in my mind. I mus' be one of his 'ciples. Dese here is mirkels I can do. Cain't nobody do dese but me. I cain't help carvin' I jes' does it . . . Jesus has planted the seed of carin' in me.[7]

These narrative constructions, however, have never conveyed the full story of William Edmondson or his sculptural practice. As artist Romare Bearden and scholar Harry Henderson suggested in their landmark survey *A History of African-American Artists: From 1792 to the Present* (1993), "Edmondson knew what people expected a black man to say."[8] The sculptor also often spoke truths that were ignored, like the fact he was not illiterate but rather could read "most printin' and some writing" but neither without his glasses.[9] Other aspects of his life, including the claim that he never left Nashville, have always been untrue but became hidden in plain sight because no one took the trouble to question them. As art historian Jennifer Jane Marshall states, these facts did not neatly fit into the established "plantation-to-plot trajectory" that formed the bedrock of such accounts. Marshall points to a story in the *Pittsburgh Courier*, archived in MoMA's clipping scrapbooks, that clearly states that Edmondson actually traveled to New York for the presentation of his work in 1937.[10]

Many have sought to elevate the stature of Edmondson and his work by crafting well-intentioned heroic narratives of a self-taught artist who rose to fame and created fine art on par with the direct carving of modern sculptors like William Zorach or Constantin Brancusi. Even these cases, however, often have the effect of flattening the complexity of his sculptural practice and the problematics of its reception. Further, it was common

6. Robert Storr, "William Edmondson," in *Self-Taught Artists of the Twentieth Century: An American Anthology*, ed. Elsa Weiner Longhauser and Harald Szeemann (San Francisco: Chronicle Books, 1998), 63.
7. "Mirkels," *Time*, November 1, 1937.
8. Bearden and Henderson, *A History*, 351.
9. Walt Logan, "Fame Leaves Him Unmoved: God Planted Him in Nashville, Says Negro Sculptor," *Nashville Tennessean Magazine*, October 31, 1937, 3, 5.
10. "'Natural Born' Sculptor Gives One-Man Show in N.Y.," *Pittsburgh Courier*, October 30, 1937, 6. Edmondson's travel to New York, Marshall notes further, was also confirmed in an oral history by Gertrude Bosley Bowling Whitworth, a former employer of Edmondson at her family's farm called Whitland. "Oral Interview with Gertrude Bosley Bowling," ca. 1960–61, Eleanor Whitworth Family Archive, Cheekwood Estate & Gardens, Nashville. Jennifer Jane Marshall, "Nashville, New York, Paris, and Nashville: William Edmondson, Mobilized and Unmoved," *American Art* 31, no. 2 (Summer 2017): 69–76. Edmondson quoted in John Thompson, "Negro Stone Cutter Here Says Gift from Lord; Work Praised," *Nashville Tennessean*, February 9, 1941.

for white curators during the interwar years to stress the working-class backgrounds of self-taught or folk artists as a means to, as Marshall writes, "promote the narrative of an artist pursuing creative self-fulfillment against all odds."[11]

There is also the issue of the labels that have been applied to Edmondson and his work since the 1930s, none of which he normally claimed for himself: primitive, modern primitive, folk, autodidact, self-taught, outsider, outlier, and simply artist or sculptor. Each carries distinct connotations and agendas that have affected and continue to affect the reception of his artistic output. As the scholar Eugene W. Metcalf wrote in a letter to collector and writer Edmund Fuller in 1984, Edmondson was a "man who created many kinds of art," and attempting to categorize his work was never really about contextualizing or understanding his work on its own terms.[12] In an oft-repeated quote, Edmondson declared, "I didn't know I was no artist till them folks come told me I was."[13] What if this statement, however, was not read through the lens of naiveté or ignorance, but instead as an avowal from an individual wholly unconcerned with labels or art-world acceptance though committed to being a carver?

Edmondson did not create art for galleries or museums, nor did he seek out critical recognition or approval. While many have tried to separate his tombstones or functional pieces—bird baths, cups, etc.—from his more figural, freestanding stonework, his entire practice was unabashedly a commercial enterprise. None of which makes Edmondson any less worthy of serious art historical consideration. This exhibition, taking its subtitle from the original sign the sculptor placed in his yard for all to see, seeks to highlight and present to a new generation the diversity, richness, and creativity of Edmondson's sculptural practice—on its own terms.

At the beginning of the Great Depression, as his primary income stream disappeared, Edmondson decided to start a new career and open a new business. He was a resourceful entrepreneur. Independent, not isolated, he worked within and for his community, drawing inspiration from a diverse range of subjects, including those from his both his spiritual life and from the world around him. Everyday people Edmondson

11. Jennifer Jane Marshall, "Find-and-Seek: Discovery Narratives, Americanization, and Other Tales of Genius in Modern American Folk Art," in *Outliers and American Vanguard Art*, curated by Lynne Cooke (Washington, DC: National Gallery of Art in association with the University of Chicago Press, 2018), 59. See also Jon Ott, "Labored Stereotypes: Palmer Hayden's *The Janitor Who Paints*," *American Art* 22 (Spring 2008): 102–15; and Katherine Jentleson, *Gatecrashers: The Rise of the Self-Taught Artist in America* (Berkeley: University of California Press, 2020).
12. Eugene W. Metcalf to Edmund Fuller, May 25, 1984. Newark Fuller Archives, Cheekwood Exhibition Files, Box 103, folder 2, Cheekwood Estate & Gardens, Nashville.
13. Edmondson quoted in John Thompson, "Negro Stone Cutter Here Says Gift from Lord; Work Praised," *Nashville Tennessean*, February 9, 1941.

knew and regularly encountered became carved stone figures, as did more famous people he would have known about, like the prizefighter Jack Johnson or the First Lady of the United States, Eleanor Roosevelt, who had visited Nashville with her husband, President Franklin Delano Roosevelt, to great fanfare in 1934 (fig. 9).

Edmondson approached the carving of a tombstone, a birdbath, or a statue of Eleanor Roosevelt as equally worthy and worthwhile pursuits. He created sculptural objects that were intended to live and be seen by all, in public spaces, whether that was his yard, someone else's garden, or the local cemetery. In bringing together this selection of objects and images, along with new scholarly perspectives on them, *The Sculpture of William Edmondson* hopes to recenter his work and let it speak its own language, not one imposed upon it.

Cat. 5. William Edmondson, *Eleanor Roosevelt*, n.d.

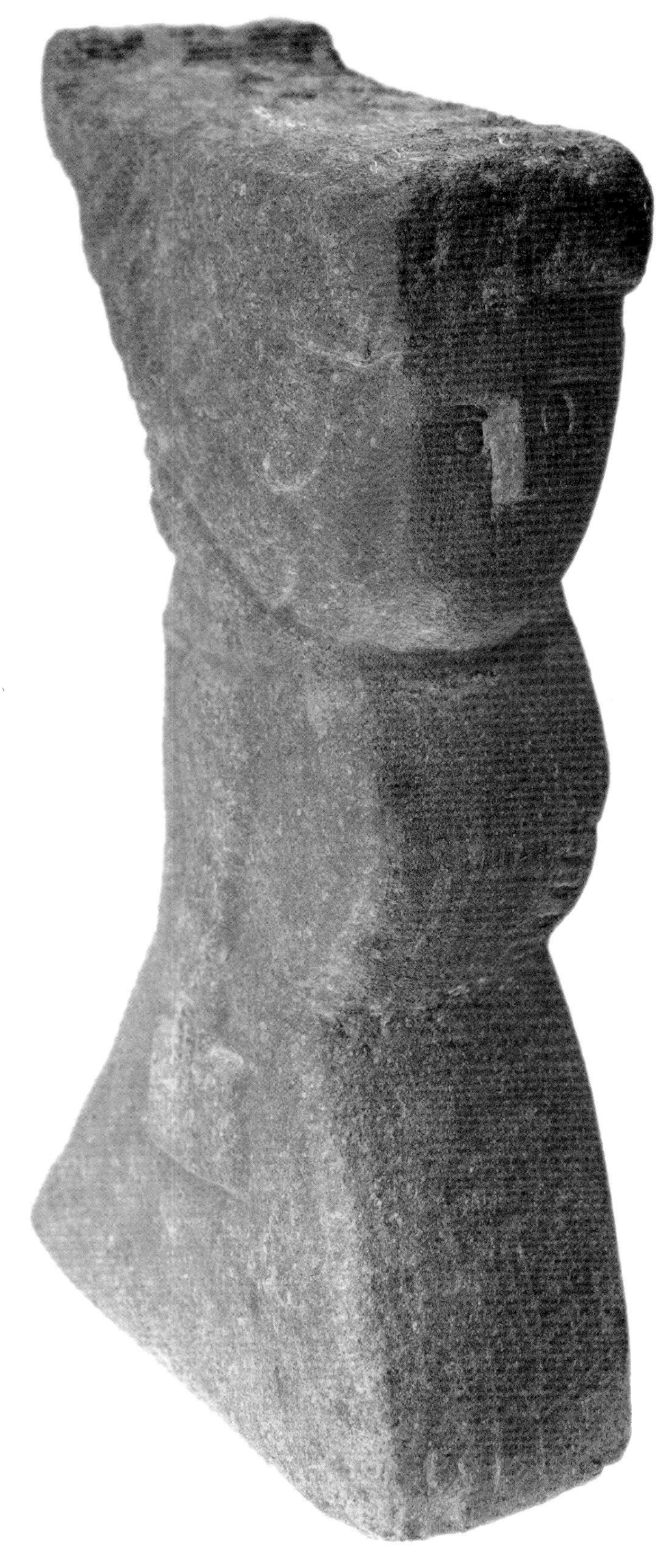

Cat. 6. (Below) William Edmondson, *Bess and Joe*, c. 1930–40

Cat. 7. (Recto, Top) William Edmondson, *Martha and Mary*, c. 1930s

Cat. 8. (Recto, Bottom) William Edmondson, *Tombstone with Bird*, 1934–41

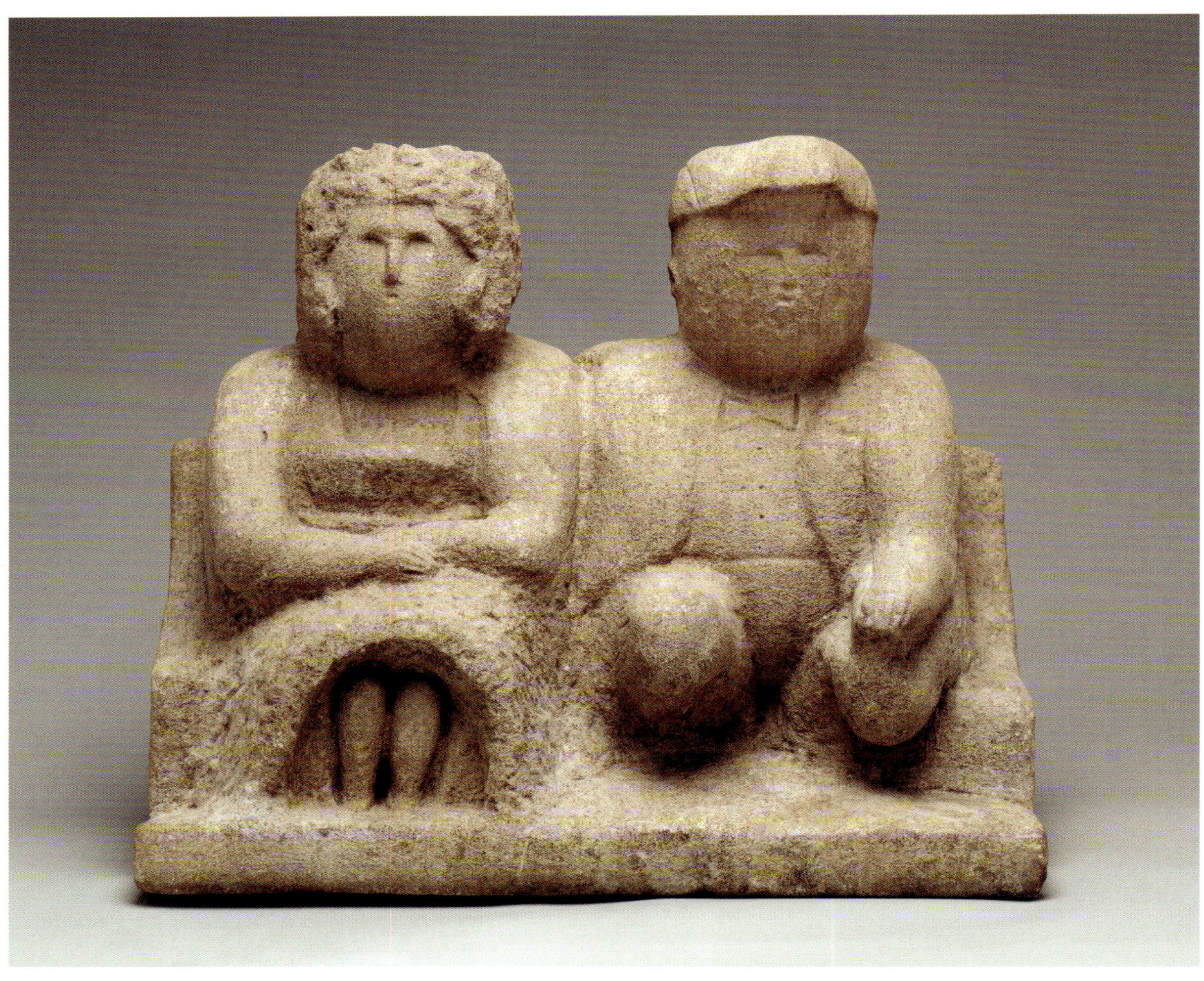

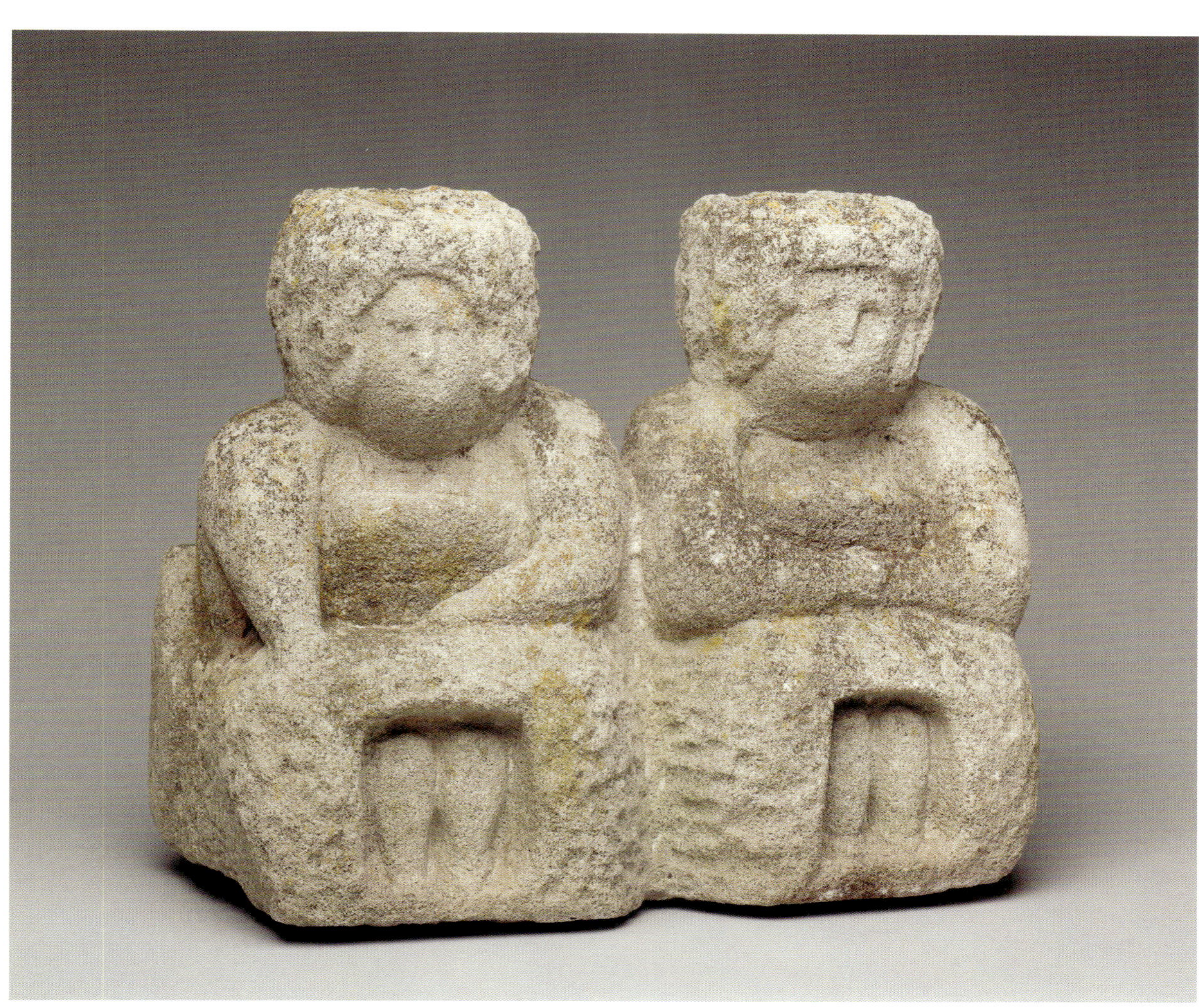

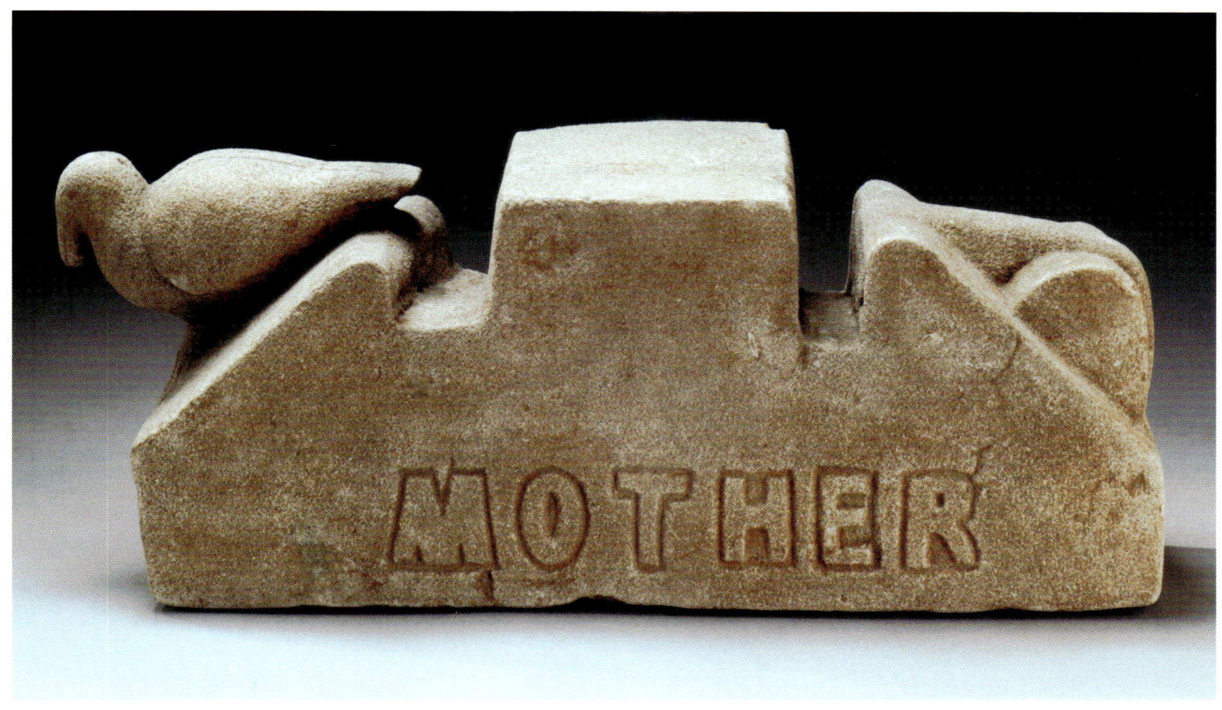
MOTHER

Cat. 9. (Top) William Edmondson, *Bowl*, 1935–40

Cat. 10. (Bottom) William Edmondson, *Garden Ornament*, n.d.

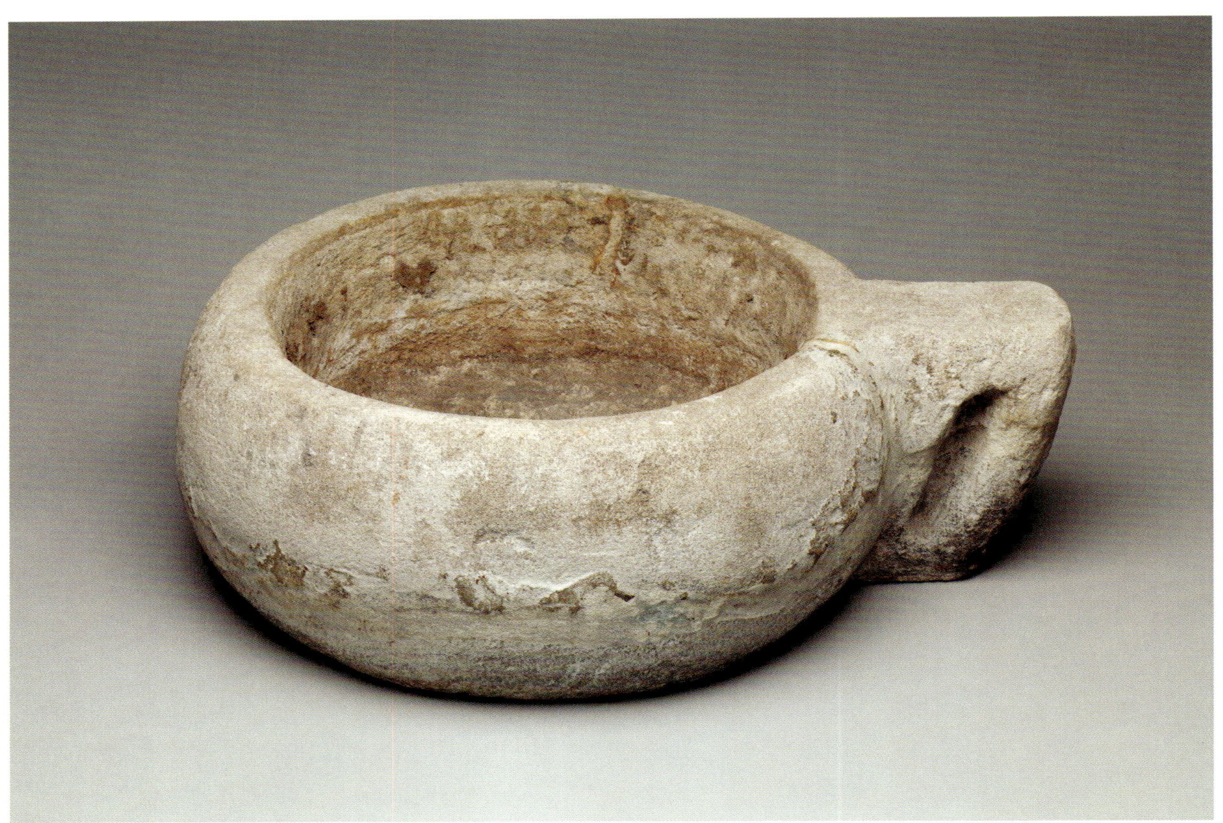

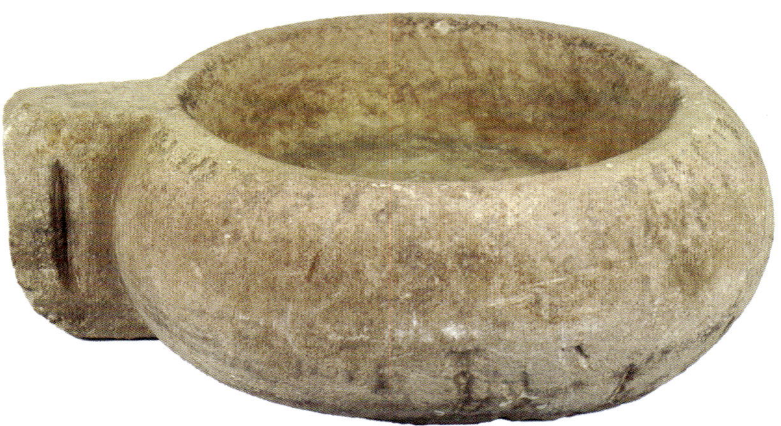

Cat. 11. Puryear Mims, *Bust of William Edmondson*, n.d.

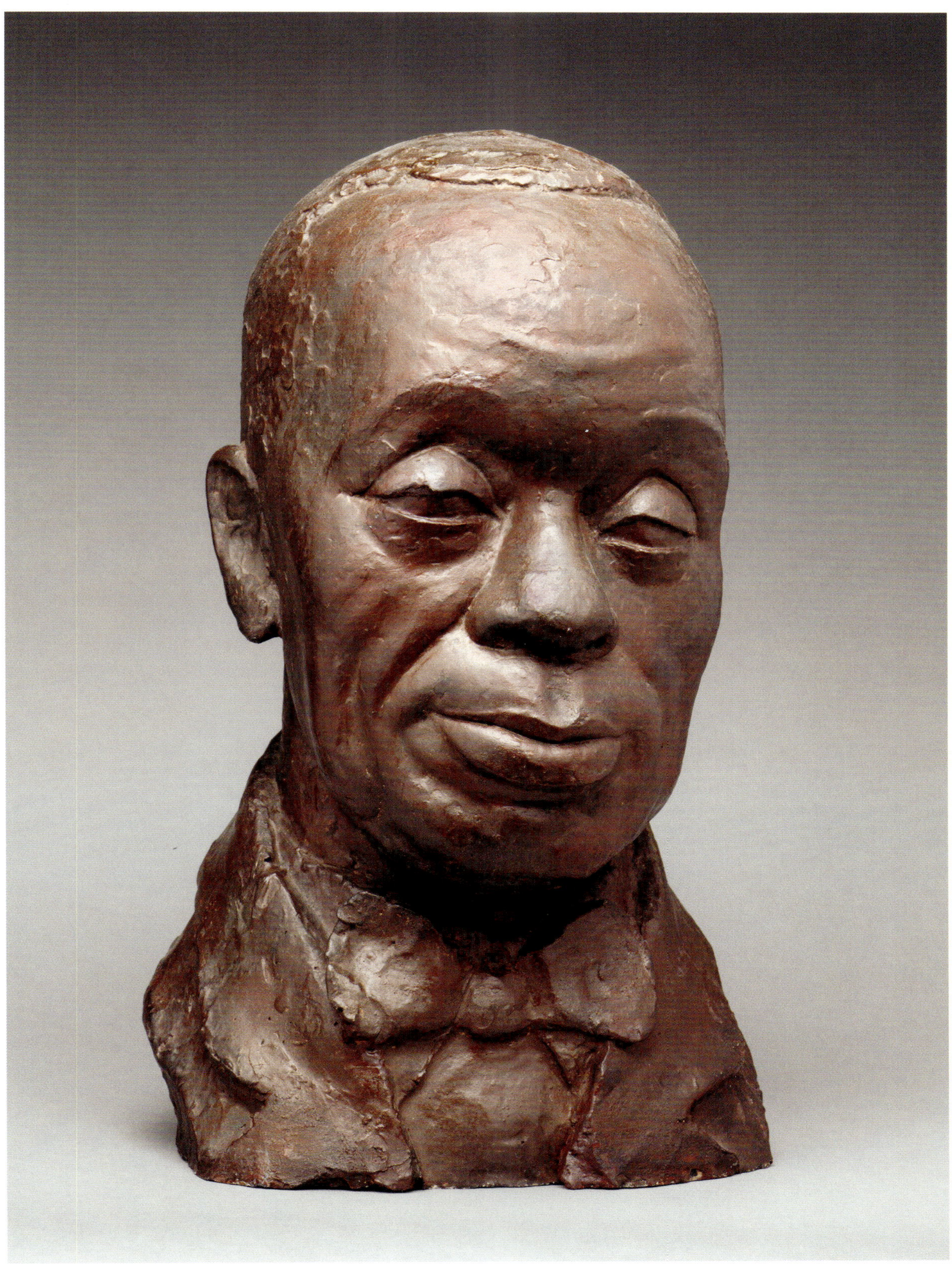

Cat. 12. (Recto) Louise Dahl-Wolfe, *Sculpture, William Edmondson (Birdbath)*, 1937

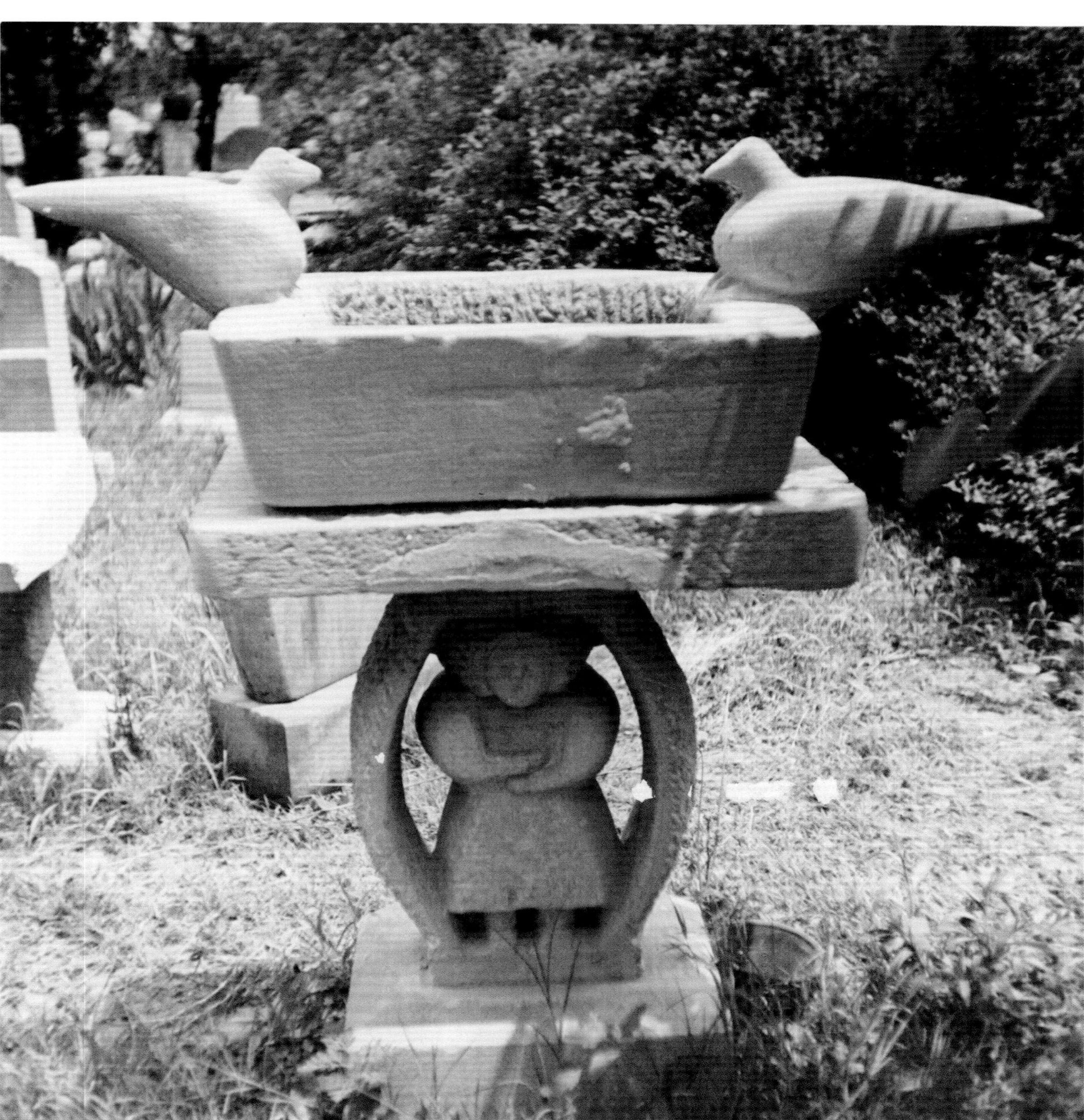

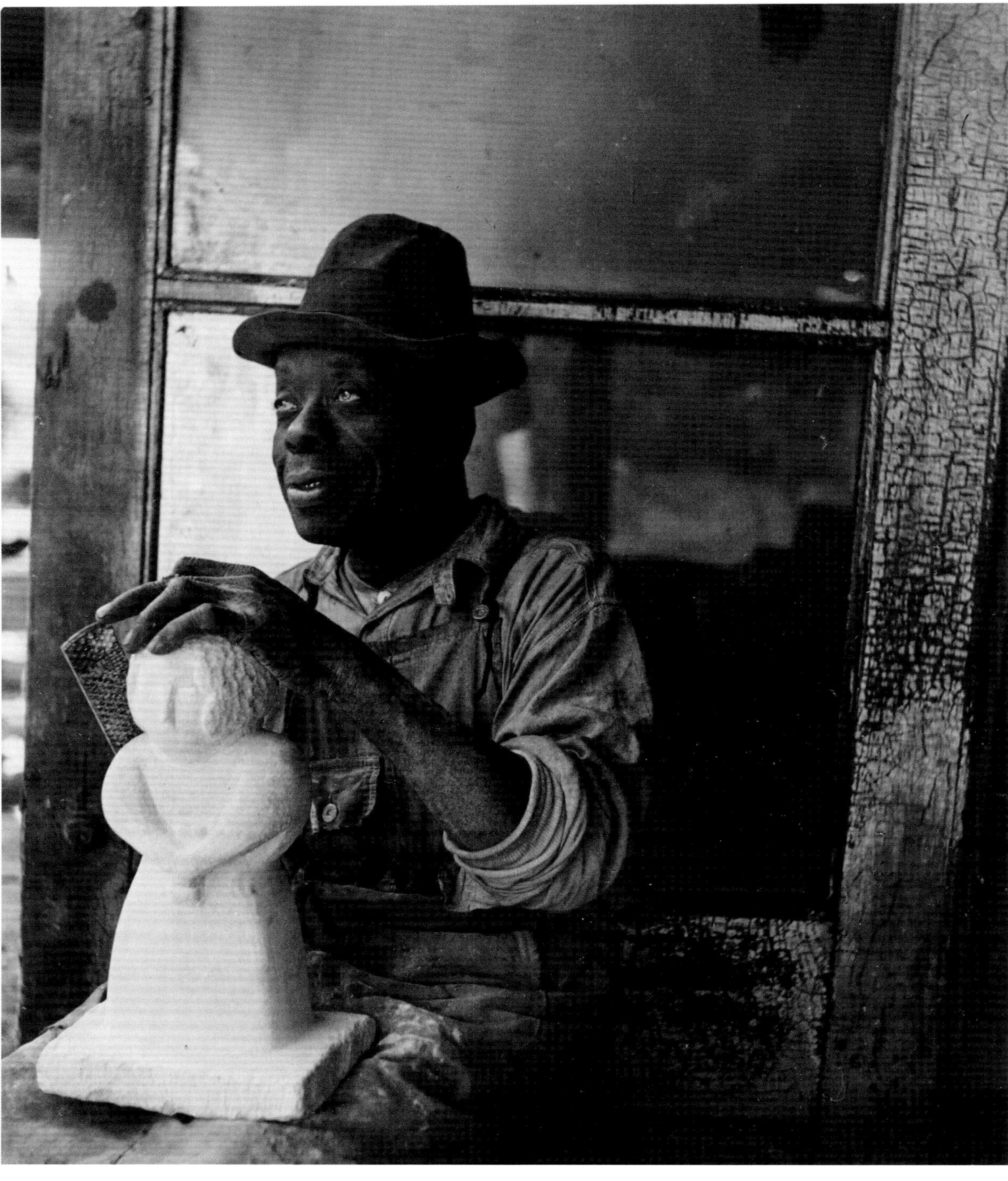

Cat. 13. Louise Dahl-Wolfe, *William Edmondson*, 1937

Hewing Stones of Hope in a City of Discarded Rocks

William Edmondson's Nashville

Learotha Williams Jr.

During the first years of the Great Depression, a visitor to Nashville taking a morning stroll up Fourteenth Avenue South between Horton and Wade Avenues would find themselves greeted by several sounds. Perhaps they might hear the chirping of a group of cardinals that had roosted nearby or the sudden roar of a Ford Model Y or the sound of children's voices off in the distance. But if the morning was calm and the wind just right, the traveler would hear what sounded like someone tapping off in the distance—a sound that was intermittent but deliberate, one that would soon dominate their senses and curiosity.

Approaching the home located at 1434 Fourteenth Avenue South, they would be met by the sight of an aging African American man sitting at what appeared to be a workbench made of two stone slabs. The senior would already likely be blanketed by a light layer of dust that morning, dressed in overalls, a well-worn hat, and a shirt with the sleeves rolled midway up his forearms. Close inspection of

Fig. 10. Edward Weston, *Stone Sculpture, Wm. Edmondson*, 1941. Gelatin silver print, 7 ⅝ × 9 ⁹⁄₁₆ in. Center for Creative Photography, University of Arizona: Edward Weston Archive.

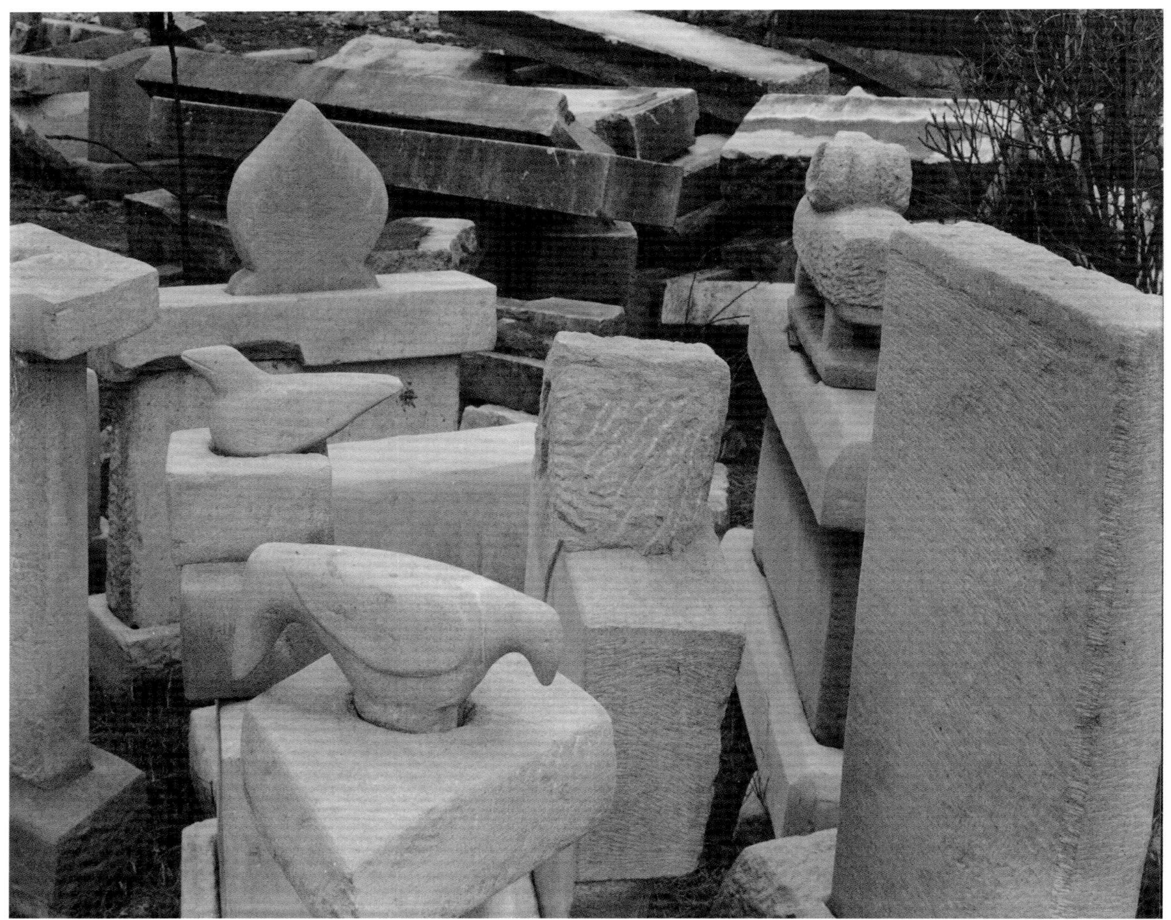

his work that morning would reveal a headstone with a dove perched at its apex. In a few days, perhaps it would sit in front of the grave of a formerly enslaved woman who had recently passed away in the city. Although she would have been unknown by the visitor to this space, the recipient would have the honor of having her final resting place adorned with the craftsmanship of one of Nashville's most prolific and unlikely sculptors, William Edmondson.

Edmondson did not start sculpting until later in his life, and he did so in a city that was firmly committed to Jim Crow. During the 1930s, African Americans made up about 24 percent of Davidson County's population, a figure that was slightly less than their number when James Robertson and his companions established what would become Fort Nashborough in 1779. Although Edmondson was among the

1. For more information about the history of Nashville's Black business class, see Bobby L. Lovett, *The African American History of Nashville, Tennessee, 1780–1930: Elites and Dilemmas* (Fayetteville: University of Arkansas Press, 1999).

first generation of Black Nashvillians to be born free from the generational curse of slavery, anti-Black racism shaped the world he lived in. White terror and the abandonment of Black Americans in the South by Rutherford B. Hayes and the Republican Party fatally undermined any gains they had made during Reconstruction. By the time Edmondson reached his twentieth birthday, lynching had become a common feature of African American life in the United States, with as many as three having occurred in Nashville since his birth. One of the most notorious was the 1892 murder of Eph Grizzard that occurred at the Woodland Street Bridge, an episode that occurred after Grizzard had been placed in police custody.

By the turn of the century, Nashville would have well-defined areas of the city where it expected its African Americans to live, often having formal and informal economic, social, and political controls to enforce these policies. These segregated parts of town—which included places like Edgehill, where Edmondson's home and shop were located—had roots in Civil War–era Nashville. They were communities where many African Americans from the periphery and neighboring states first settled and defined what freedom would mean to them and their descendants. These segregated parts of town would continue to draw African Americans to Nashville. The new arrivals—like their forebears who came here seeking freedom—were often poor and destitute, but they did not arrive in Nashville empty handed. Their culture, skill, and desires would contribute to creating Nashville's identity as the Music City and the Athens of the South throughout the twentieth century. Indeed, by the time Edmondson began working on his first sculpture, Black Nashville could boast of having three institutions of higher learning in the city, a Black-owned bank, two Black-owned publishing houses, and scores of other Black businesses and churches that contributed to the city's cultural and intellectual vitality.[1] By the time Edmondson had begun carving his vision into discarded stones, the city had produced exemplary Black political leaders such as James C. and Nettie Napier, Preston Taylor, Juno Frankie Pierce, and others. They also created organizations to better Black life in the city such as the numerous Colored

Women's Clubs, African American Lodges, business leagues, and scores of Black churches, many of which had congregations with roots dating back to the second generation of African Americans to call this city home.

Although these achievements were laudable, their successes were diminished by the city's commitment to Jim Crow. By the time Edmondson had received his divine commission to begin his work, the Athens of the South was a study in paradoxes when it came to race relations. The city had separate libraries, with the facility for African Americans receiving less support and having fewer volumes than its white counterparts. Black Nashvillians could access the titles in the white libraries, but only after going through an elaborate and somewhat frustrating process that whites were not subjected to. Nashville's public park system was also segregated. In 1912, the city opened Hadley Park at the site of what had once been a plantation at the end of Jefferson Street. Celebrated as the first park in America to be created for the exclusive use of African Americans, Hadley Park opened to serve as an example of the efficacy of Jim Crow in the Volunteer State.[2]

Although different motives led to the creation of Hadley Park, its final form was unlike anything African Americans had hoped for and fell short of what white Nashvillians hoped they would be willing to accept. Noted Nashville publisher Henry Allen Boyd wrote of the park's neglect, "During the summer months, Jimson Weeds and Dogfennel hold high carnival in the confines of the so-called park, while horse weeds and Sweet Annie run riot at will."[3] The "Nashville Way" during Edmondson's life was to offer African Americans the bare minimum of the best things the city had to offer while demanding applause and gratitude for these half-hearted overtures.

As America's economy boomed during the 1920s, Edmondson and his neighbors found steady employment in the service industries. While he worked as a janitor at the Woman's Hospital, located at 301 Spruce Street, his neighbors worked as stewards, cooks, laundresses, and general laborers for public and private employers throughout the city. The continued growth of its premier institutions bore witness to the success of African Americans during this period, with

2. "Democracy a Dead Issue in Nashville," *Pittsburgh Courier*, April 3, 1948.
3. *Nashville Globe*, November 9, 1917.

Cat. 14. William Edmondson, *Whitlow Tombstone*, 1944

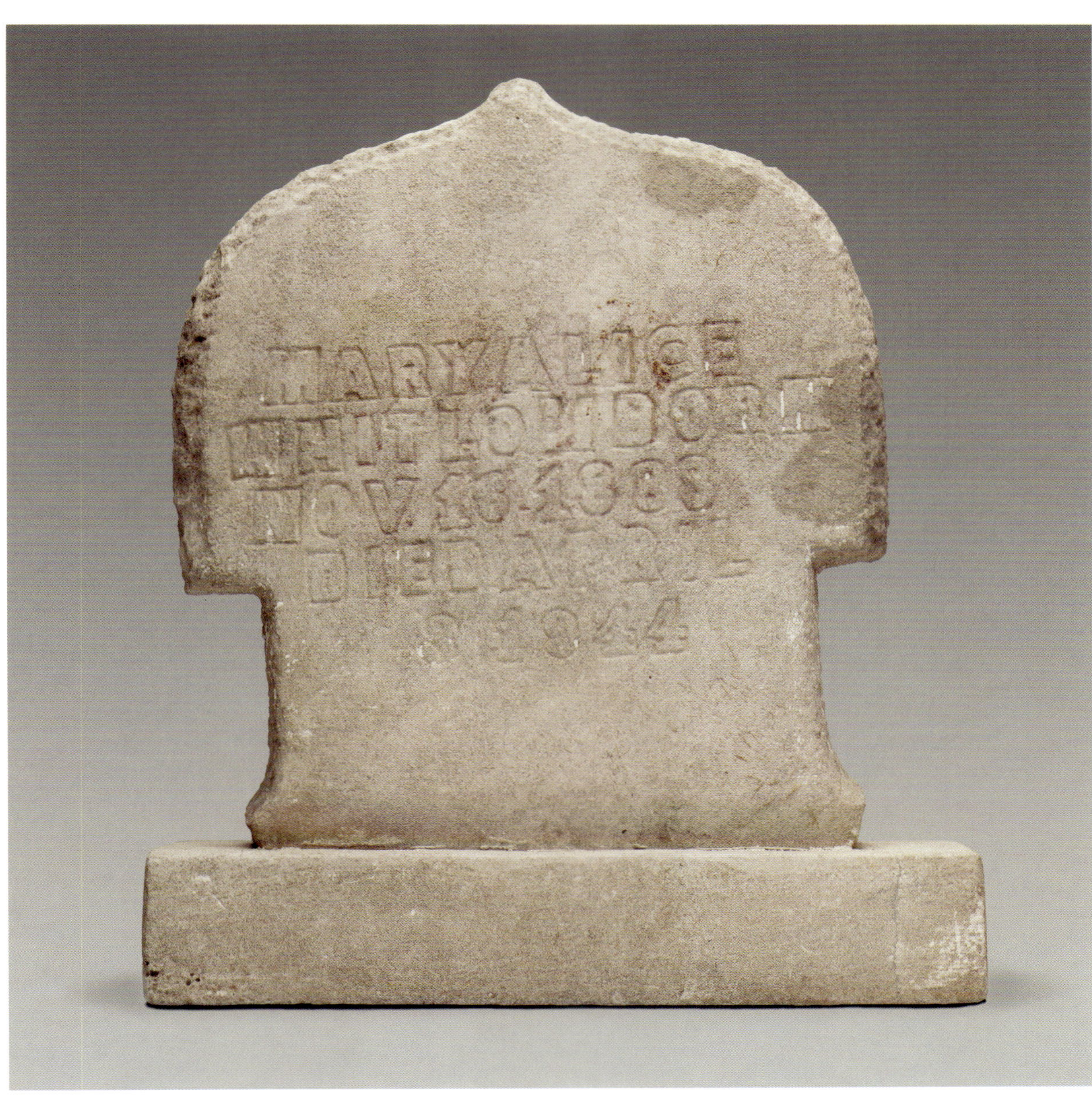

4. US Census. 1920. Nashville Ward 22, Davidson, Tennessee; Roll: T625_1735; Page: 7A; Enumeration District: 85.

Tennessee Agricultural and Industrial State College enjoying unprecedented growth and Meharry Medical College making plans to move to North Nashville by the decade's end. While not all Nashville's African Americans desiring a college education could attend these or the other Black colleges in the city, the doctors, nurses, teachers, and engineers the schools produced helped raise the quality of life for themselves and other African Americans around the country.[4]

Cat. 15. William Edmondson, *Reclining Man (Sidney Hirsch)*, n.d.

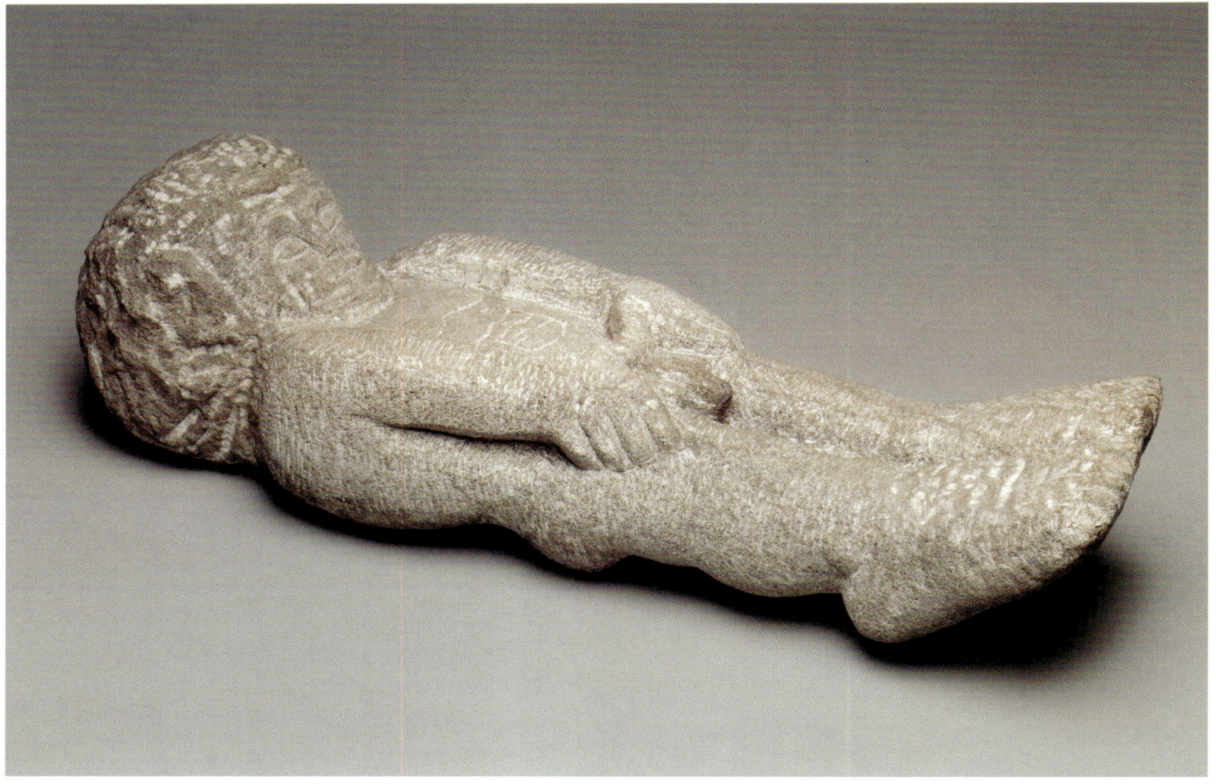

The decade of the 1930s would be one that was transformative for Edmondson and all of Black Nashville. As the Great Depression set in and challenged the idea of uninterrupted prosperity in American life, Edmondson—like many other African Americans in the city—fell on hard times. This was a particularly difficult time for him as a middle-aged man with declining health, and he lost his janitorial position at the hospital. It was during this period in his life when Edmondson received his calling and began his career as a sculptor. Using discarded pieces of limestone, stones that the people of the Music City had rejected, Edmondson began carving headstones. He would transform this refuse into powerful pieces of African American material culture and become one of the greatest autodidacts Nashville has ever produced.[5]

Throughout the 1930s and '40s, Edmondson's workspace would become his gallery, and the taps of his hammer striking a chisel would serenade the residents of Fourteenth Avenue South, but early in his career the only Nashvillians that

5. David Driskell and Los Angeles County Museum of Art, *Two Centuries of Black American Art (Exhibition)* (Los Angeles: Los Angeles County Museum of Art and A.A. Knopf, 1976).

appreciated his genius were the families whom he blessed with headstones. Nonetheless, his work would languish in obscurity until Sidney Mttron Hirsch, an art professor from George Peabody College for Teachers, discovered his yard and was impressed with what he saw. While it is uncertain if this was a chance encounter or if Hirsch was out for a walk and was drawn to the site by the sound of Edmondson working on the carving of an angel, preacher, or one of the many "critters" that dotted his worksite, this meeting would lead to Edmondson receiving international acclaim as an artist and becoming the first African American to have a solo exhibit at the prestigious Museum of Modern Art.

Many accolades and exhibits would follow, and today William Edmondson is recognized as one of the city's most significant artists. Although he was not formally trained, he became a sculptor whose works leaned heavily on the themes and culture of his forebears who had been enslaved in the Volunteer State. His limestone sculptures became representations of what his ancestors spoke and sang during times of joy and trouble. His sculptures consoled bereaved African Americans and offered a positive vision for the future to those who viewed and received his work. In many ways, his ingenuity, versatility, labors, and drive were representative of the African American experience in Nashville from its late eighteenth century founding to the present day.

Cat. 16. Louise Dahl-Wolfe, *William Edmondson*, 1937

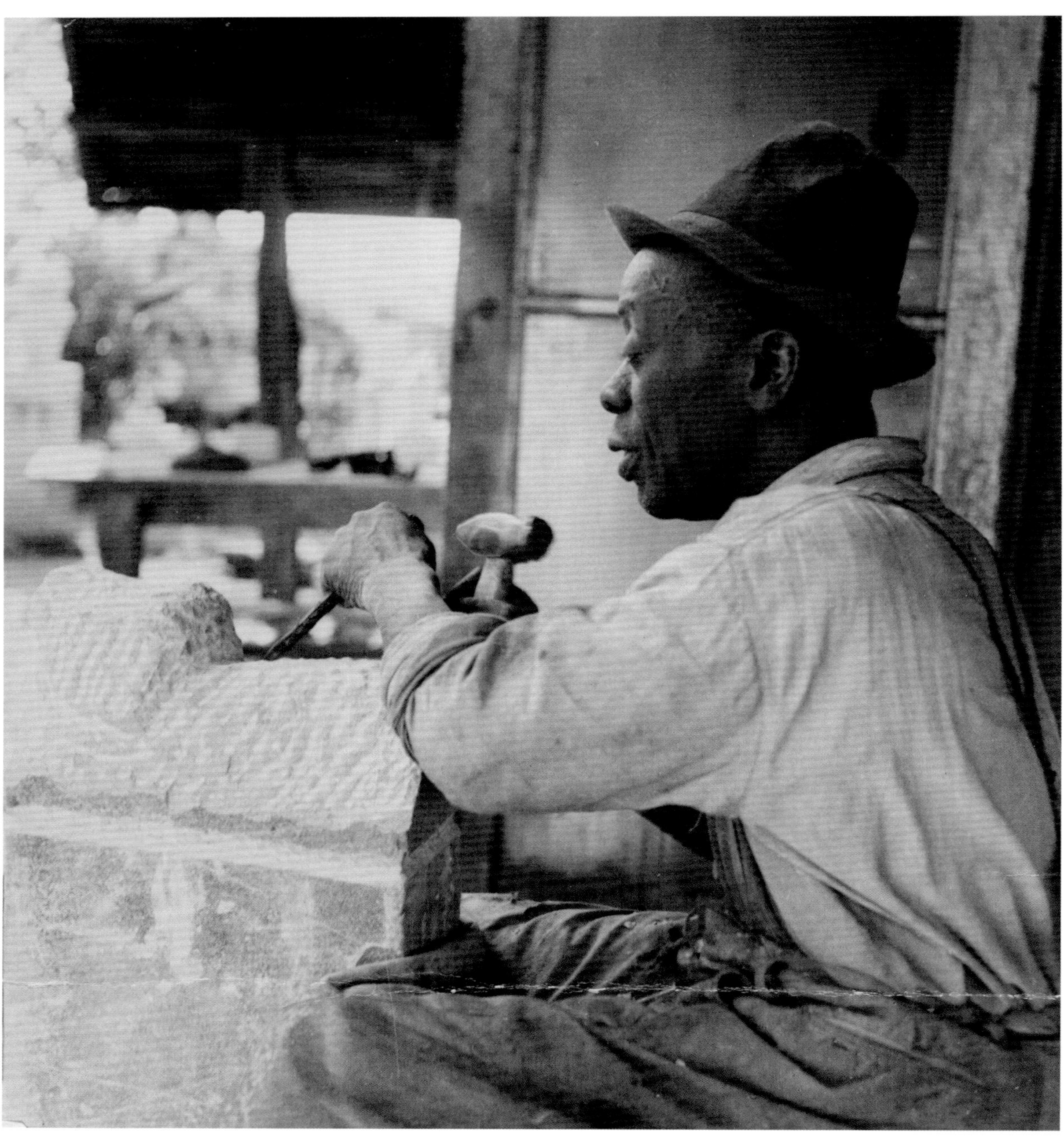

Cat. 17. Louise Dahl-Wolfe, *Sculpture, William Edmondson (Eleanor Roosevelt; Crucifix)*, 1933–37

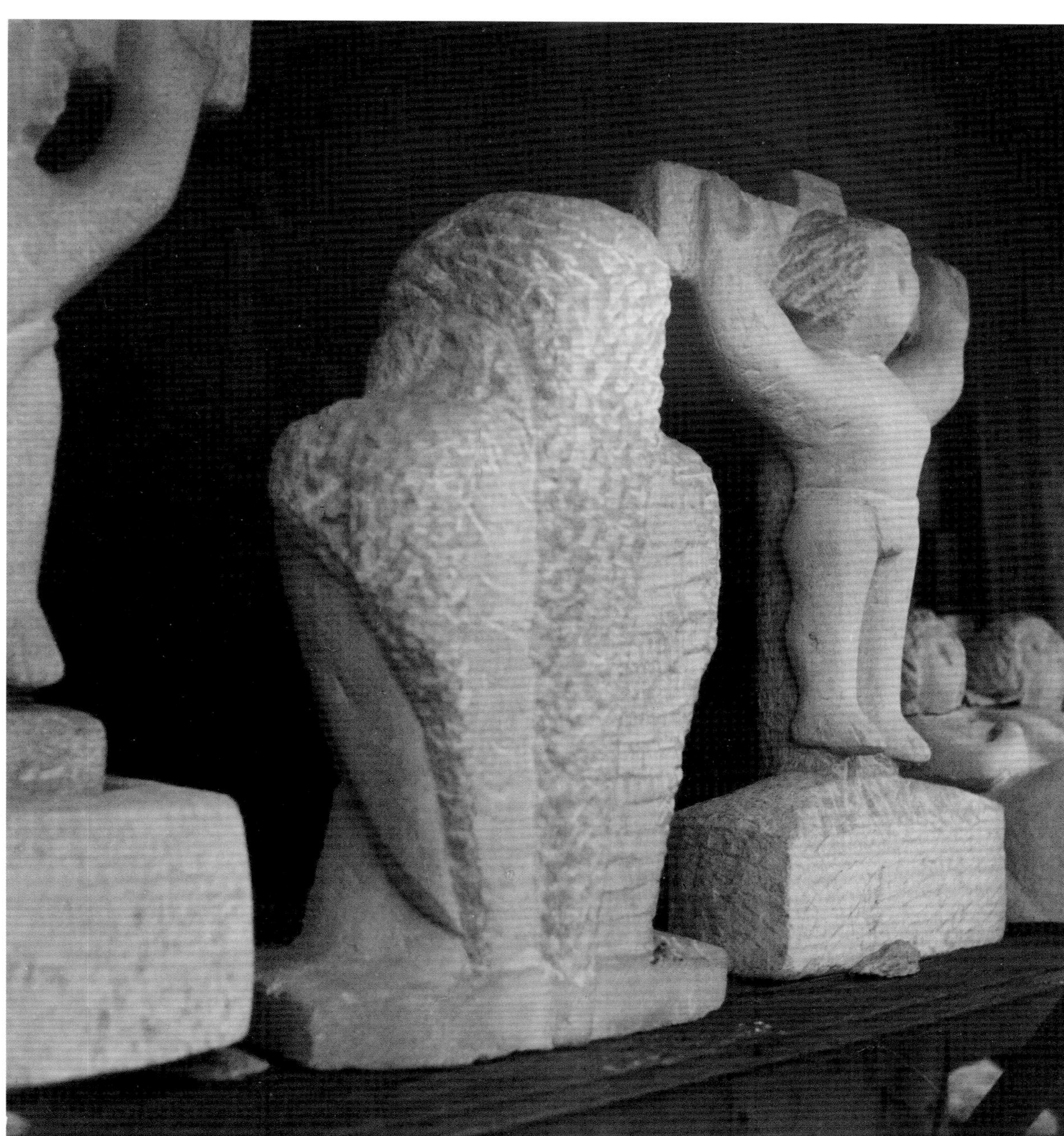

32

Cat. 18. (Recto) Louise Dahl-Wolfe, *William Edmondson, Sculptor, Nashville, Tennessee*, 1937

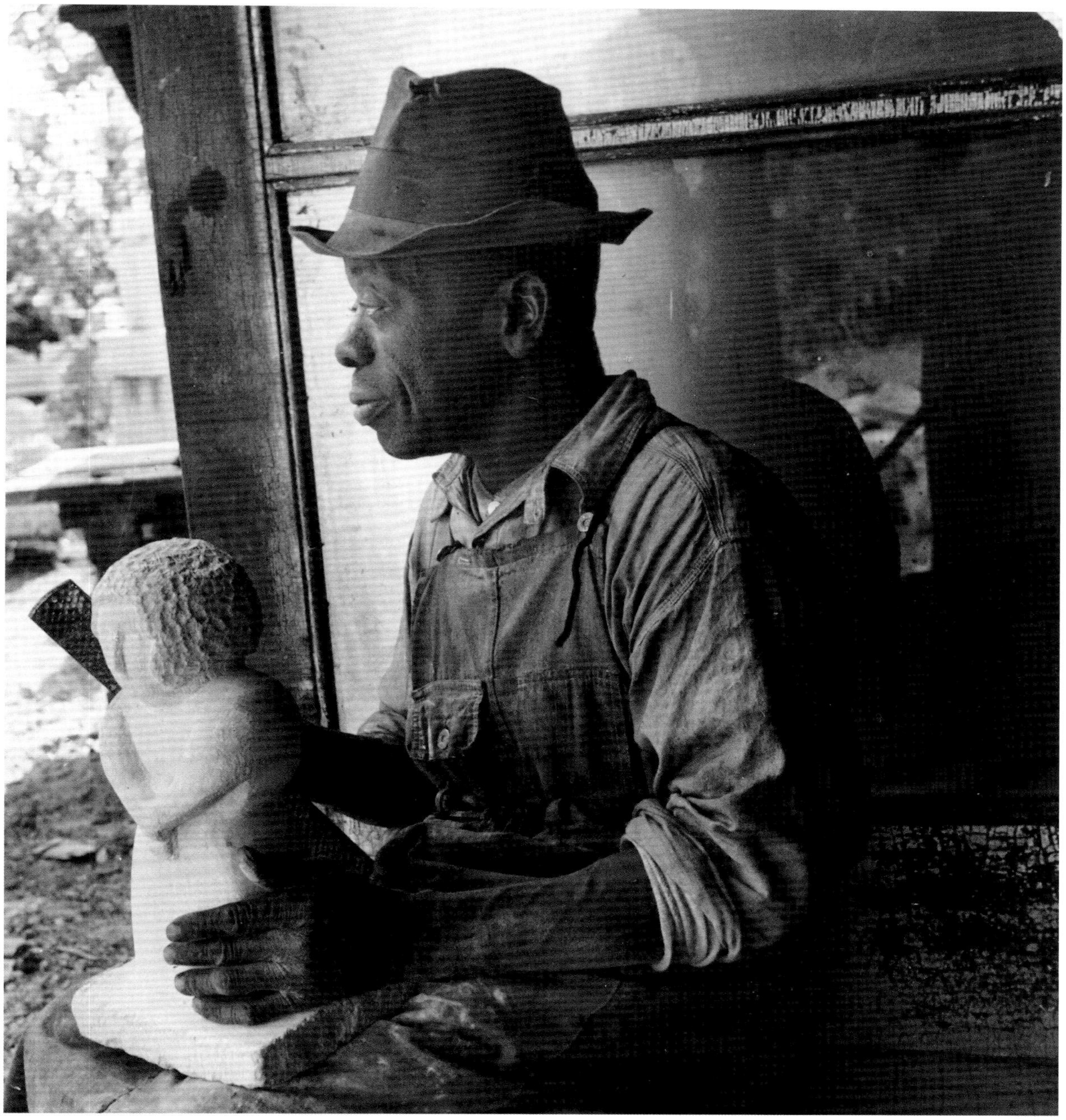

Cat. 19. Meyer Wolfe, *Vanderbilt Clinic*, 1939

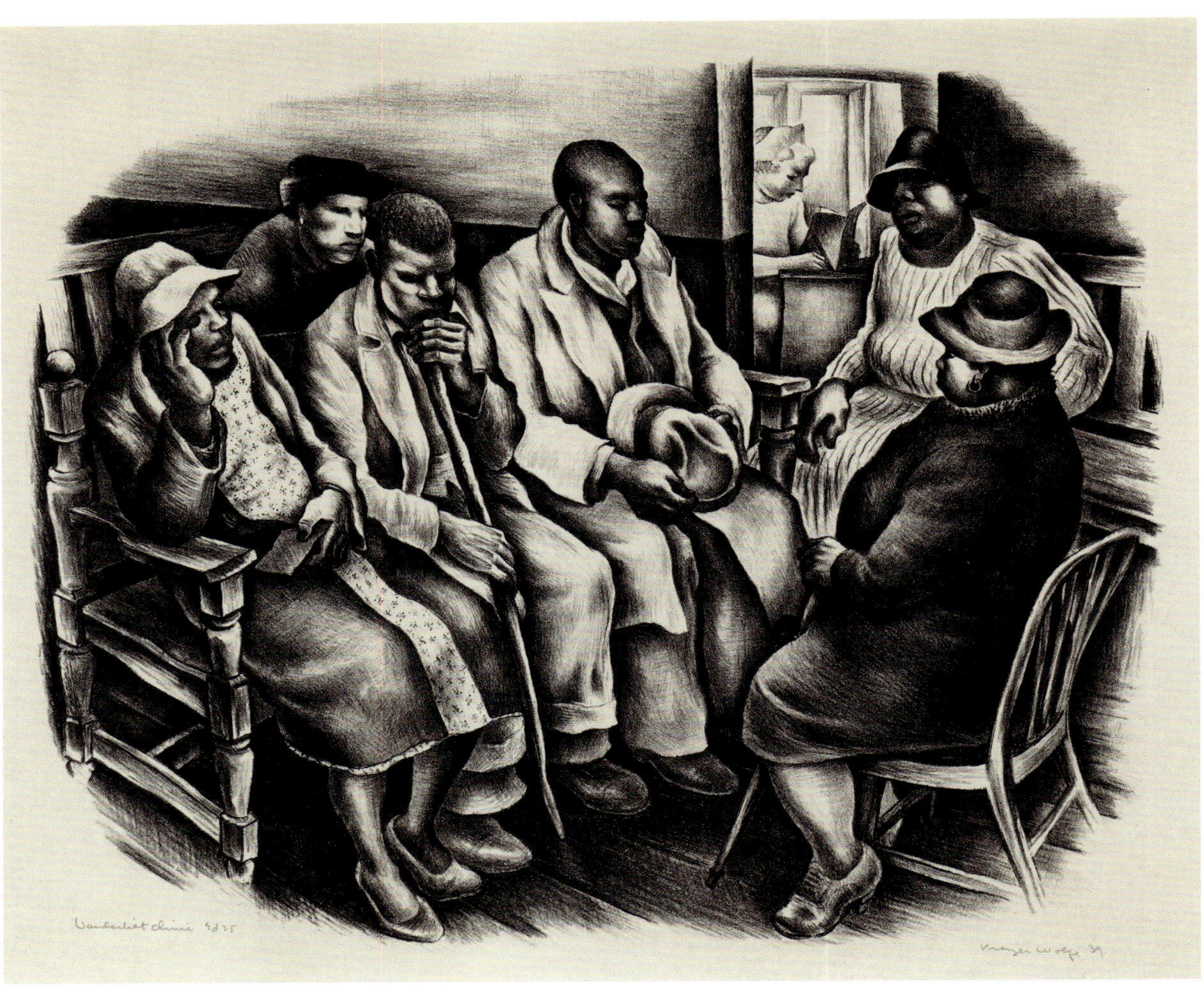

Cat. 20. Meyer Wolfe, *Brother Matthew Preaching*, 1941

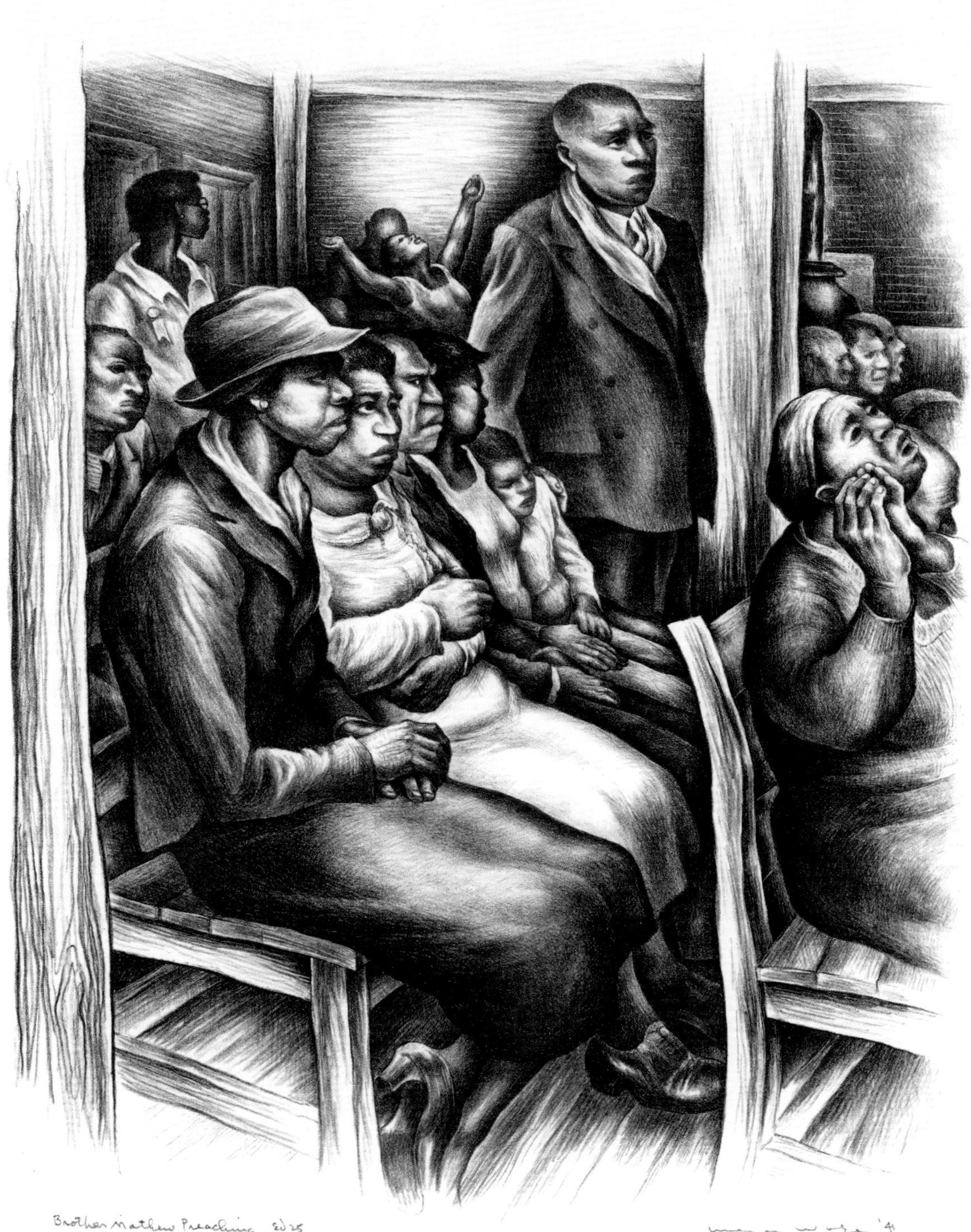

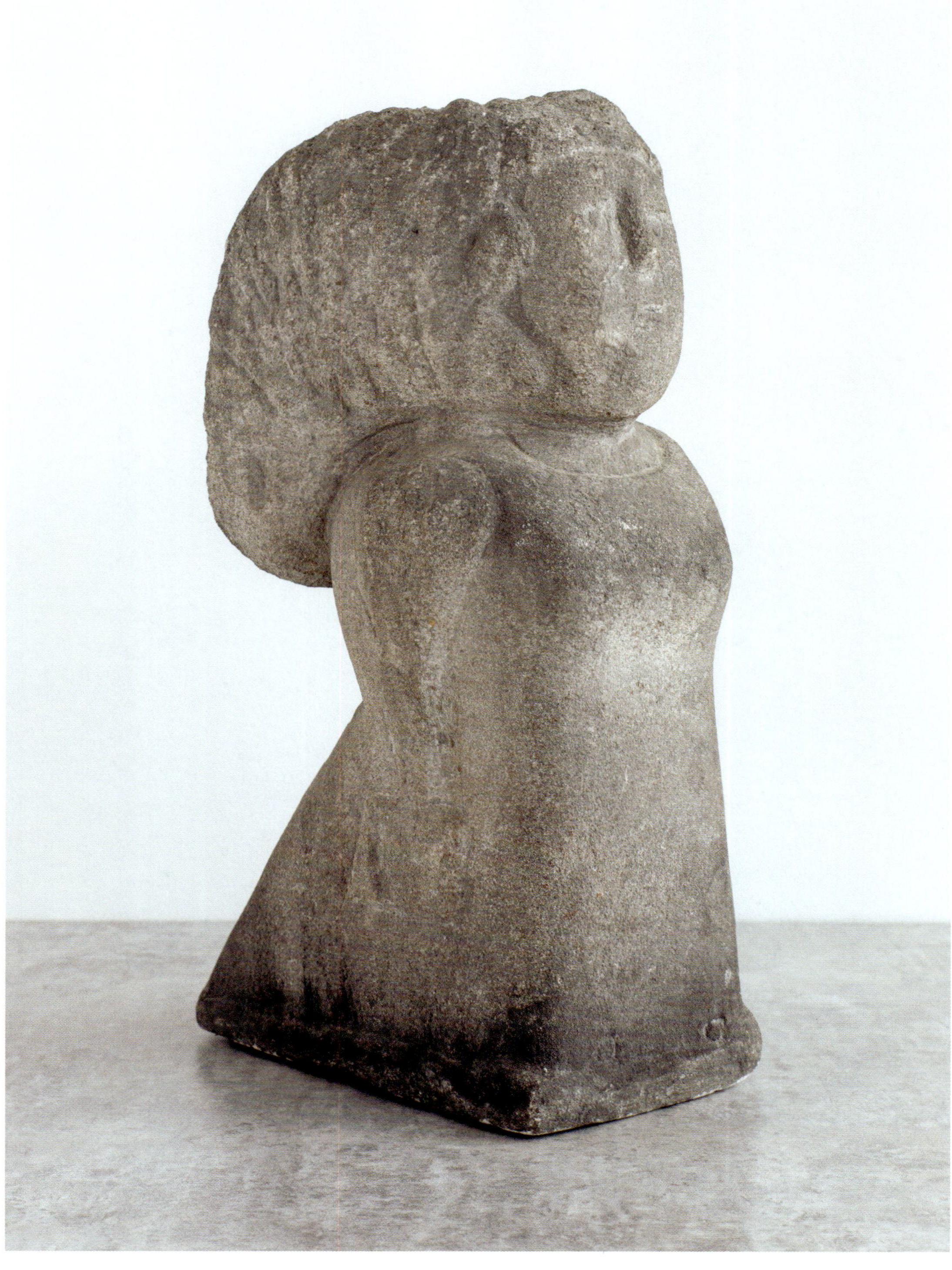

Cat. 21. William Edmondson, *Untitled (Schoolteacher)*, c. 1930–40

Edmondson's Stone Women

Renée Ater

Both secular and biblical representations of women populate the sculpture of William Edmondson: seated nudes, teachers, brides, nurses, church ladies, women in capes, women sitting on porches, numerous female angels, a singular Eve, and Martha and Mary sitting on sofas. In discarded blocks of limestone, Edmondson suggested women in motion going about their everyday activities, whether it be in the real or celestial realm. In 1937, Edmondson exhibited his sculpture in New York City at the Museum of Modern Art (MoMA). With interpretative clarity underscored by the cultural elitism of his time, Edwin Alden Jewell, the art critic for the *New York Times*, wrote of the MoMA exhibition, Edmondson's direct carvings, and the crossover between the secular and profane in his subject matter:

> Though all of them, no doubt, were done, in a sense, at Heaven's behest, some of the forms are purely secular—such, for instance, as the delicious "Two Women Seated on a Sofa," the forcefully, if crudely, stylized "Lady with a Cloak" and "Woman with a Bustle." . . . There appears, at any rate, no salient difference between mundane and celestial subjects; between the strong-minded "Bride" and the "Angel," whose strange pair of wings attached somewhere to the back alone denotes membership in the hierarchy of the skies.[1]

1. Edwin Alden Jewell, "Tennessee Negro Shows Sculpture: William Edmondson Displays Small Exhibition at Museum of Modern Art," *New York Times*, October 20, 1937.

Cat. 22. William Edmondson, *Lady with Two Pocketbooks*, n.d.

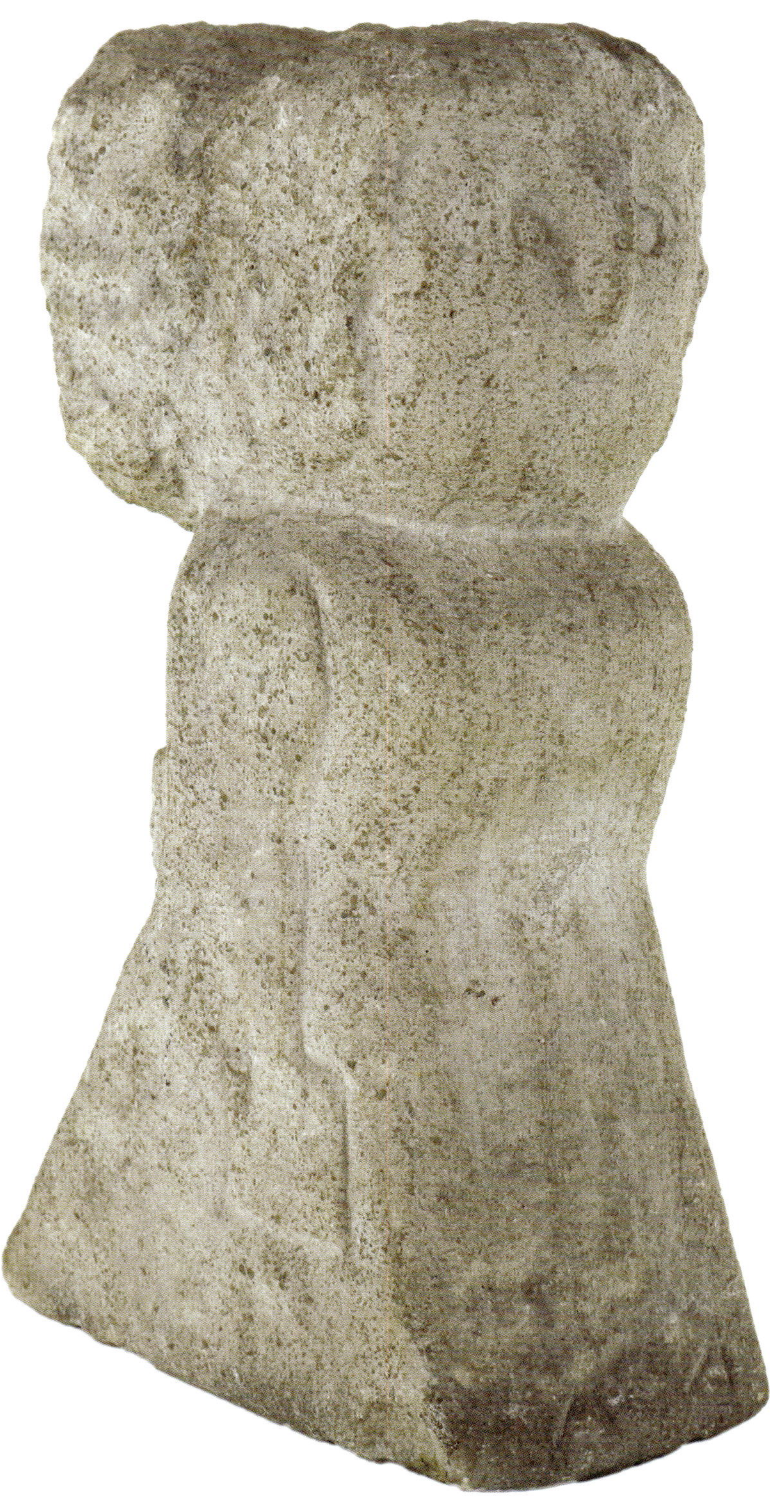

2. Alfred Barr quoted in "Modern Museum to Show Negro Art: Work of Unlettered Tombstone Cutter of Nashville, Tenn., to Be in One-Man Show," *New York Times*, October 9, 1937.
3. Bobby L. Lovett, "From Plantation to the City: William Edmondson and the African-American Community," in *The Art of William Edmondson* (Nashville, TN: Cheekwood Museum of Art, 1999), 20–21.

In another review of the MoMA exhibition, Alfred Barr, the first director of the museum, points to the importance of limestone as Edmondson's material and his ability to work directly in the material that is partially soluble: "Usually, the naïve artist works in the easier medium of painting. Edmondson, however, has chosen to work in limestone, which he attacks with extraordinary courage and directness to carve out simple, emphatic forms."[2] From the chalky limestone, Edmondson chiseled out the essential character of his sacred and everyday women: strong, forward moving, weighty, and determined.

I engage these stone women to talk about their visual impact and abundance in Edmondson's body of work. Riffing off Jewell's discussion of them as profane and sacred imaginings, I am interested in the ways Edmondson captured Black womanhood in his corner of Black Nashville: the church ladies, teachers, and neighbors who lived in the Vanderbilt-Belmont area along Edgehill Avenue (Fourteenth, Thirteenth, Eleventh, and Tenth Avenues South). Edmondson's neighborhood also included a number of all-Black congregations: Mount Sinai Primitive Baptist Church, Kayne Avenue Baptist Church, and the Bethel African Methodist Episcopal Church. Edmondson, as well as members of his family, was an active member of the Primitive Baptist Church.[3] On any given Sunday, Edmondson would have seen the women of his neighborhood finely dressed and heading to church, as well as women dressed in all white who were ushers and/or members of the church's nurses auxiliary. Reading through the lens of familial relations, I propose that Edmondson's ties to his sisters and nieces as well as his daily encounters with Black women in his community led to the abundance of representations of women in his work and reveal his appreciation and celebration of their difference from him.

Edmondson had strong relationships with the women in his family. He had four siblings as well as a half-sister: Sarah (b. 1869), Richard (b. 1875), Orange Jr. (b. 1879), James (b. 1881), and Ellen Brown (b. 1864). Once the siblings moved from the former Compton plantation to Nashville in 1890, they worked as domestic and manual laborers. They also maintained intimate ties to each other, living in close proximity, attending church together, and even sharing the raising of children.

After the death of his mother in 1922, William's sister Sarah moved in with him to keep house as Edmondson never married. Sarah has been described as "an expert cook who loved to have barbecues" and someone who thrived on her big family: "she frequently invited the entire Edmondson clan and friends to walk over for an evening of eating, drinking, laughter, cards, and storytelling in William's huge yard." [4] Ellen Brown's youngest daughter, Mary Jane Johnson, also lived with William and Sarah, and they both helped to raise her. Deep affection and commitment shaped the Edmondson family.

Curator Rusty Freeman points to the power of Edmondson's work within his community, writing, "Edmondson's work is filled with folk motifs, real people, and mythological characters that reveal him to be a vibrant voice of his community ideals and an immortalizer of its most important heroes."[5] Edmondson's renderings of teachers and nurses highlight the importance of these women within the Black community. As historian Carter Julian Savage writes, African Americans came together in post–Civil War Nashville to found Black schools in the city and in the surrounding rural areas because they were restricted from attending white schools: "Many Nashville schools turned their attention to developing an army of African American teachers who would move into the countryside to teach literacy and morality to the freed men and women. The normal schools programs at Fisk, Central Tennessee State, Walden, and Roger Williams Universities sent scores of their graduates to teaching positions in surrounding counties of Middle Tennessee." [6] Education became one tool by which Black Nashville sought to transform itself on the way to middle-class standing.

Edmondson's limestone teachers reveal this rise of the Black teacher in Nashville and the surrounding areas. Although diminutive, *Schoolteacher* (Cat. 24) conveys Edmondson's appreciation for these professional women educators. Carved with tight curls around her face, the Black teacher wears a long dress with a lace collar. In one hand, she holds the attribute of her labor: a book or sheaf of papers. Despite its small size, the stone sculpture conveys the agency of the teacher and her power to educate despite racism, Jim Crow, and unequal

4. Lovett, "From Plantation to the City," 22.
5. Rusty Freeman, "Community Heroes in the Sculpture of William Edmondson," in *The Art of William Edmondson* (Nashville, TN: Cheekwood Museum of Art, 1999), 33.
6. Carter Julian Savage, "'Because We Did More with Less': The Agency of African American Teachers in Franklin, Tennessee: 1890–1967," *Peabody Journal of Education* 76, no. 2 (2001): 171.

Cat. 23. Louise Dahl-Wolfe, *William Edmondson, Sculptor, Nashville, Tennessee*, 1937

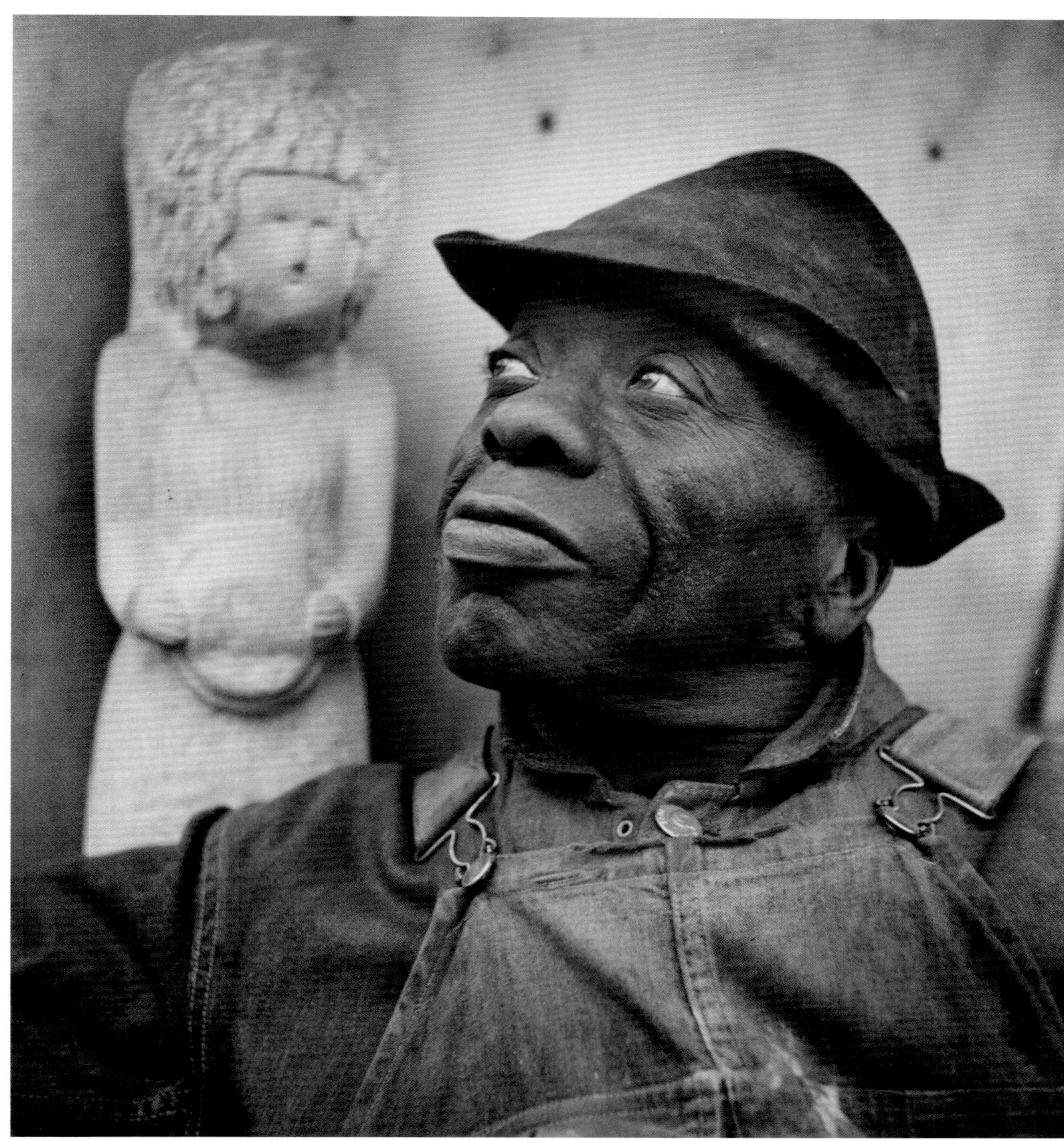

allocation of resources. These Black women educators were the heroes of their communities and faced insurmountable odds to achieve their goals. "Answering the community's call, African American teachers embarked on a journey that required them to combat the impact of segregation and oppression at a variety of levels," states historian Sonya Ramsey.

Cat. 24. William Edmondson, *Schoolteacher*, c. 1937

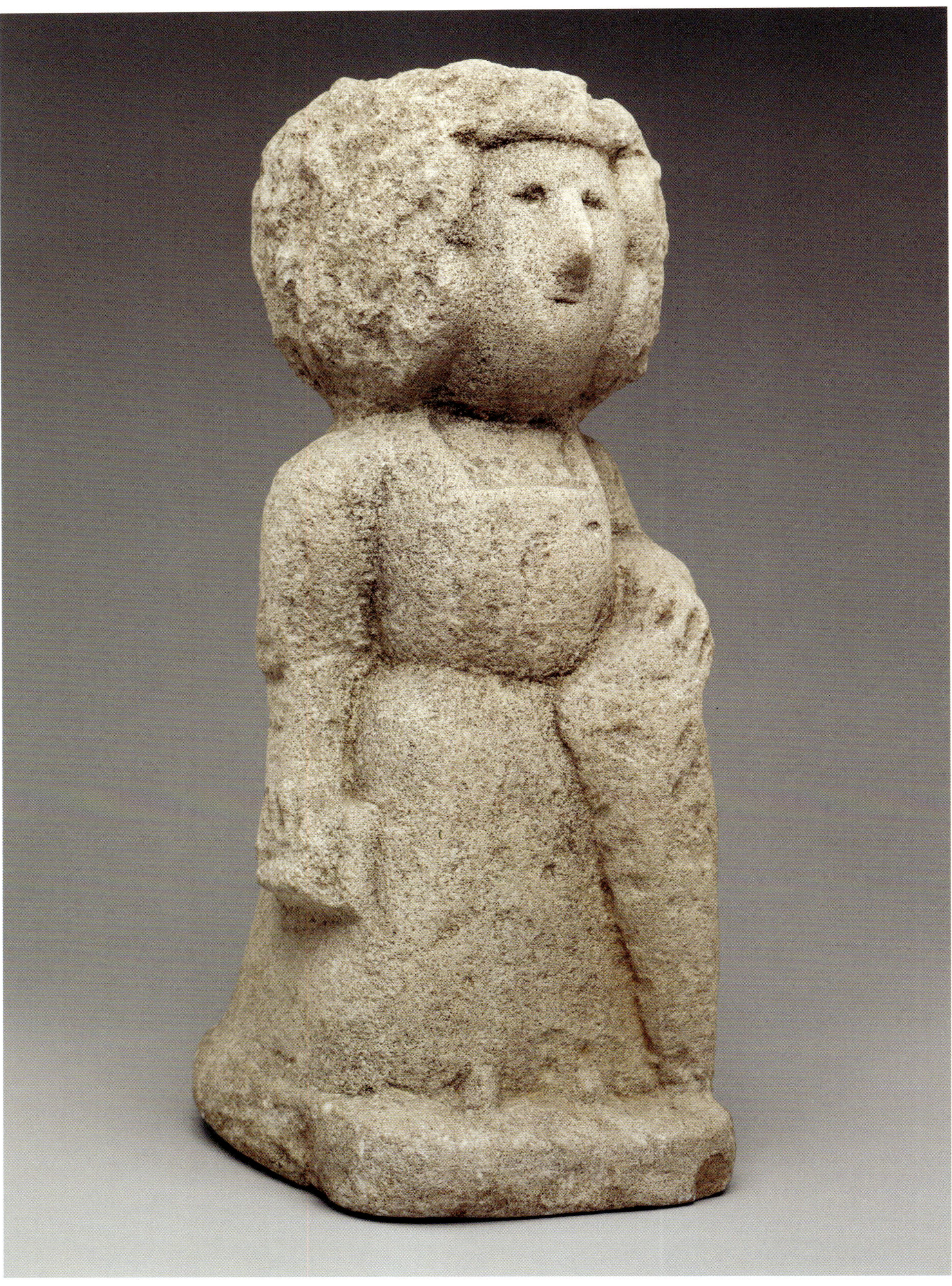

7. Sonya Ramsey, *Reading, Writing, and Segregation: A Century of Black Women Teachers in Nashville* (Urbana: University of Illinois Press, 2008), 2.
8. Evelyn Brooks Higginbotham, *Righteous Discontent: The Women's Movement in the Black Baptist Church, 1880–1920* (Cambridge, MA: Harvard University Press, 1993), 2.
9. Darlene Clark Hine, *Black Women in White: Racial Conflict and Cooperation in the Nursing Profession, 1890–1950.* (Bloomington: Indiana University Press, 1989), 9.

"Working against overwhelming circumstances, black women teachers . . . offered the black community the comfort of knowing that its children had caring and accountable instructors."[7] By the 1930s, Black female teachers were the majority of Black professional women in the city, visible in the classrooms and streets of Black Nashville. Edmondson's numerous sculptures mark these women educators as proud and dedicated leaders of the Black community.

Church ladies and nurses are also well represented in Edmondson's body of work. Sundays were important days in the Black community, and certainly for the Edmondson extended family, allowing them time to participate in service through song and worship, to share a meal together, and to prepare for the coming week. Most importantly, the Black church in the early twentieth century served as a key space for the work of racial self-help. Historian Evelyn Brooks Higginbotham writes of the importance of Black women in the transformation of the Black Baptist church, who, she argues, were engaged in "everyday forms of resistance to oppression and demoralization."[8] Black women assisted with fundraising efforts to build schools, to clothe and feed the poor, to establish orphanages and nursing homes, and to provide a variety of other social welfare services. Edmondson's *Church Lady* (fig. 12) reveals such a woman of faith. Attired in a dress with bow and long coat, *Church Lady* holds a purse in one hand and a Bible in the other. Resting jauntily atop her short wavy hair is a hat with a snood. Here, with economy of carving, Edmondson has captured not only a Black churchgoer in her finery but also a woman of integrity: dedicated and stalwart in her faith.

Nurses abound in his work and can be seen in the numerous photographs of his yard. For nearly twenty-five years Edmondson worked at Nashville's Woman's Hospital. During the 1890s and into the early twentieth century, a dozen Black hospitals and nurse training schools were founded, including the Hubbard Hospital and School of Nursing at Meharry Medical College in Nashville.[9] As nursing became professionalized and moved from a low-status occupation "too frequently associated with domestic drudgery and with uneducated and unrefined women," more Black women entered the

Fig. 11. William Edmondson, *Schoolteacher*, 1935. Limestone, 14 ⅛ × 4 ⅝ × 7 ¾ in. National Gallery of Art, Washington, DC, Corcoran Collection (Gift of David and Renee McKee), 2015.19.3920

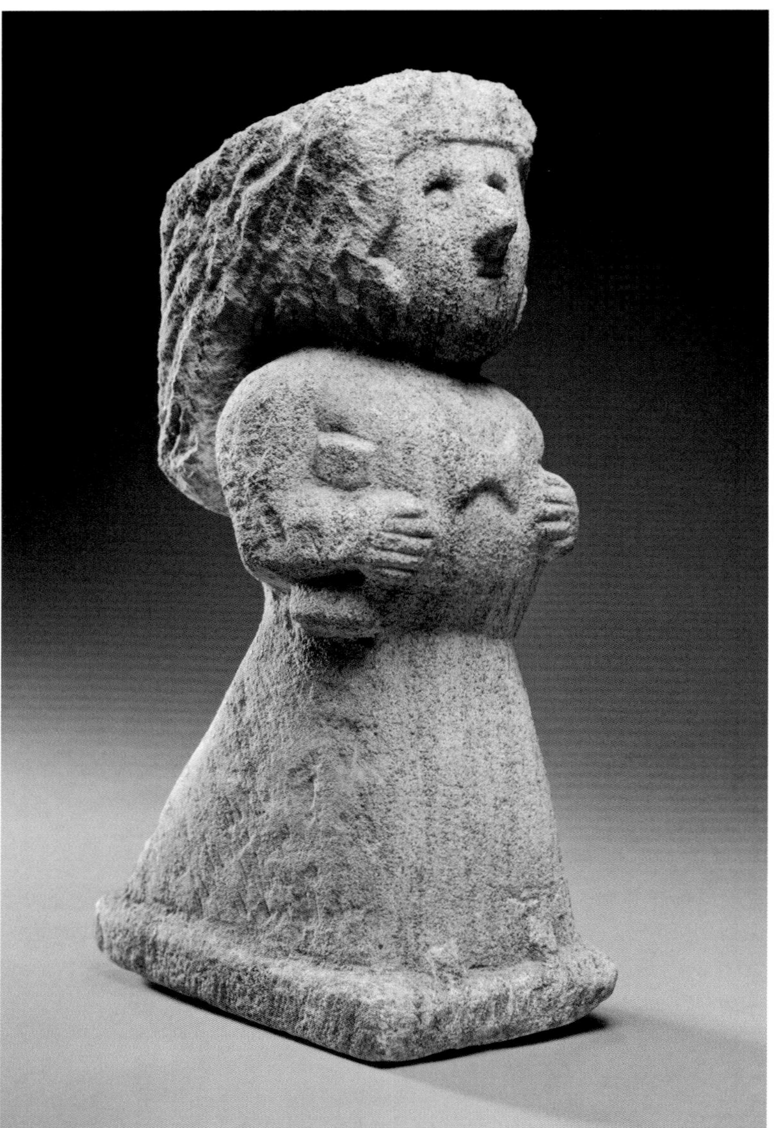

profession.[10] Black nurses fought hard and long for professional status, and as Stephanie Shaw notes, the Black community was the first to recognize these women.[11]

Edmondson's statues of nurses certainly indicate this admiration; I am suggesting here that many of his nurses are Black women due to their hairstyles.[12] In *Nurse* (fig. 13), Edmondson used the block of limestone to honor the seated nurse. With a white nurse's cap on her curly head, she sits in full uniform with one hand across her stomach, her gaze resolutely frontal. In another *Nurse* statue (fig. 14), Edmondson revels in

10. Hine, *Black Women in White*, 89. See also Stephanie J. Shaw, *What a Woman Ought to Be and to Do: Black Professional Women Workers during the Jim Crow Era* (Chicago: University of Chicago Press, 1996), 138–55.
11. Shaw, *What a Woman Ought to Be and Do*, 149.
12. See Freeman, "Community Heroes," 37. He reproduces pages from the *Nashville Globe* that show a range of Black women's hairstyles.

Fig. 12. William Edmondson, *Church Lady*, c. 1933–37. Limestone, 19 ½ × 7 ⅞ × 7 ⅞ in. Art Institute of Chicago, Through prior acquisition of the George F. Harding Collection, 2014.4.

Fig. 13. William Edmondson, *Nurse*, late 1930s. Limestone, 22 × 7 × 11 in. High Museum of Art, purchase with Fay and Barrett Howell Fund. High Museum of Art, Atlanta, 1983.61.

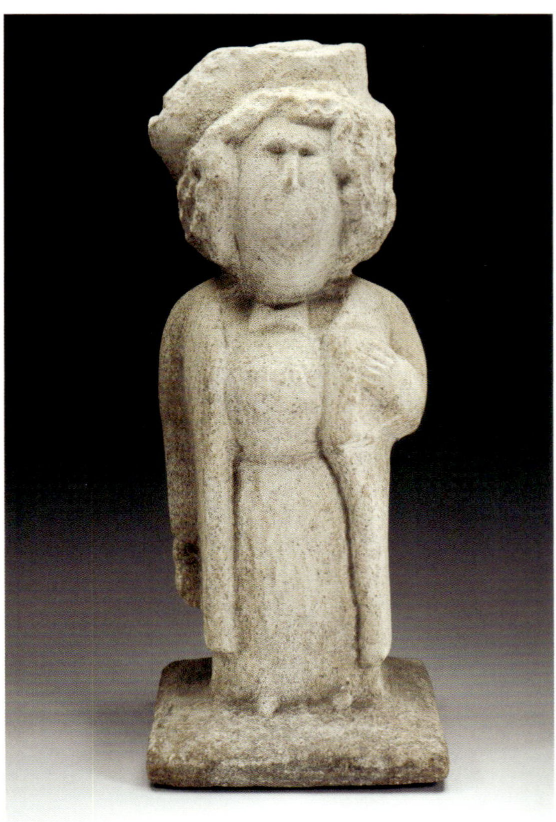

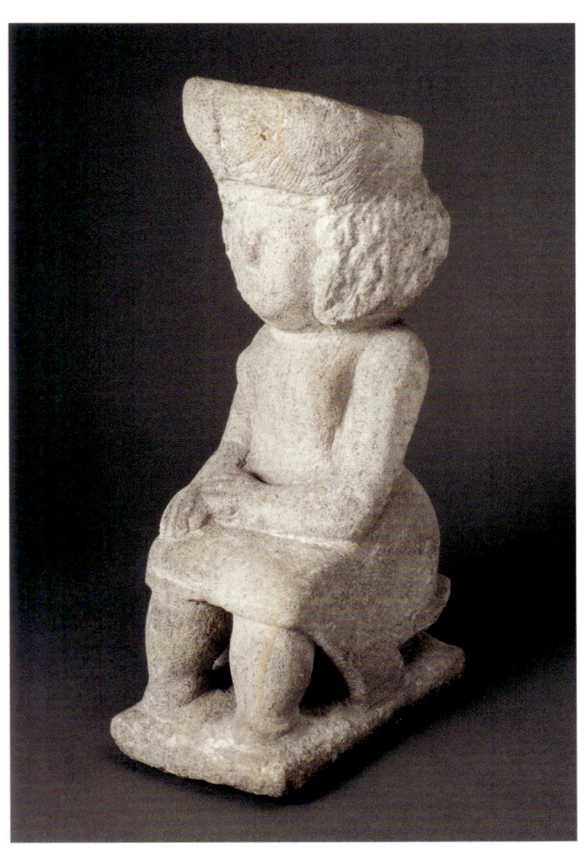

her geometric form. Maintaining the rectangular shape of the block, he carved the woman with her arms flattened to her side; in one hand she carries a clipboard or medical file. Her clothing is suggested by the rectangular shape of her breasts and the triangular shape of her skirt. Her oversized head is covered in drilled curly hair and what appears to be a bun at the back of her head. She is small and contained, conveying self-possession.

As Jewell observed, Edmondson often blurred the line between "the mundane and celestial." His quotidian angels with their curly, kinky tresses and weighty wings, some carrying pocketbooks and wearing short skirts, share much with his teachers and nurses. Modest and demure with their arms crossed in front, the angels' physicality in limestone suggests a worldly realm and the dignity of Black woman. Historian Robert Farris Thompson has noted that these are no ordinary angels of innocence and eternity. He writes, "Edmondson's angels sustain their role differently. Their stare is frontal. . . .

Fig. 14. William Edmondson, *Nurse*, c. 1940. Limestone, 11 ½ × 2 ¾ × 6 ¾ in. Museum of Fine Arts, Boston, The John Axelrod Collection—Frank B. Bemis Fund, Charles H. Bayley Fund, and The Heritage Fund for a Diverse Collection, 2011.1811.

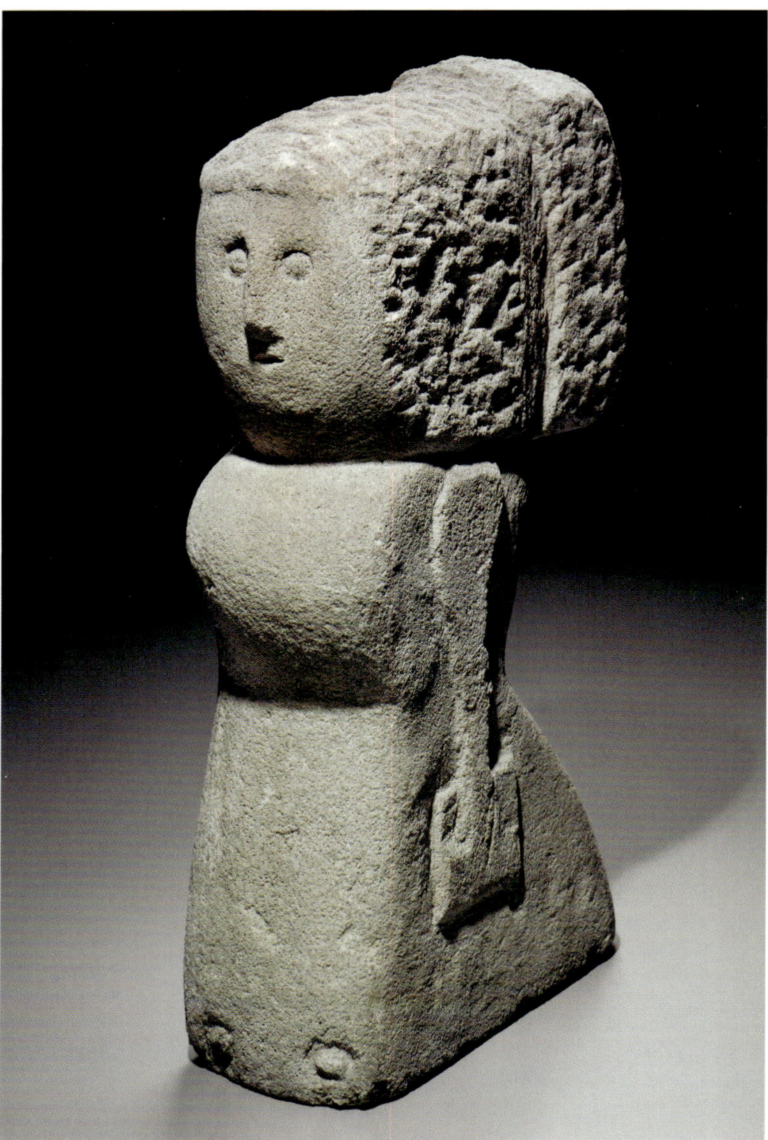

Feathered wings disappear. In their place are textured shield-like structures or textured caves of space. Draped clothes become cylinders. Edmondson's angels confront the world as solid ministers of protective grace."[13] He continues by proposing that these angels are "old-time religion angels, earthily realized, right now messengers of God." Although solemn representations of supernatural beings, these angels also suggest that Black women are the everyday attendants of God, as are his numerous teachers and nurses. In his yard, Edmondson placed Black women front and center, part of the essential social fabric of Black life in Nashville.

13. Robert Ferris Thompson, "Edmondson's Art," in *The Art of William Edmondson* (Nashville, TN: Cheekwood Museum of Art, 1999), 9.

Fig. 15. William Edmondson, *Angel*, 1932–38. Limestone, 25 × 13 ⅞ × 6 ⅝ in. Newark Museum of Art, Newark. Bequest of Edmund L. Fuller Jr., 1985, 85.30.

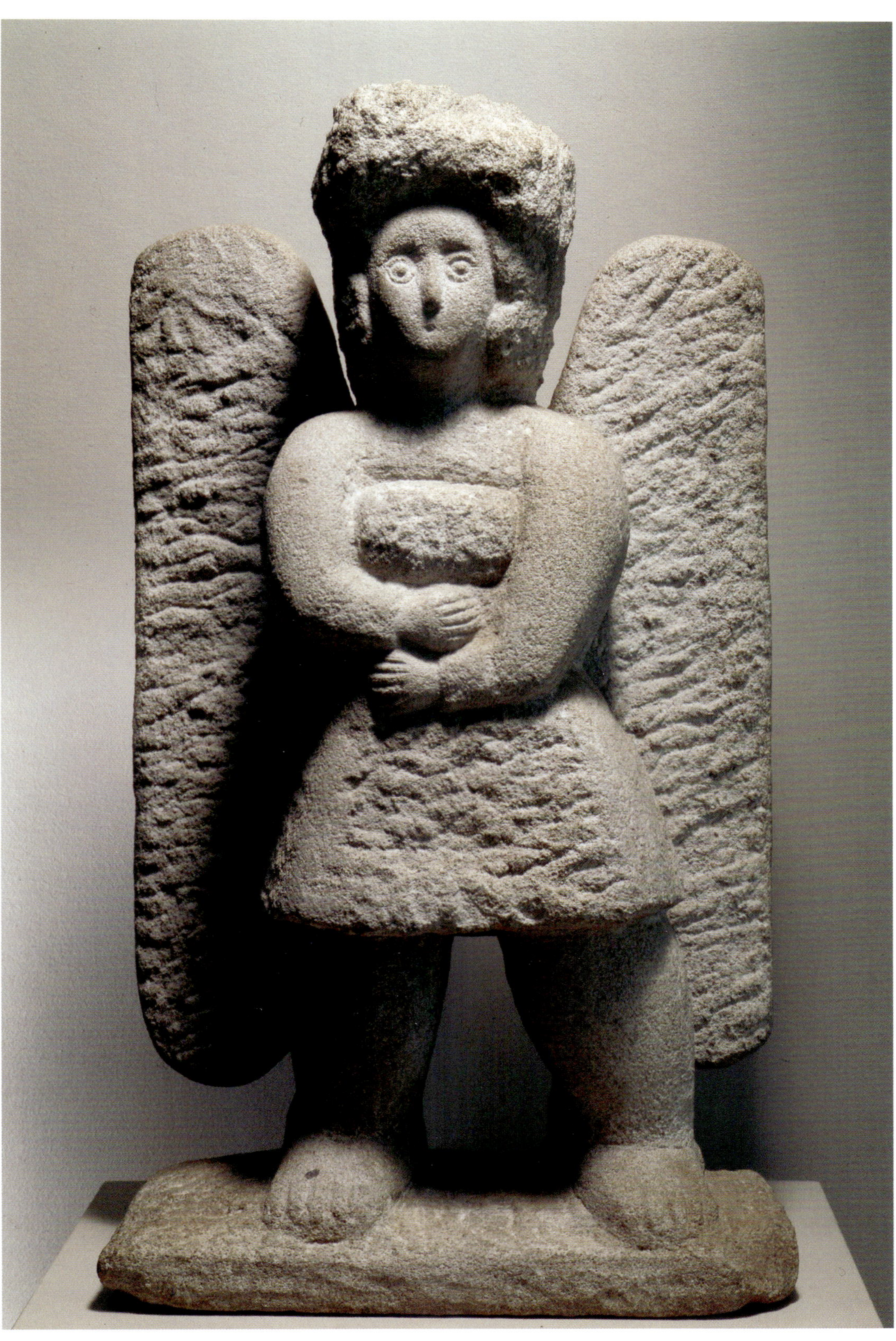

Cat. 25. William Edmondson, *Angel*, 1937–39

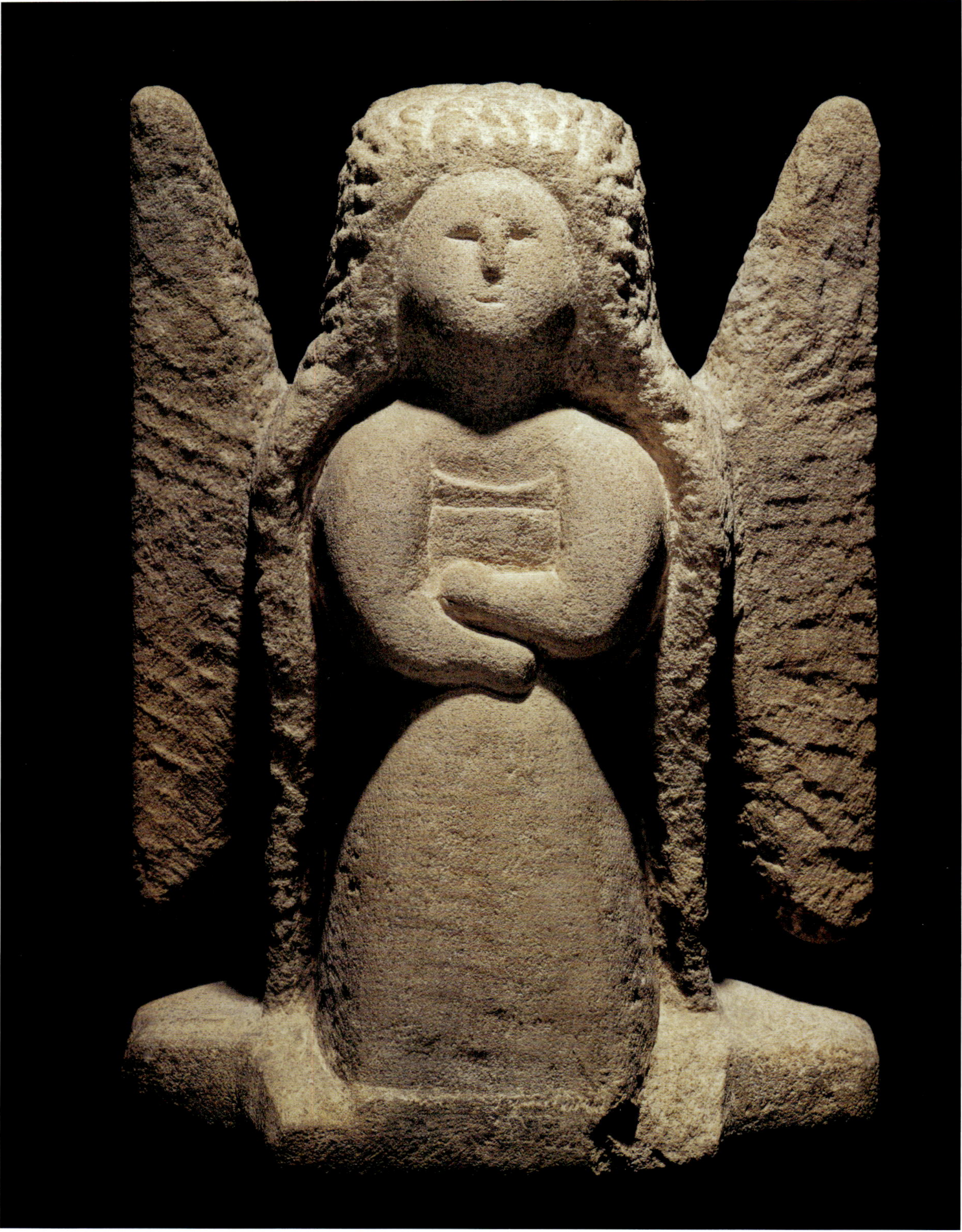

Cat. 26. William Edmondson, *Seated Girl with Folded Legs*, 1934–41

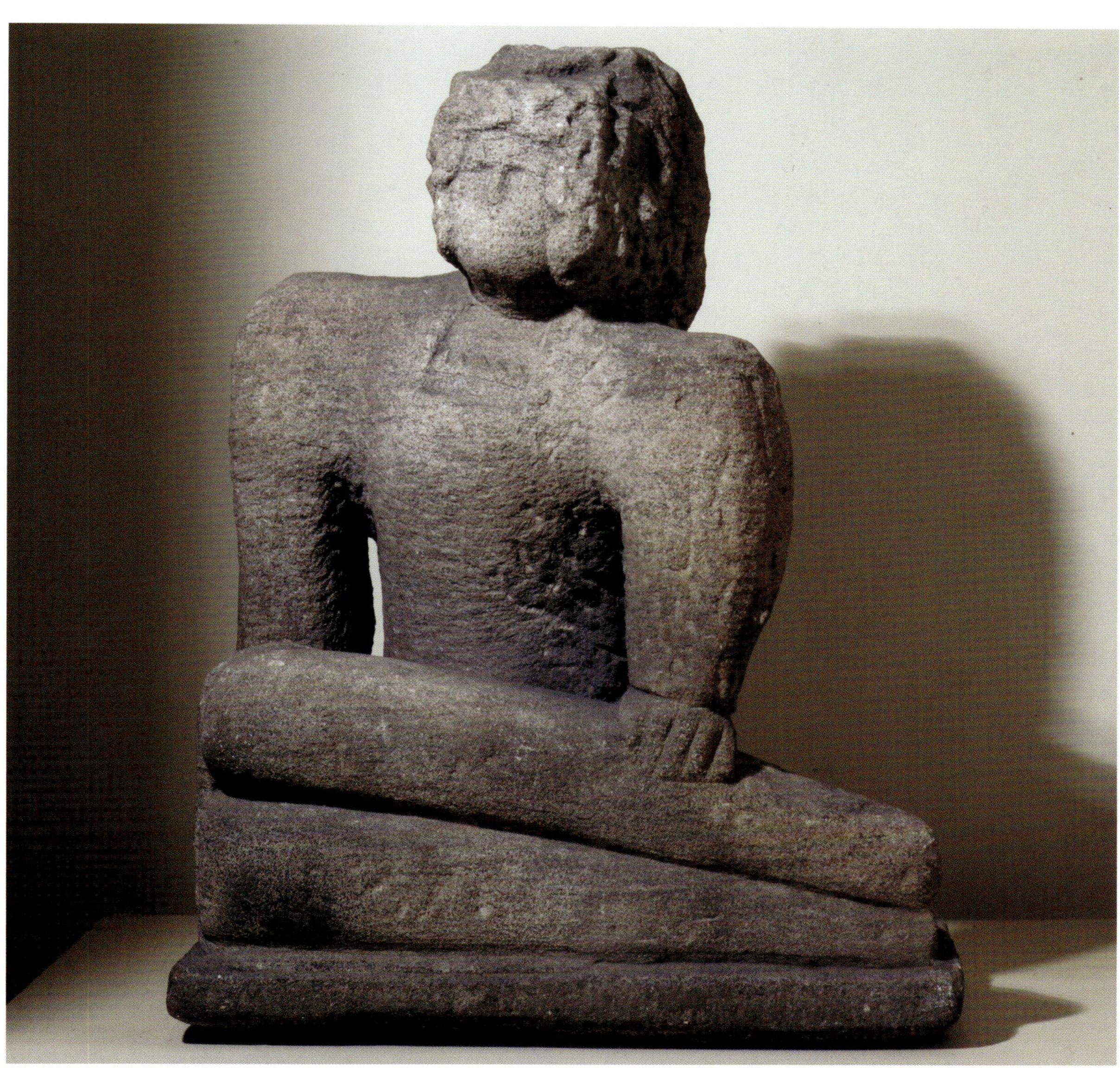

Cat. 27. William Edmondson, *Untitled (Seated Girl)*, c. 1940

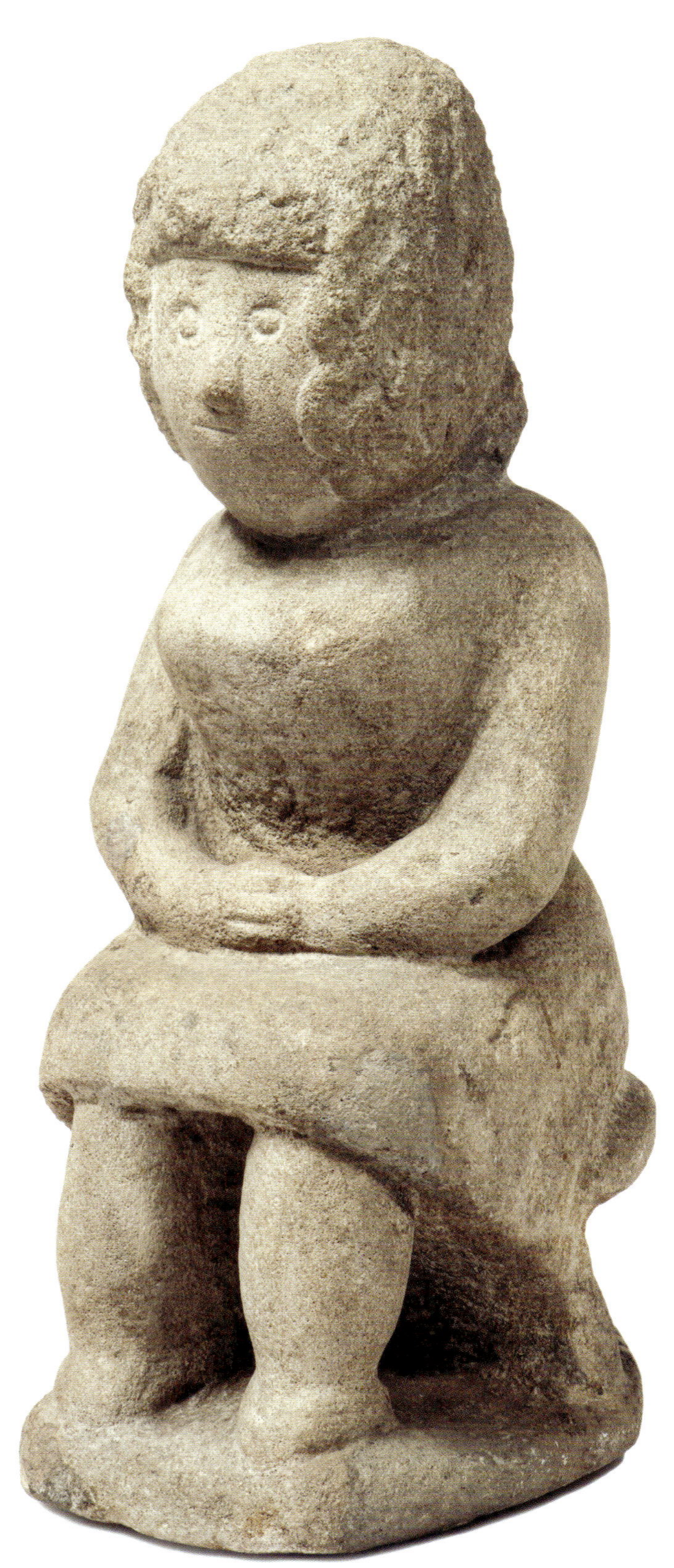

Cat. 28. William Edmondson, *Girl with a Cape*, n.d.

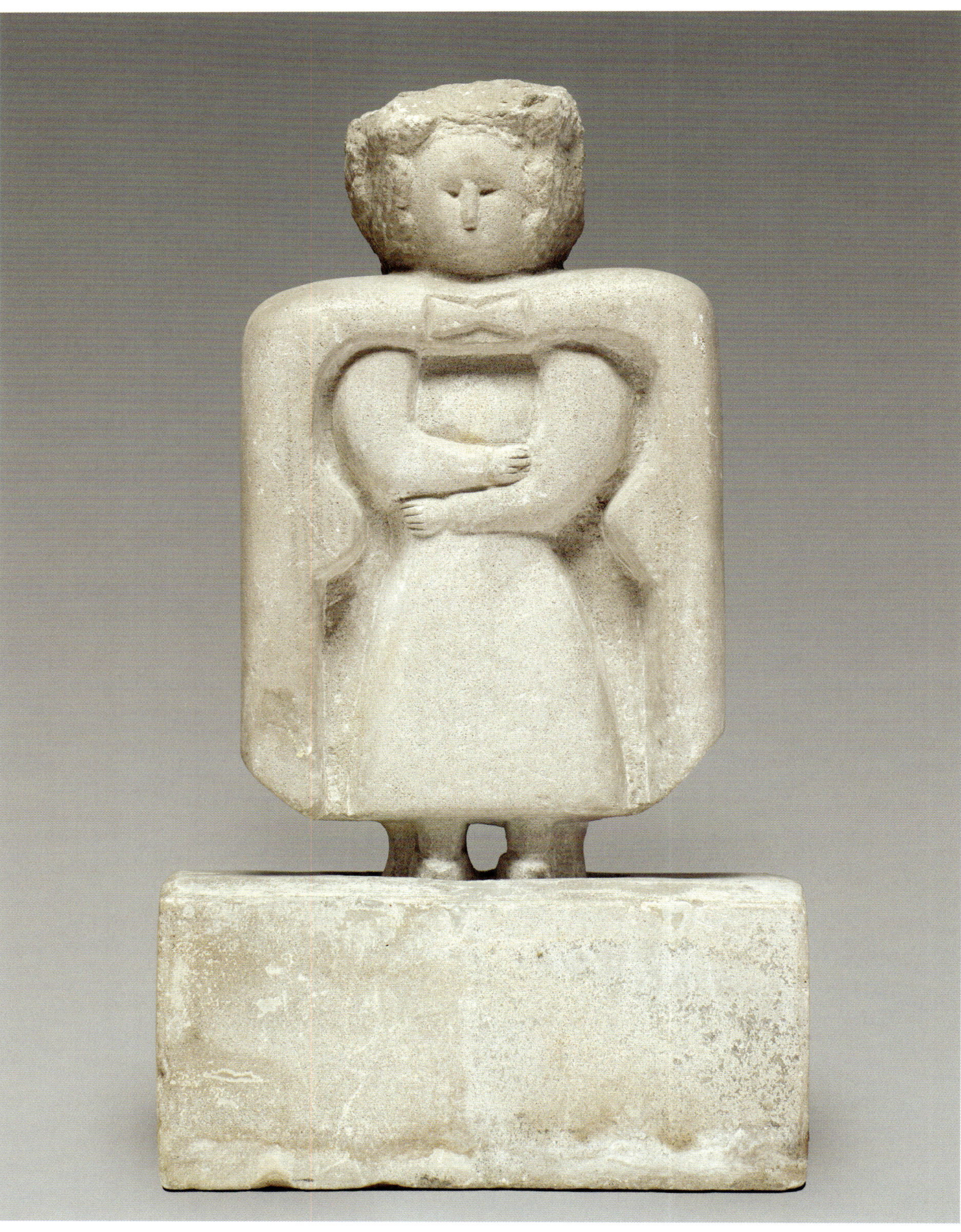

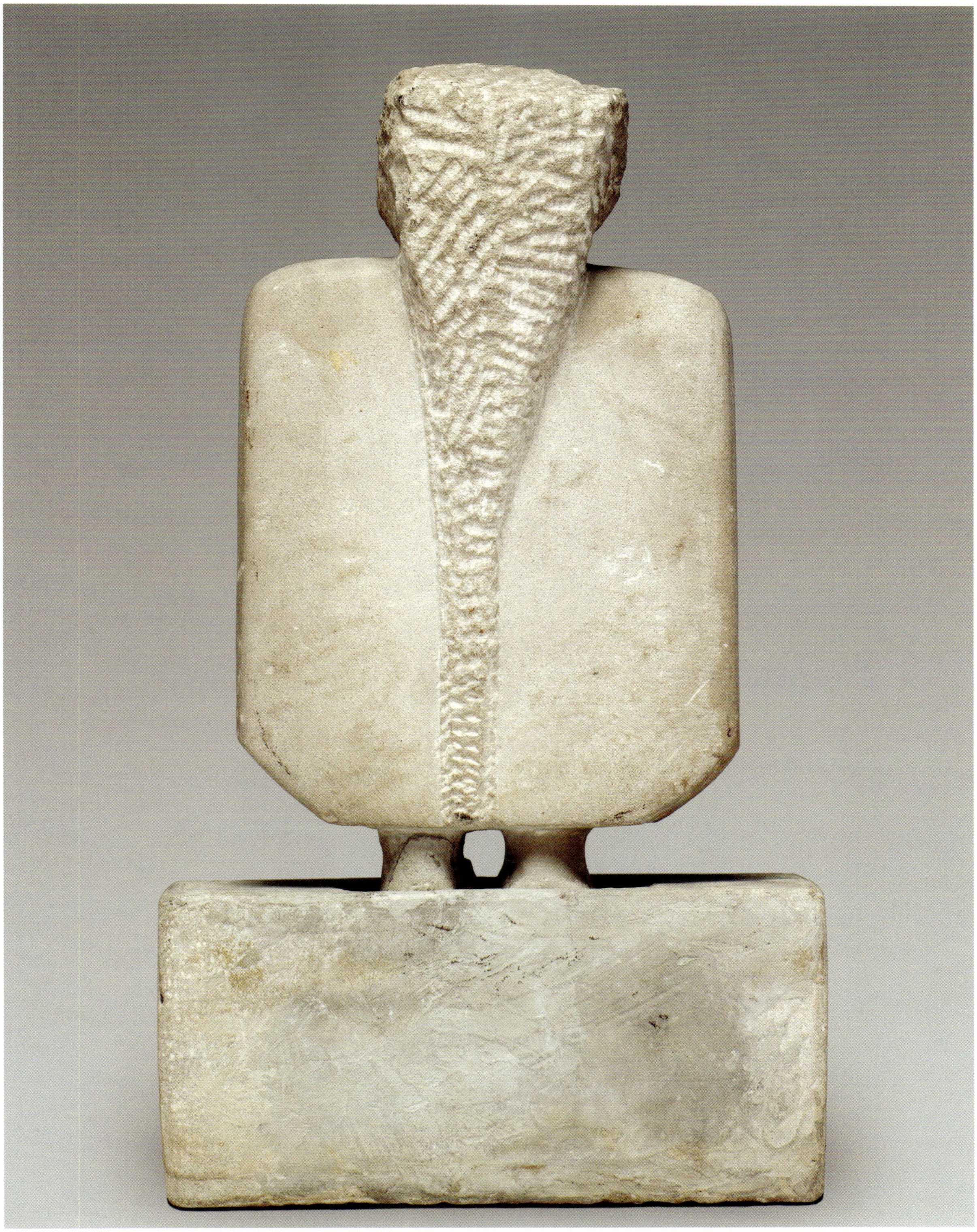

Cat. 29. Louise Dahl-Wolfe, *Sculpture, William Edmondson (Girl with a Cape)*, 1937

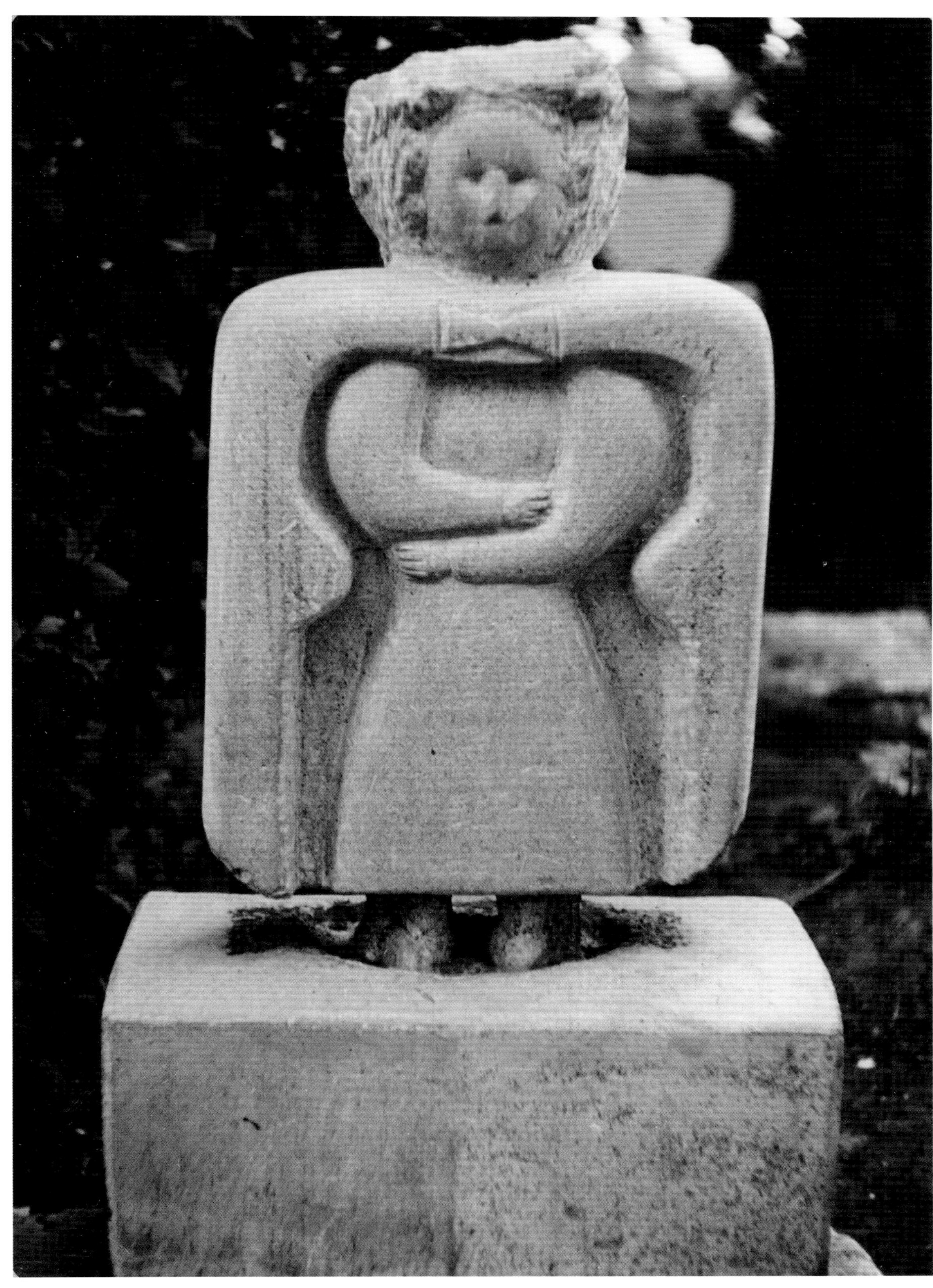

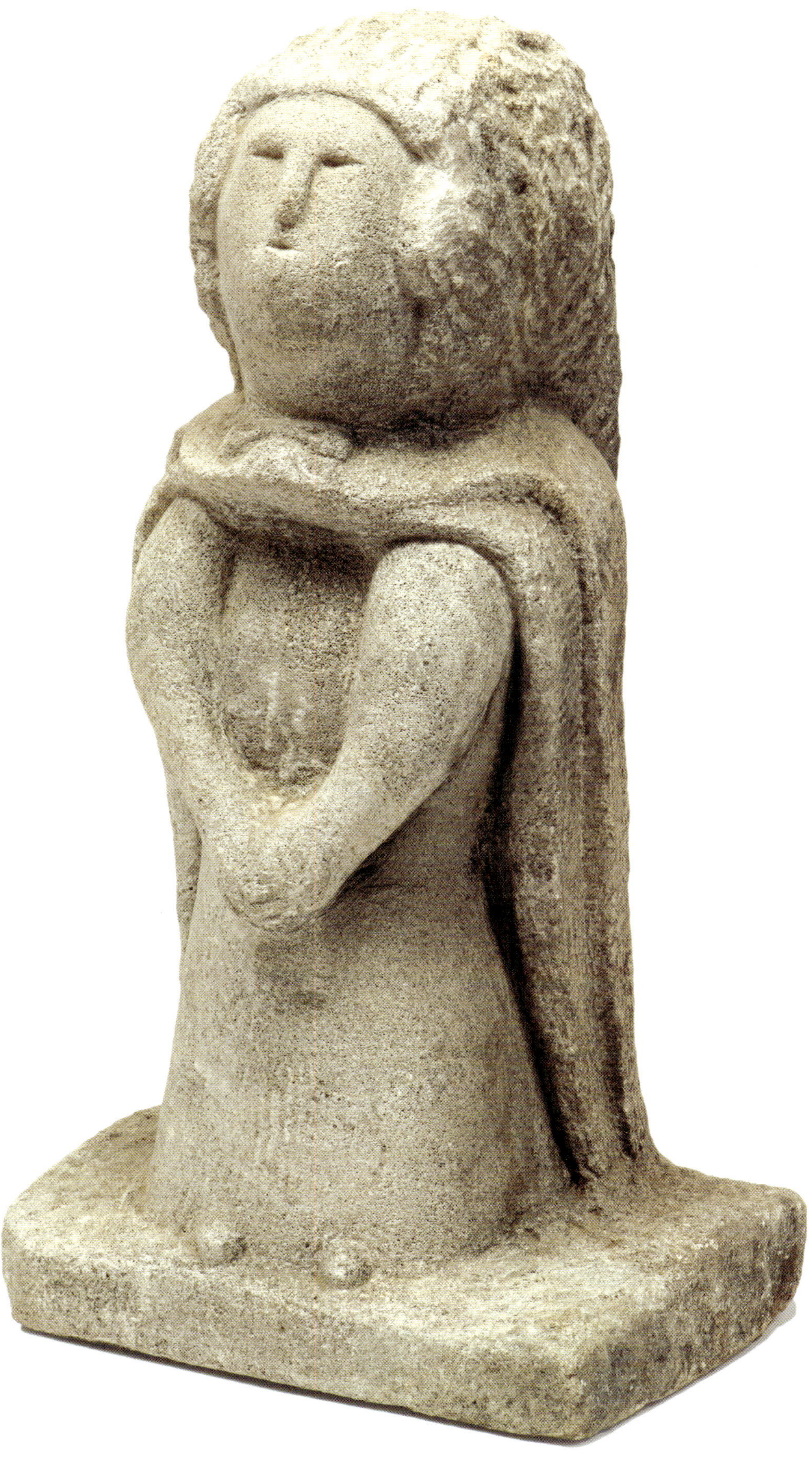

Cat. 30. (Verso) William Edmondson, *Lady with Cape*, c. 1935–40

Cat. 31. (Below) William Edmondson, *Lady with Muff*, c. 1940

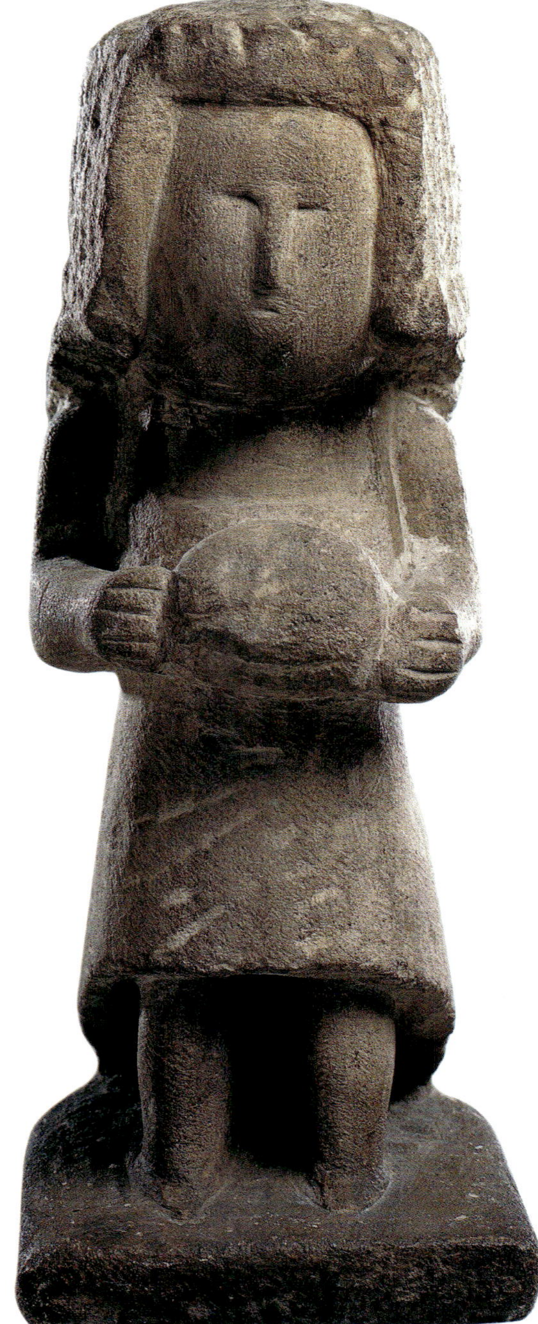

Cat. 32. William Edmondson, *Miss Amy*, c. 1935

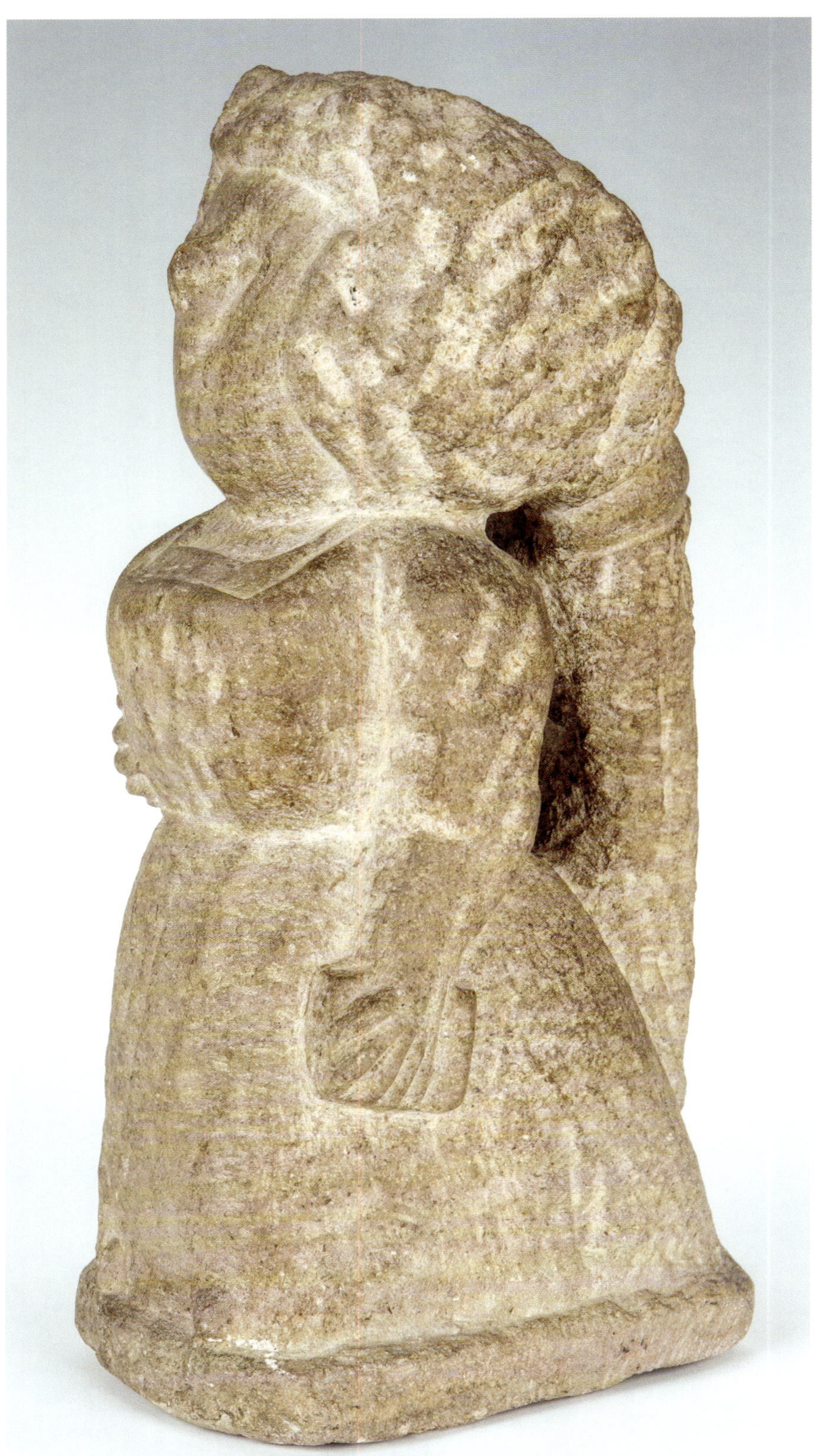

Cat. 33. William Edmondson, *Untitled*, n.d.

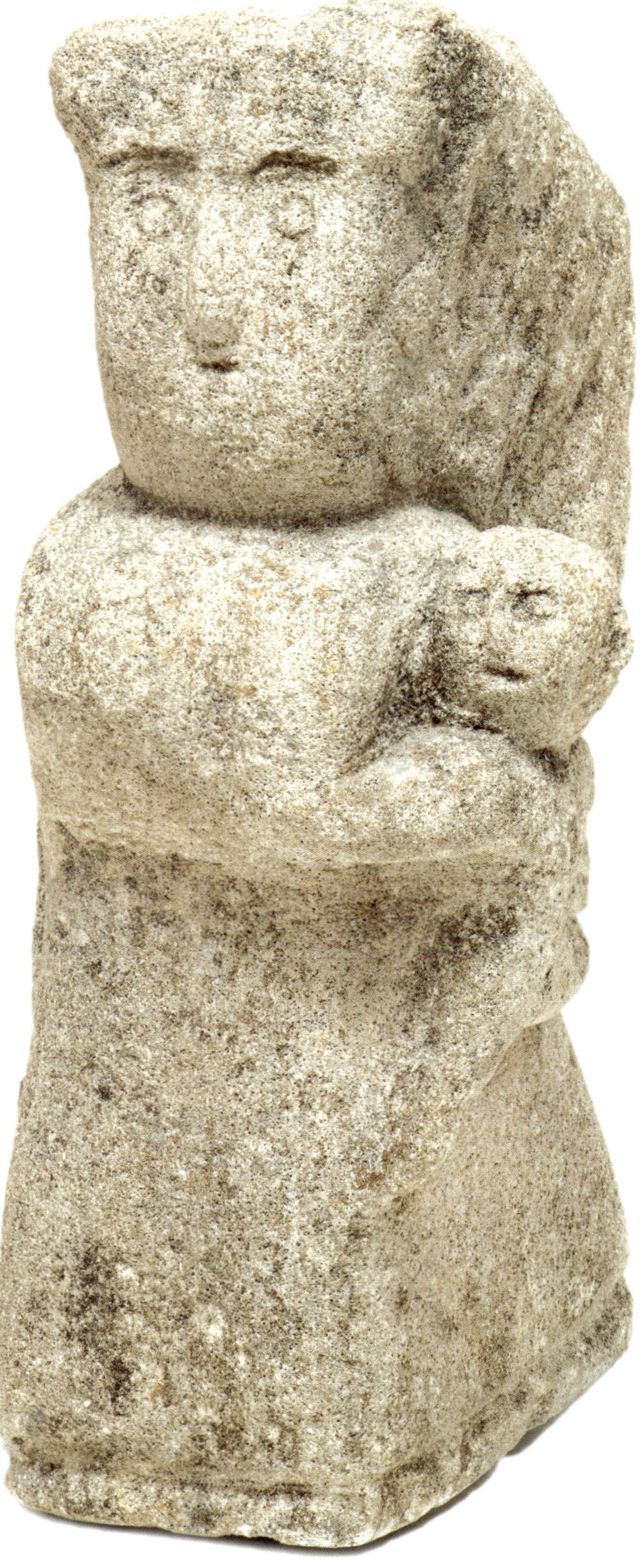

Cat. 34. William Edmondson, *Bride*, n.d.

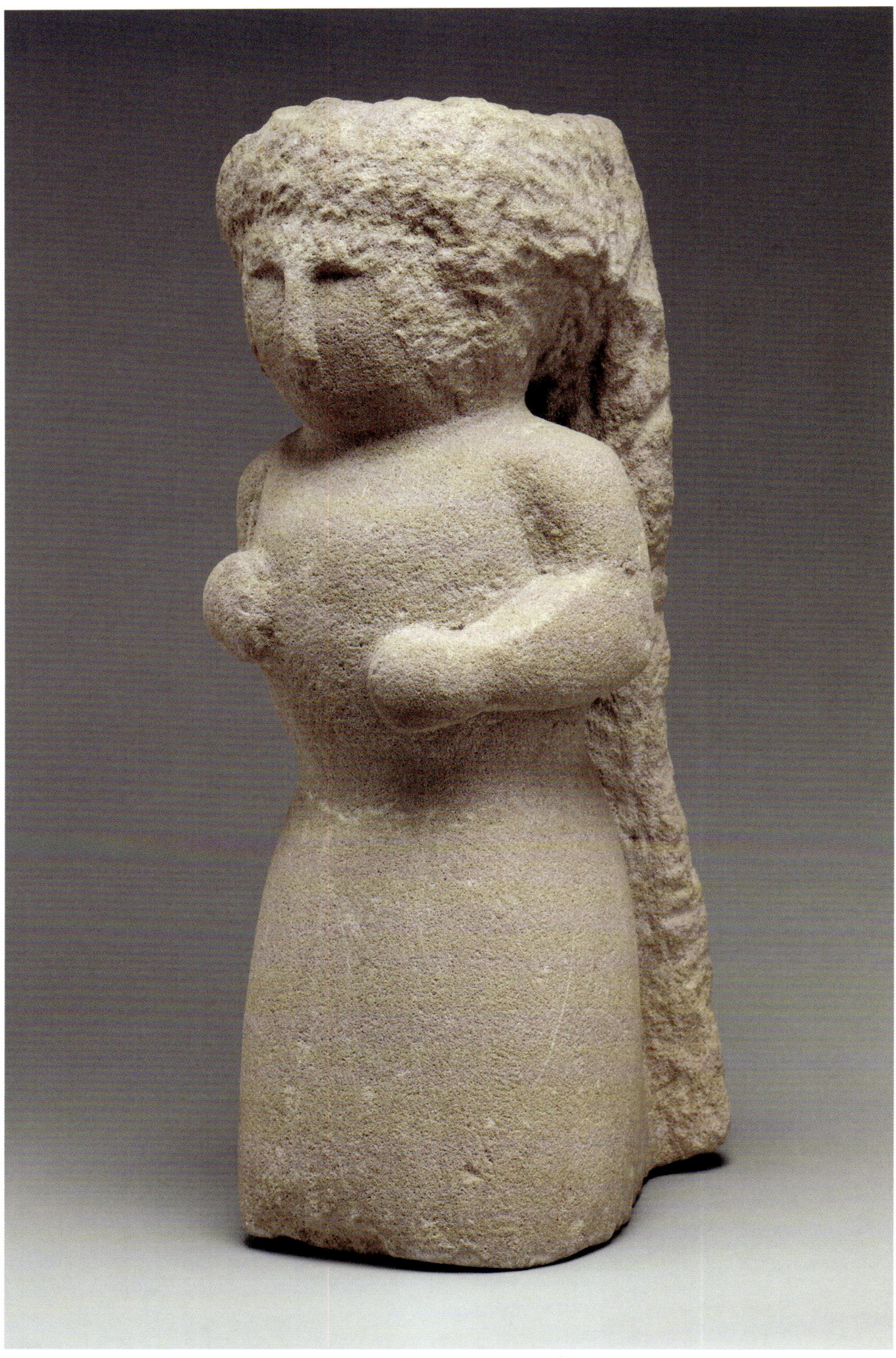

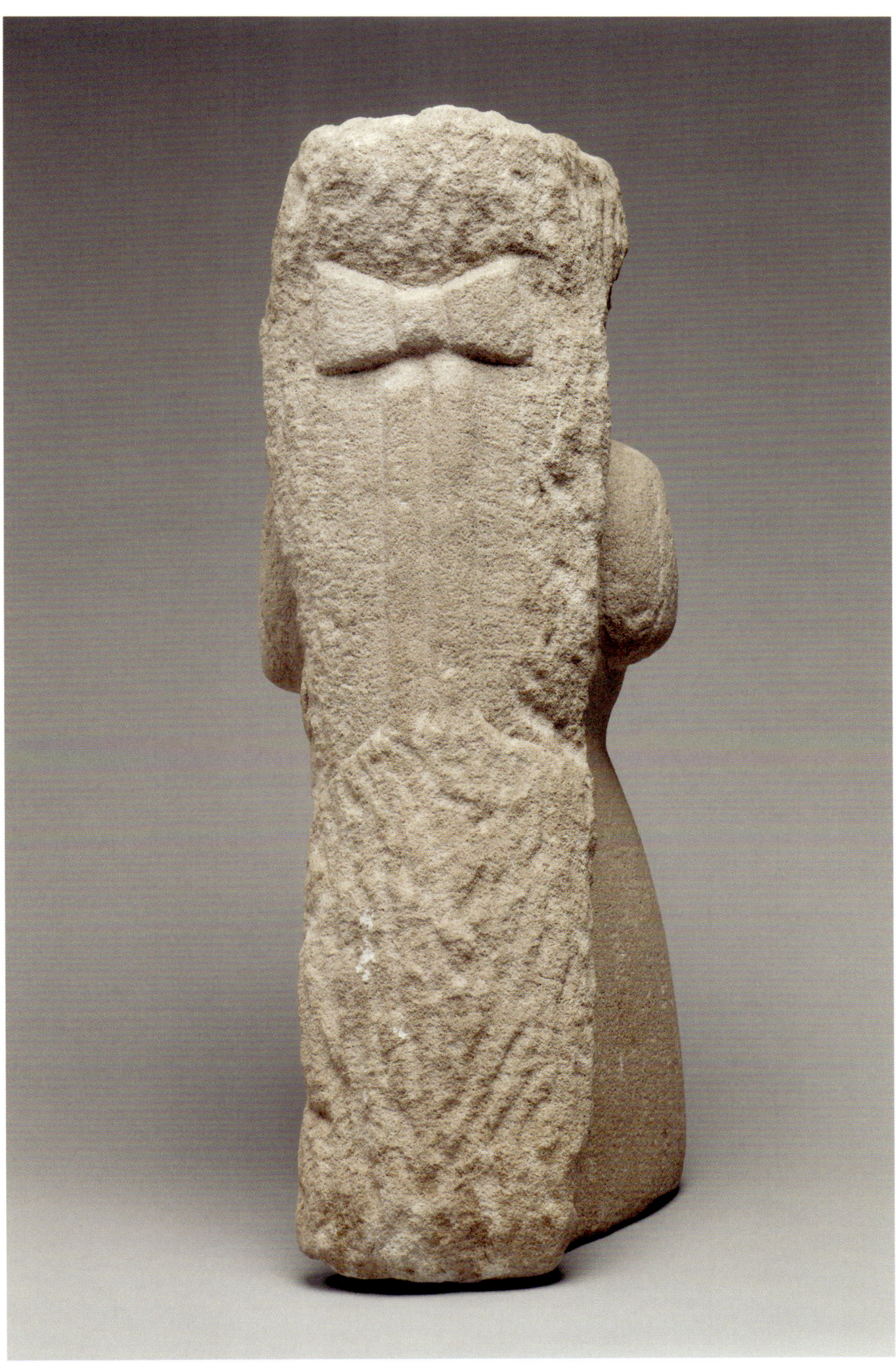

Cat. 35. William Edmondson, *Bride*, n.d.

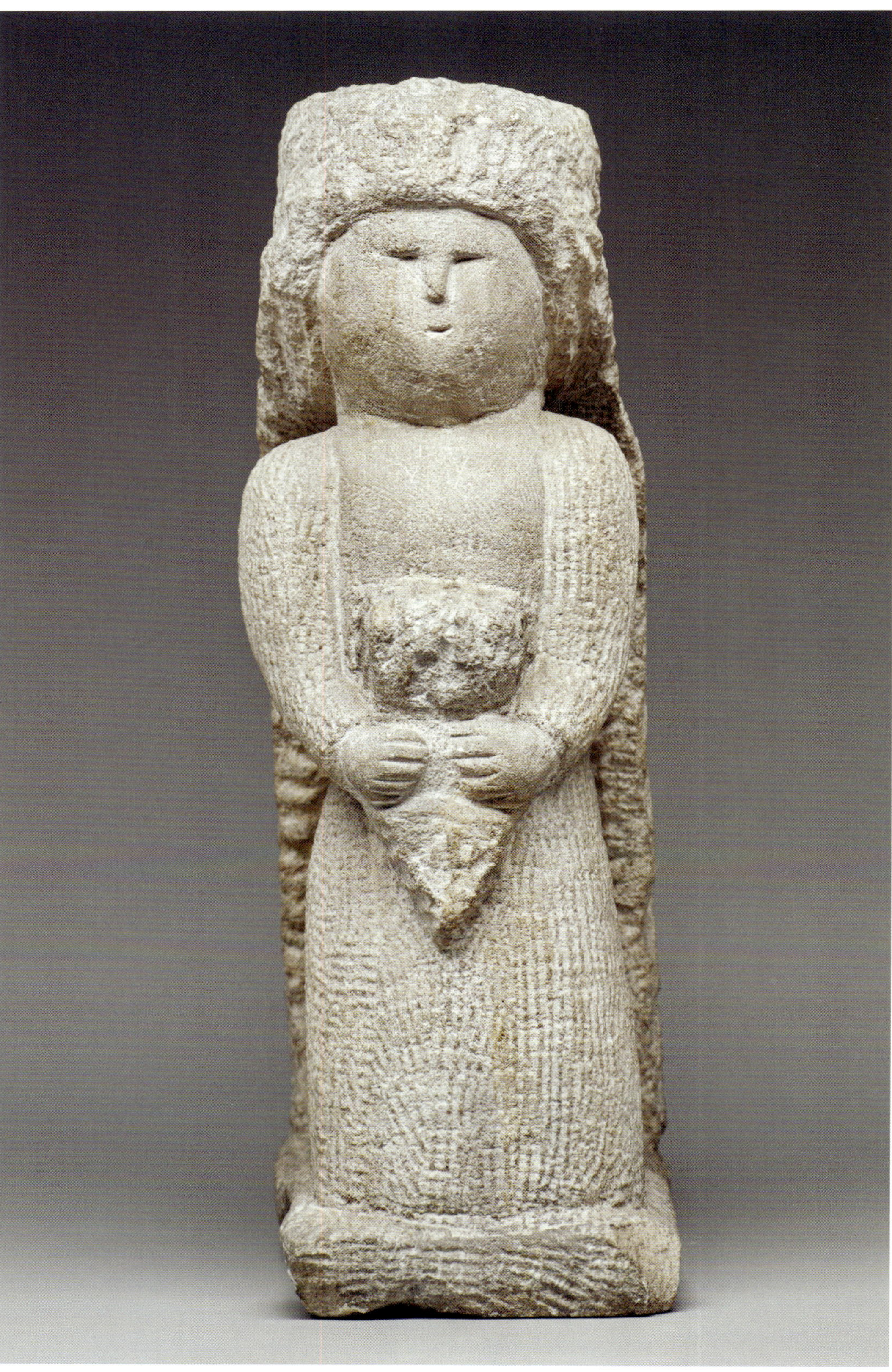

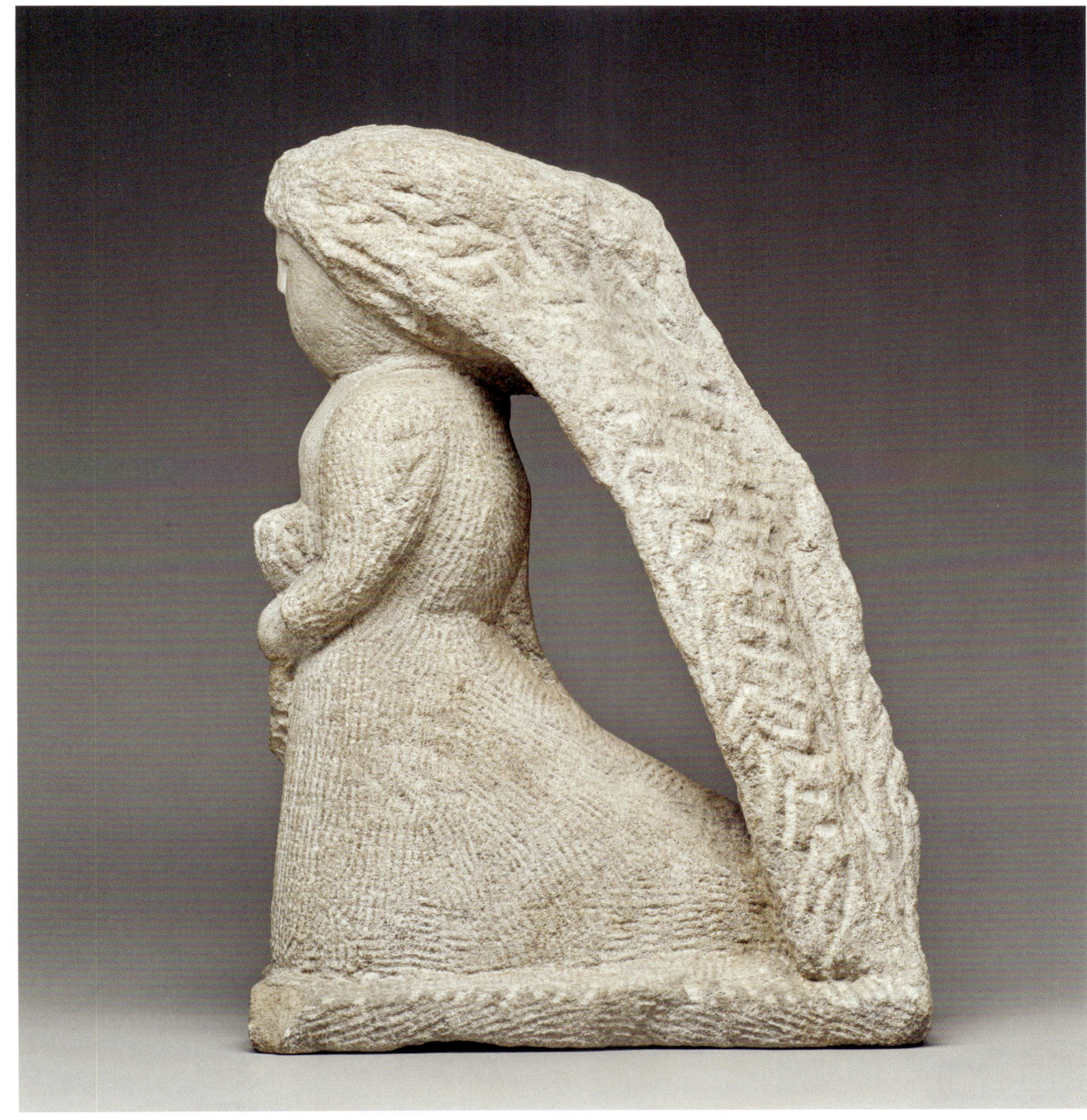

Cat. 36. Louise Dahl-Wolfe, *Sculpture, William Edmondson (Bride)*, 1933–37

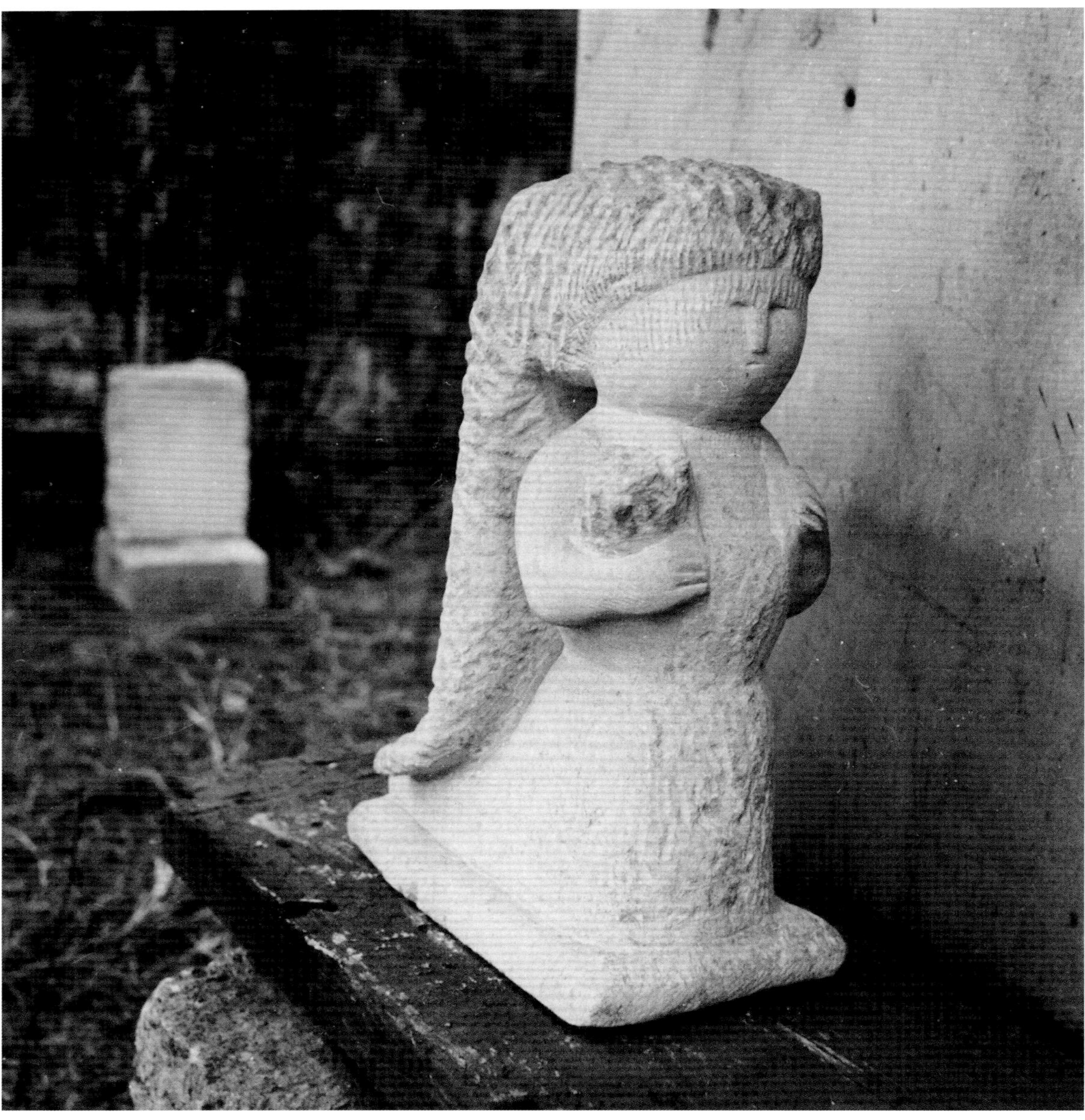

Cat. 37. Louise Dahl-Wolfe, *Sculpture, William Edmondson (Lady with Uplifted Skirts)*, 1937

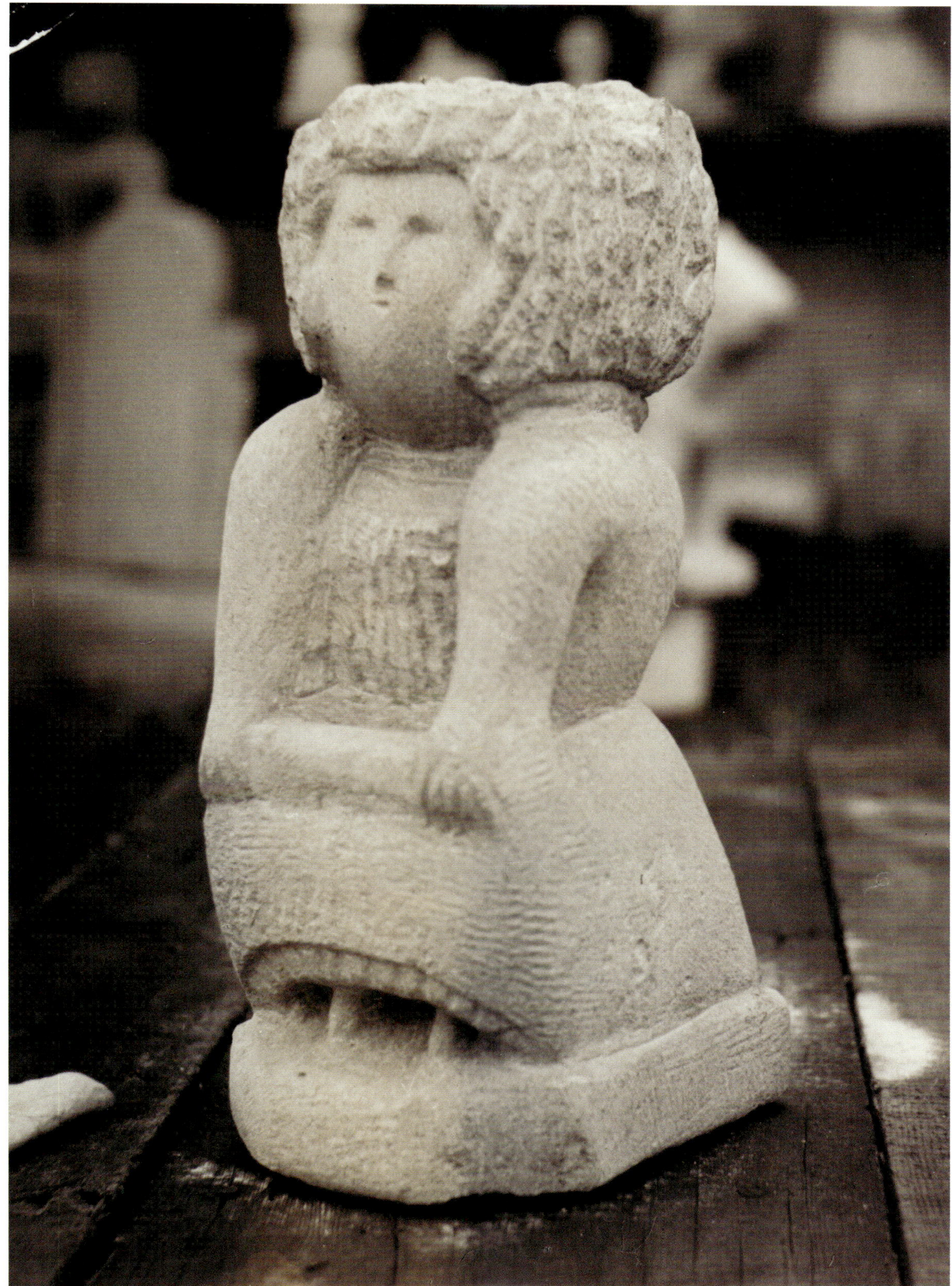

Cat. 38. (Recto) Louise Dahl-Wolfe, *Sculpture, William Edmondson (Miss Lucy)*, 1937

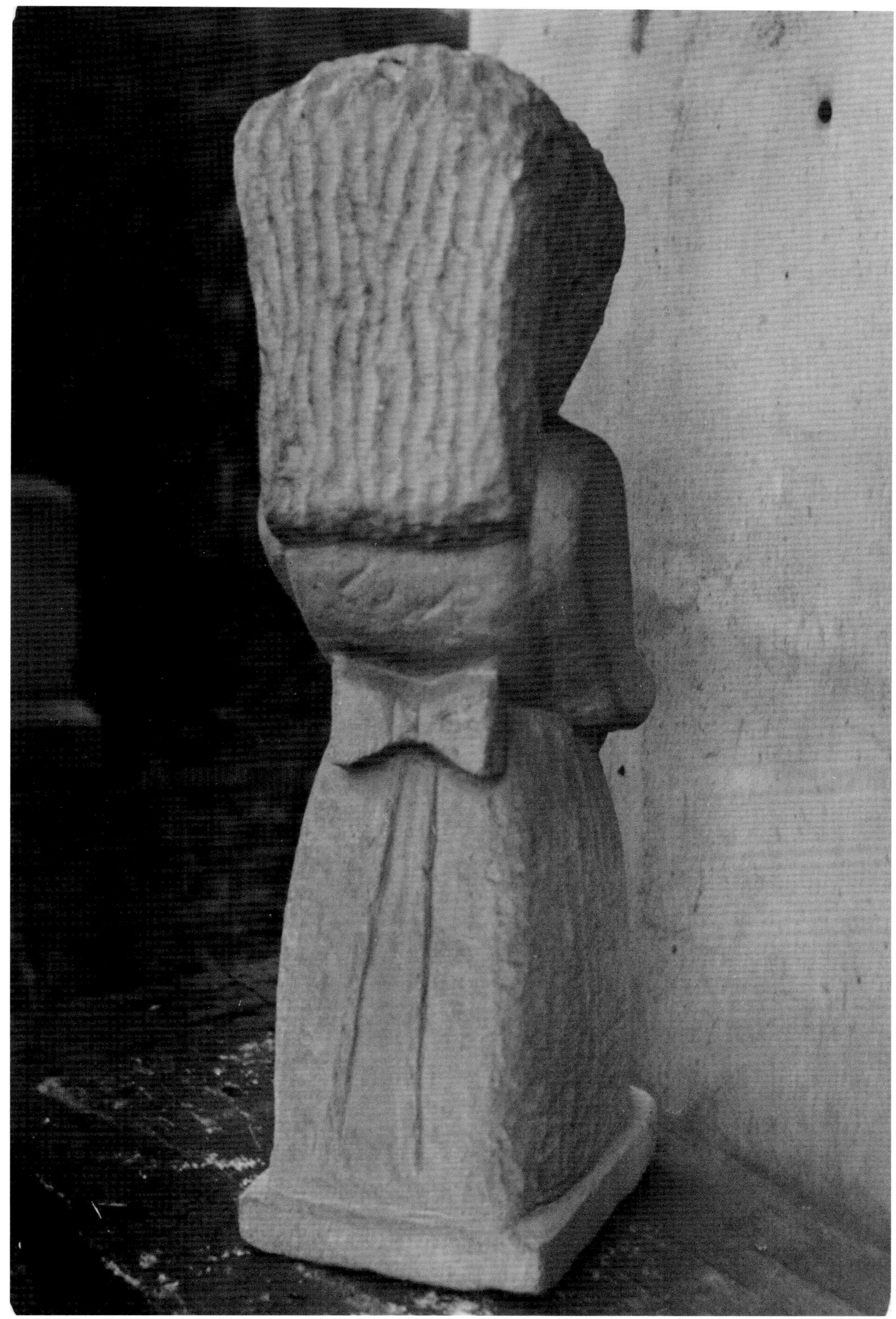

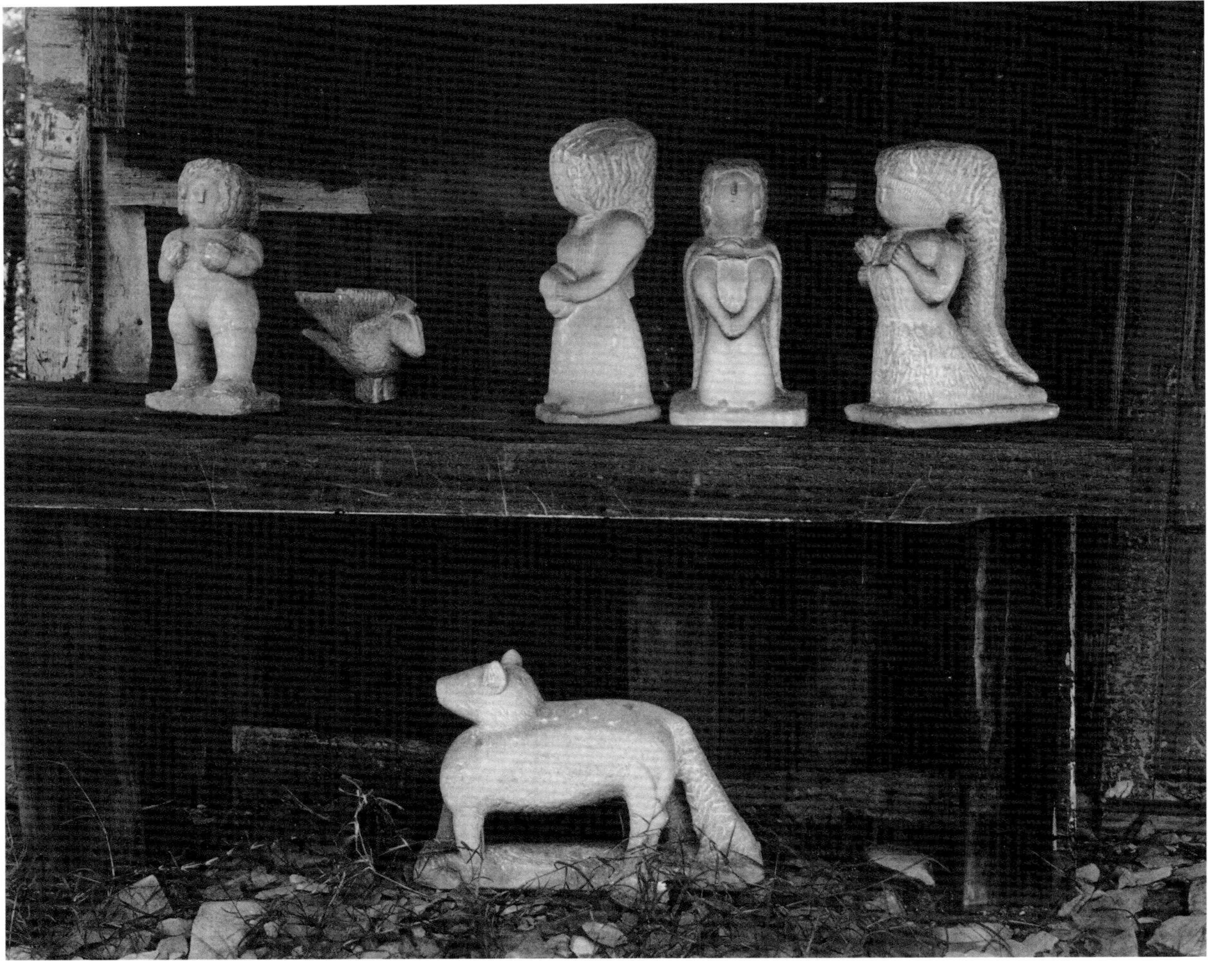

Fig. 16. Edward Weston, *Stone Sculpture, Wm. Edmondson*, 1941. Gelatin silver print, 7 9⁄16 × 9 5⁄8 in. Center for Creative Photography, University of Arizona: Edward Weston Archive.

Quotidian Monumentality

Practices of the Everyday in the Art of William Edmondson

Kéla B. Jackson

I was out in the driveway with some old pieces of stone when I heard a voice telling me to pick up my tools and start to work on tombstone. I looked up in the sky and right there in the noon daylight He hung a tombstone out for me to make . . . God was telling me to cut figures. First He told me to make tombstones; then He told me to cut figures. **William Edmondson**

William Edmondson's home was nestled between a local quarry, Peabody College, and Ward-Belmont College (now Vanderbilt and Belmont universities). As his great-niece Evelyn Edmondson Hill recounts, a lone dirt road carved an entrance toward his backyard studio and a vast bed of his ornamental and funerary sculpture. The two-story craftsman home he shared with his sister Sarah Edmondson served as a nexus of religious and artistic activity brimming with monuments to animals, angels, and prominent figures within the community.[1] Edmondson's yard overflowed with sculptural objects. For those unaware of Edmondson's story and divine guidance, the yard seemed to be a repository for an aimless hobby. Some figural objects rested prominently on his porch while others sat on modestly crafted pedestals or buried in the overgrown grass. Now only noted by a couple of historical markers, the former site of Edmondson's home currently hosts the Murrell School, and only a small collection of photographic works help contemporary audiences recall the experiential aspects of Edmondson's yard. Photographers Louise Dahl-Wolfe,

Epigraph. Edmond L. Fuller, *Visions in Stone: The Sculpture of William Edmondson* (Pittsburgh, PA: University of Pittsburgh Press, 1973), 8.

1. Judith McWillie, "William Edmondson with Edward Weston and Louise Dahl-Wolfe, 1934–1941," in *The Art of William Edmondson* (Nashville, TN: Cheekwood Museum of Art, 1999), 48–49.

Consuelo Kanaga, and Edward Weston captured the abundance of Edmondson's sculptural craftsmanship, while also cementing his image as a lone folk artist within larger modernist art discourse. The photographic and sculptural remains together constitute fragments of Edmondson's yard as a space of inquiry into his practice of monument-making.

The work of French philosopher and sociologist Henri Lefebvre offers a possible alternative framework in which to consider Edmondson and his artistic activity. Lefebvre argues the essence of monuments and monumental spaces to be locations of repression where hegemonic narratives thrive through a disavowal of the lived experience and the everyday. In reading Edmondson's yard as counter-monumental space in which the contradictions of the everyday and the spectacular are overcome, the importance of Edmondson's craft as not merely artistic but spatial becomes quite evident. Thus, the counter-monumental works to disrupt the pervasive narratives of the state by emphasizing the everyday. Edmondson's yard and choice of figural subjects articulate a vision of quotidian monumentality that runs counter to Western notions of monumentality. Edmondson monumentalized his community not only in carving out prominent figures, but also by giving them space. In delineating the mundane and monumental, sacred and profane, Lefebvre asserts the mutability of signs and objects, for any object can be transformed or rather uplifted to the monumental.[2] Edmondson's yard and sculptural works, as they existed during Edmondson's lifetime, represent vernacular monuments, motifs, and traditions imbued with a collective memory that entered into public discourse. The marriage of aesthetic and thematic vernacular of African American folk traditions and the sentimentality and command of the monumental within Edmondson's sculpture create a productive friction that demands more scholarly attention. Edmondson's work truly embodied the world around—from his honorific sculptures of community figures to his sourcing of limestone from a nearby quarry. He transformed the ruins of the cityscape into humble monuments, primarily featuring prominent figures of the African American community. Thus, Edmondson's yard was his own Parthenon—sculptural garden and ode to the everyday.

2. Henri Lefebvre, *The Production of Space*, trans. Donald Nicholson-Smith (Oxford, UK: Blackwell, 1991), 220–26.

Fig. 17. Consuelo Kanaga, *Untitled (Sculptures in William Edmondson's Yard)*, 1950. Gelatin silver photograph, Image: 4 ⅞ × 3 ¾ in. Brooklyn Museum, Gift of Wallace B. Putnam for the Estate of Consuelo Kanaga, 85.65.2119a-g.

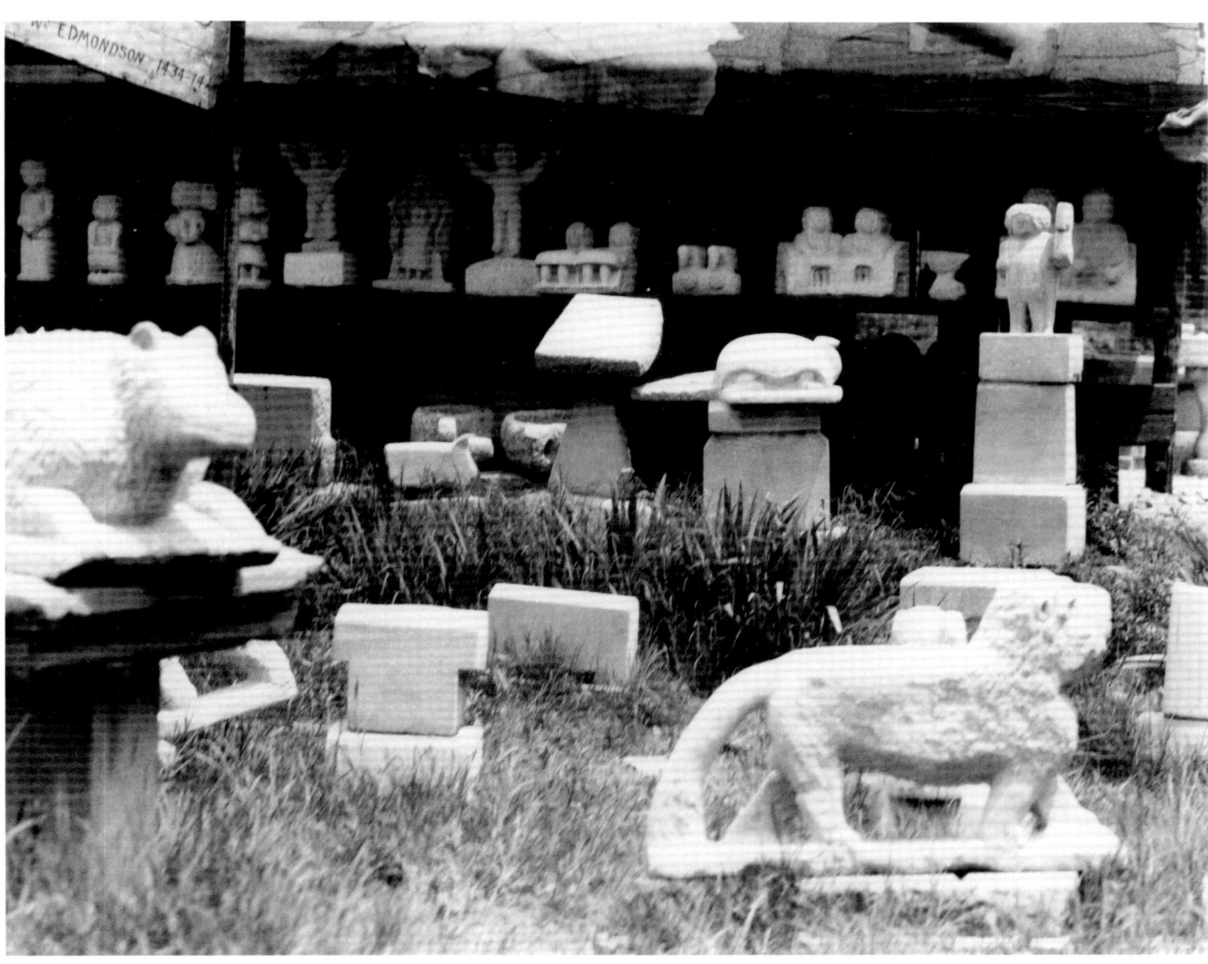

A photograph by Consuelo Kanaga taken in 1950 provides a glimpse of how one might have encountered Edmondson's yard. Varying in tone and texture from warm-hued and granular aggregate to smoothly finished white stone, Edmondson's sculptural congregation evidences his commitment to God's vision. What God placed in the sky, only Edmondson's clairvoyant eye could ascertain—he materialized God's sight, transforming divine vision into sculptural monuments.[3] He fervently crafted tombstones before subsequently turning to sculptures of humans, angels, and animals, tarrying between the realms of the living and the dead. While Edmondson was not a preacher in the traditional sense, his practice was that of a devout apostle. Rife with angels, heavenly birds, and biblical scenes, his yard stood testament to the works of God. Although I emphasize Edmondson's spiritual conviction to foreground the impetus of such a prolific artist, I

3. Fuller, *Visions in Stone*, 12.

Cat. 39. William Edmondson, *The Preacher*, 1934–41

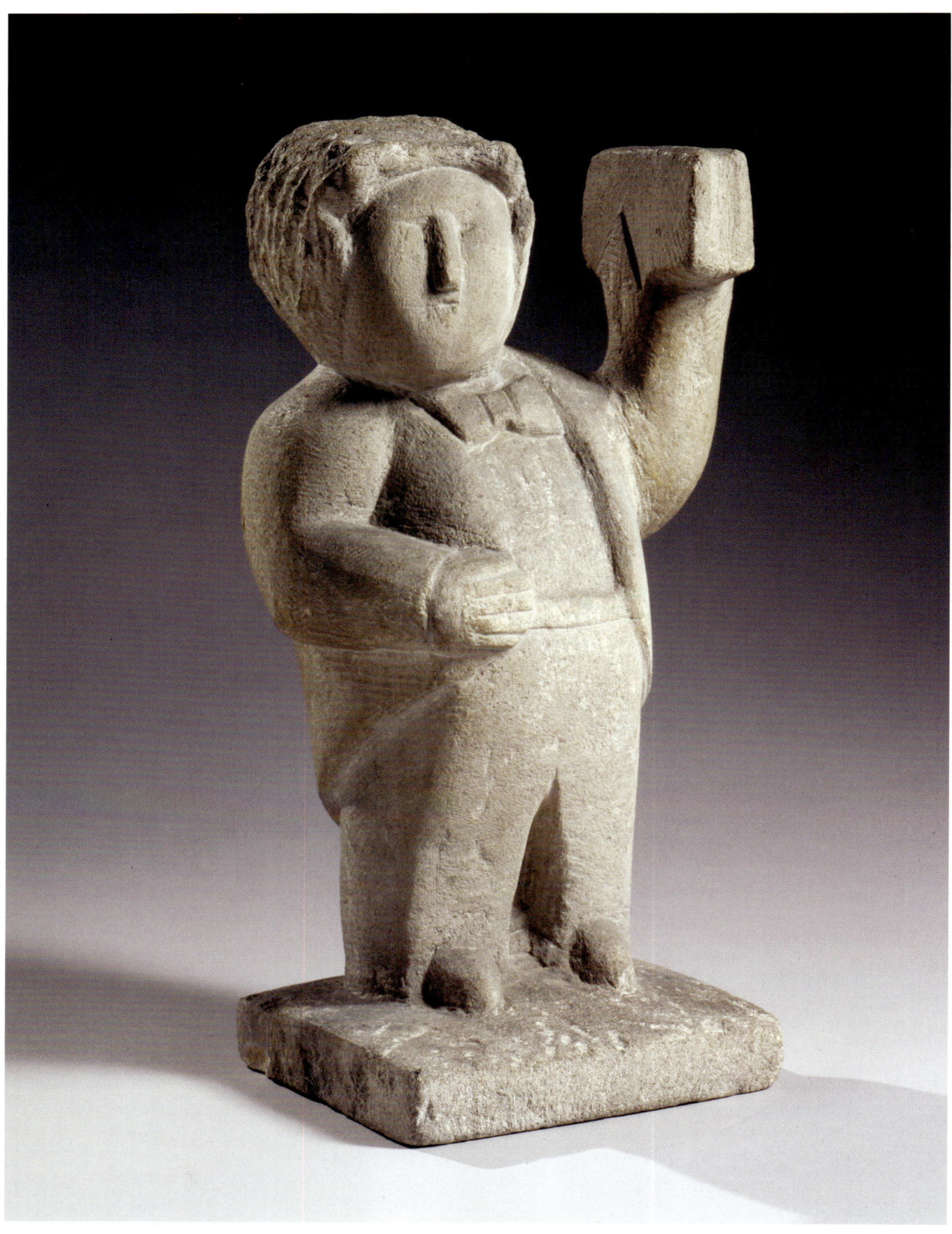

would be remiss to allow Edmondson's visions to overshadow his own artistic negotiations.

Kanaga's image offers an intimate view of the density of Edmondson's monumental yard space. Perched atop a three-tiered modular plinth, *The Preacher* (Cat. 39) commands the attention of viewers with his left hand gesturing toward the sky. *Preacher* wears a three-piece suit accented by a bow-tie. The tail of his coat brushes across his calves and his right hand grips the opening of the coat. As in this specific rendering, Edmondson's preachers often toted a copy of the Gospel in their hands, an emblem of both devotion and wisdom. With his left hand raising the Bible toward the sky, we can almost imagine his bellowing voice reverberating in a sanctuary. The sculptures lined along the porch and situated in the weeds compose the preacher's congregation of human and animals alike. In seeing *The Preacher* as a monument, it is critical to understand the importance of Edmondson's thematic choices as indicative of his own social analysis. During the periods of Reconstruction and Jim Crow in the late nineteenth and first half of the twentieth century, preachers were lauded as both religious and civic leaders within the African American community.[4] The prominence of preachers within Edmondson's oeuvre—rivaled only by that of teachers and nurses—cements their presence as pillars of Edmondson's community.

Female figures make up a great deal of Edmondson's sculptures, a result of his surroundings and everyday life. The corpus of nurse figures marks his time as a custodial worker at the Nashville Woman's Hospital, and there is lore that one of Edmondson's loves was a schoolteacher. Teachers, like preachers, embody tenants of leadership that Edmondson so clearly admired. Edmondson's *Schoolteacher* (Cat. 24) is of modest size, and the highly porous texture of the stone resembles that of a city curb or building foundation. Edmondson did not always repress the traces of his materials' former lives, leaving surfaces raw and unfinished, or in this case yielding to the mass's rectangularity. The teacher's hair curves just below the suggestion of a jawline. While he meticulously rendered the coils of the teacher's tightly coiffed hair, Edmondson "stingily" carved out the remaining elements of the work.[5]

4. Rusty Freeman, "Community Heroes in the Sculpture of William Edmondson," in *The Art of William Edmondson* (Nashville, TN: Cheekwood Museum of Art, 1999), 40.
5. Fuller, *Visions in Stone*, 16.

As a result, the teacher's face appears relatively flat with small lines as eyes and a mouth and crescent-shaped protrusion for a nose. The nose and slight recession of the eyes demonstrate Edmondson's play with depth, but the weight of his skill lies in his relief lines that give form to the teacher's dress. Similar to *Preacher*, Edmondson envisions the teacher in her finest garments. A delicate lace collar accents her floor-length dress, which barely covers her pointed-toe shoes. In her left hand, the teacher holds a ream of paper or a book to solidify her role as an educator, while the other arm bends as she gathers a portion of her dress. The recurrence of the teacher and preacher within Edmondson's yard foregrounds an African American vernacular conception of counter-monumental space that envisages the pedestrian and mundane as imbued with spiritual and communal significance.

Curator Rusty Freeman assiduously notes that Edmondson's sculptures were plaudits to heroes within the African American community, such as Jack Johnson and the lesser-known figures of teachers and preachers whose heroic deeds need not go unnoticed. Freeman works to situate the recurring motifs of the teacher and preacher within Edmondson's practice, but also within African American history as a whole.[6] Edmondson's practice is preservationist in nature, lending to readings of the monumental as it figures within the objects and the space they inhabited.[7] *Teacher* and *Preacher*, as monuments to the quotidian, and more specifically of an African American vision of everyday life, require that we be more capacious in our readings and understandings of monumental works. Resounding both throughout the past of his yard and in the extant body of work, Edmondson's sculptures demonstrate a subversion of Western conventions of monumentality. Edmondson disregarded the monumental aesthetics of grandeur; instead, he chose to imbue the vernacular—space and materials—with the commemorative power typically reserved for official monuments. Edmondson, with chisel in hand and eye on God, carved out a niche in the burgeoning urban landscape of Nashville where his stories and those of his community could rest in stone.

6. Freeman, "Community Heroes," 35–39.
7. Kobena Mercer, "Tropes of the Grotesque in the Black Avant-Garde," in *Popular Art and Vernacular Culture*, ed. Kobena Mercer (Cambridge, MA: MIT Press, 2007), 142.

Cat. 40. William Edmondson, *Preacher,* n.d.

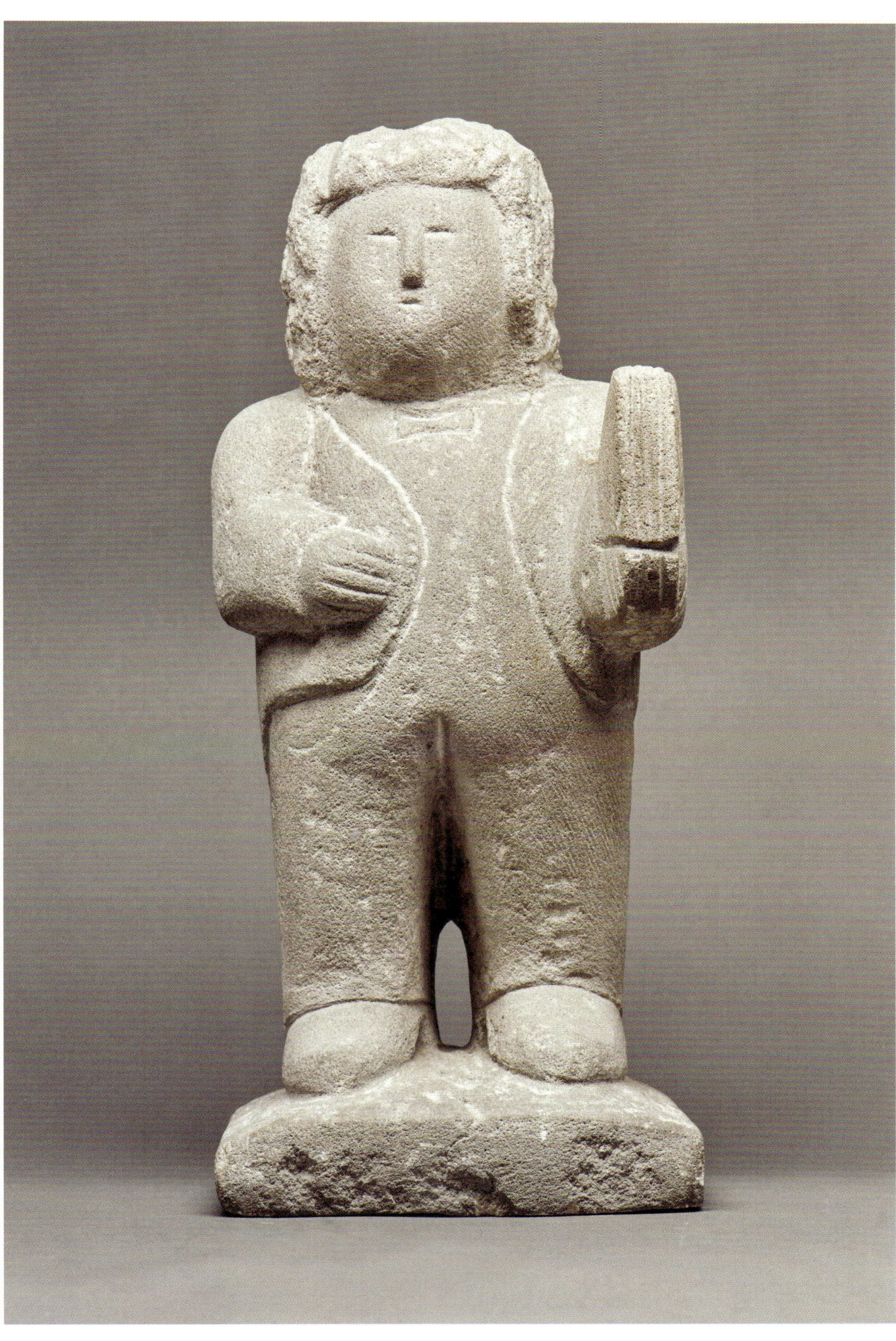

Cat. 41. William Edmondson, *Critter*, c. 1935

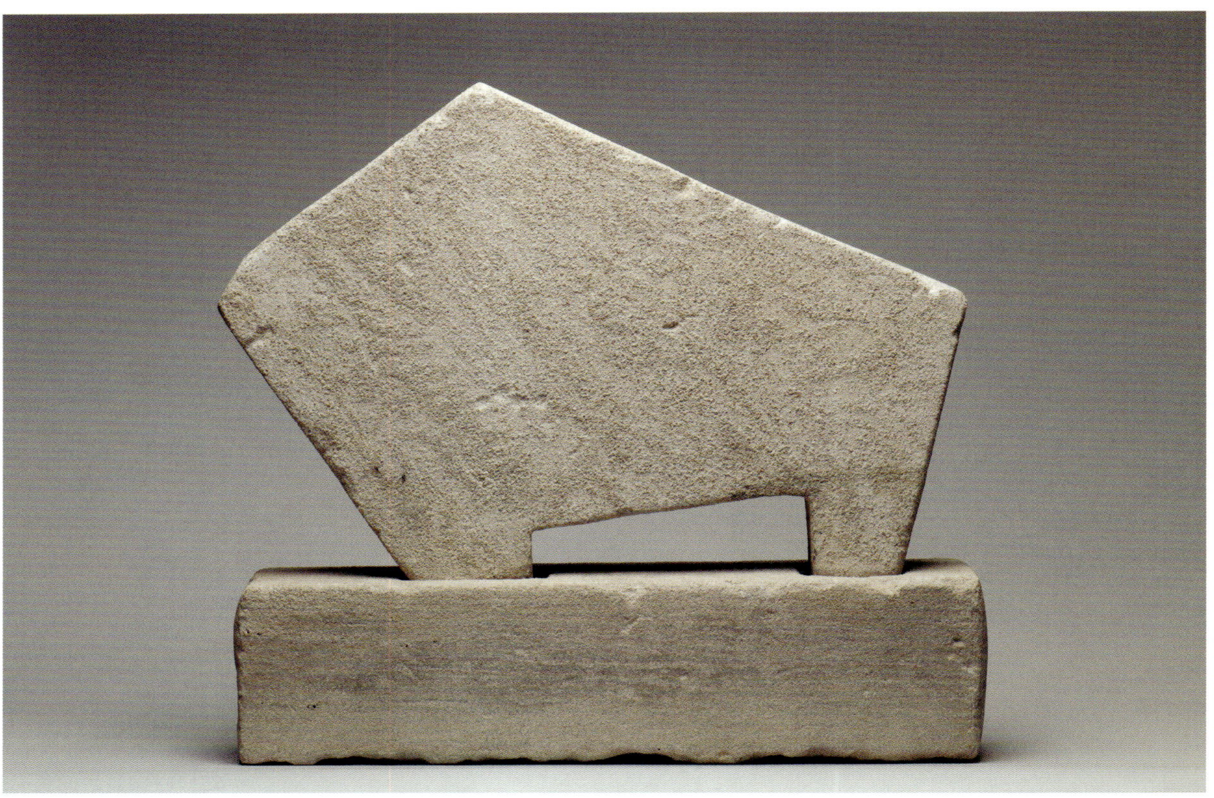

Cat. 42. William Edmondson, *Critter*, n.d.

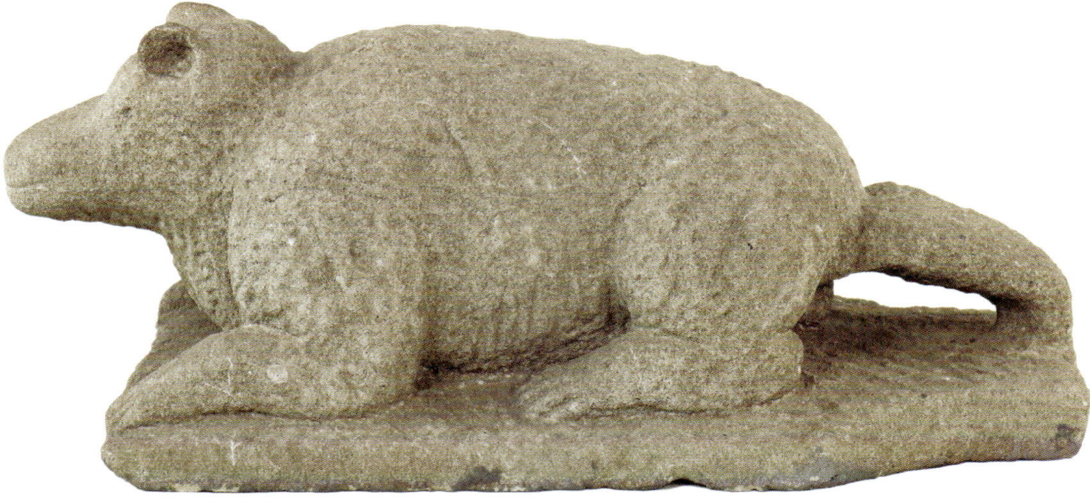

Cat. 43. Louise Dahl-Wolfe, *Critter*, 1933–37

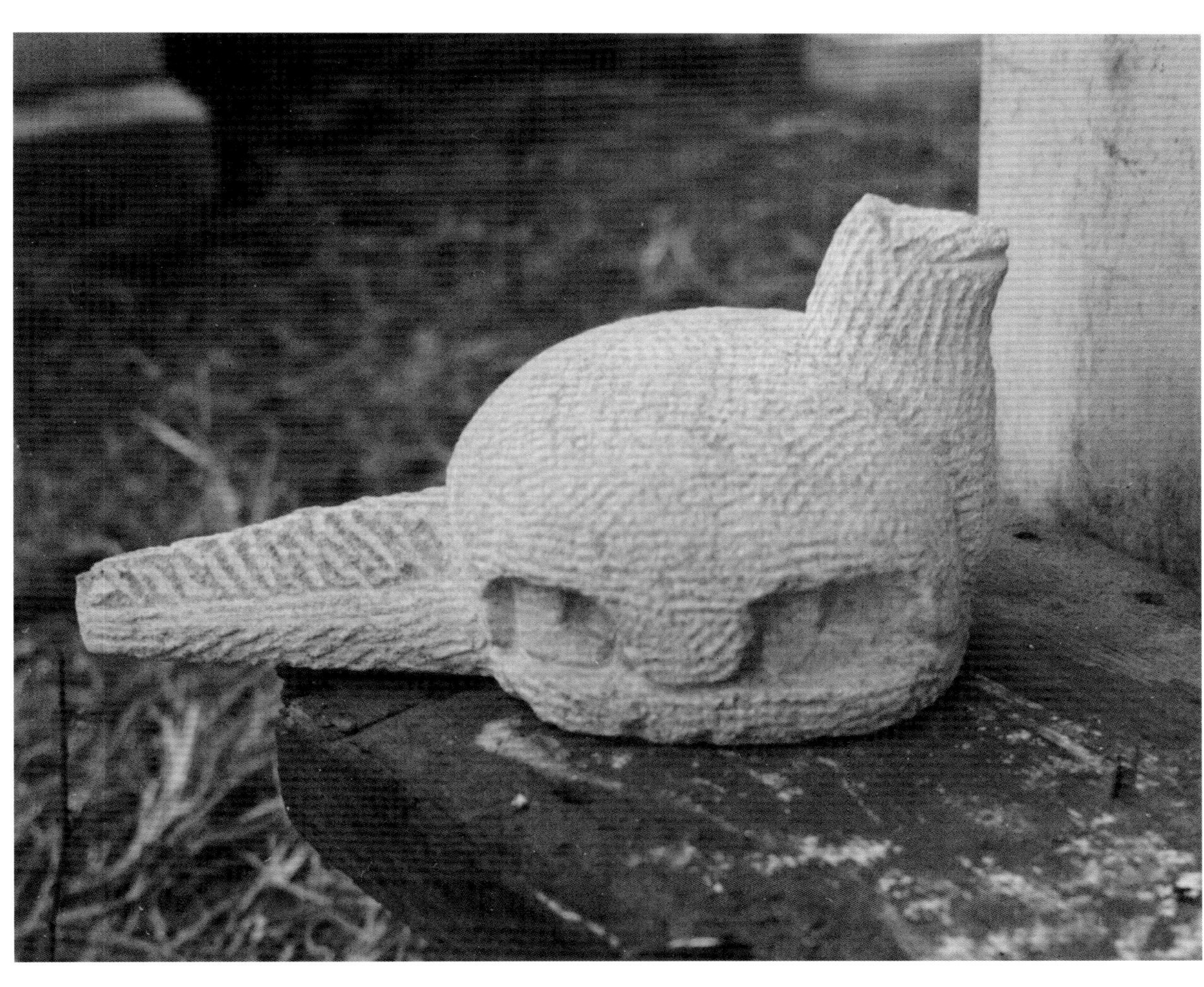

Cat. 44. (Below) William Edmondson, *Horse*, c. 1930–40

Cat. 45. (Recto) William Edmondson, *Eagle*, c. 1930–40

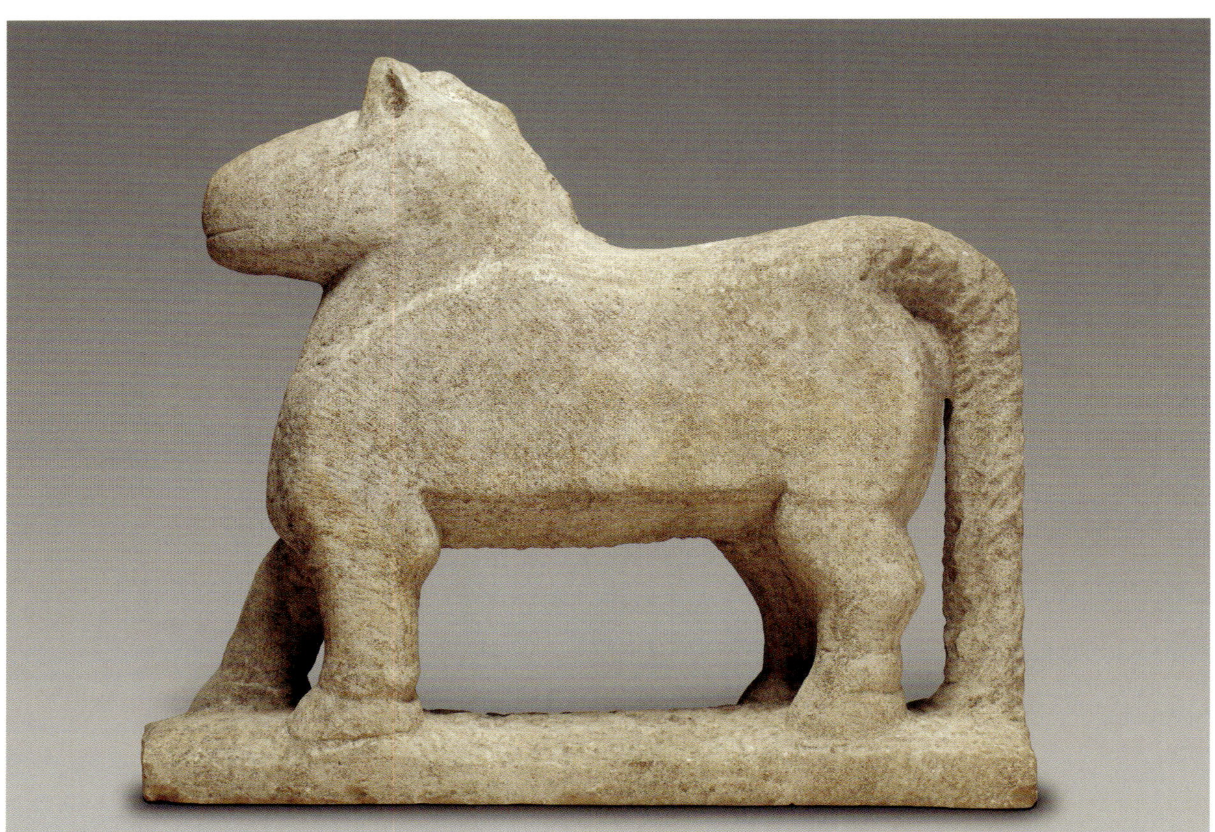

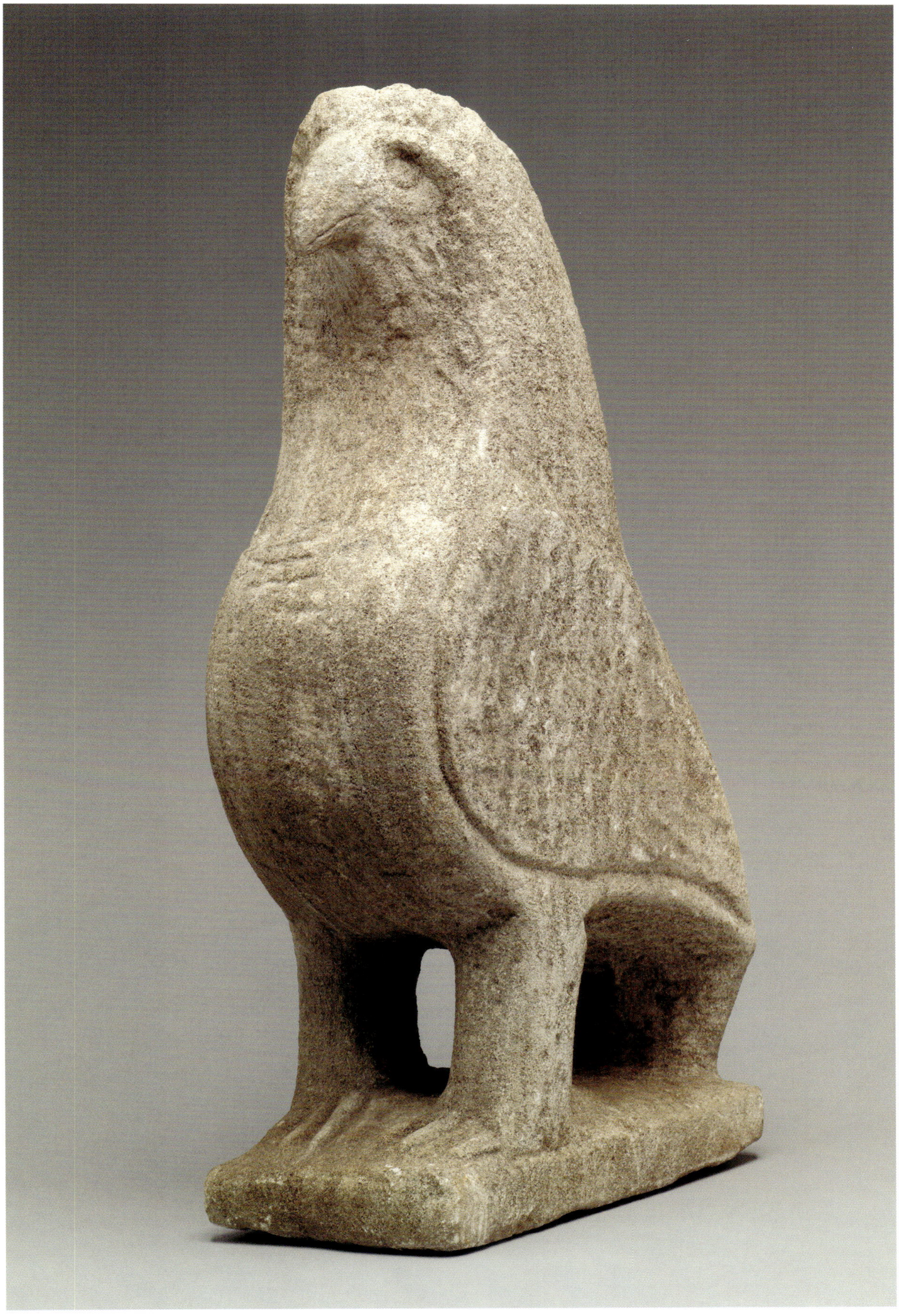

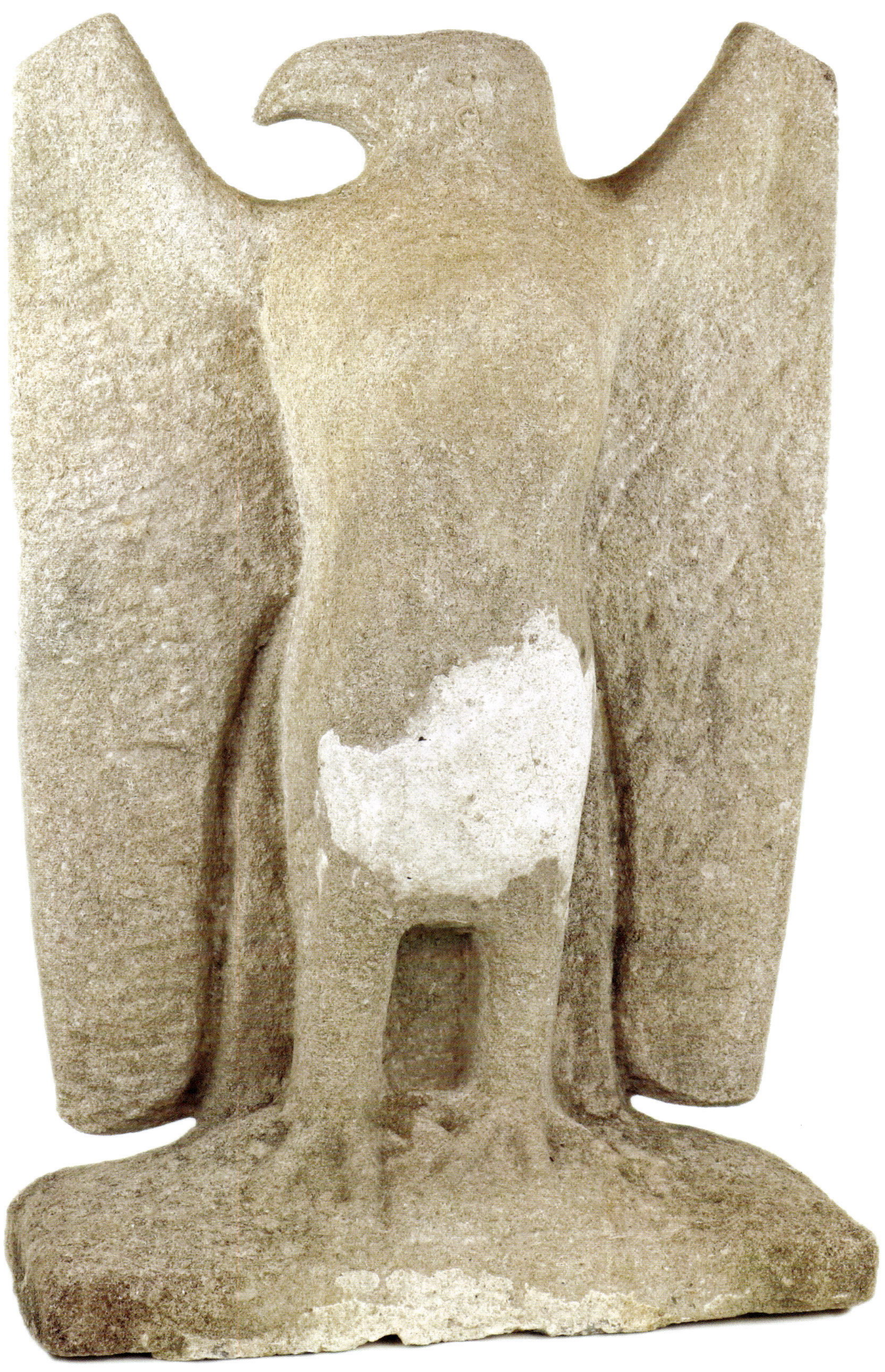

Cat. 46. (Verso) William Edmondson, *Eagle*, n.d.

Cat. 47. (Below) William Edmondson, *Untitled (Three Doves)*, c. 1930–40

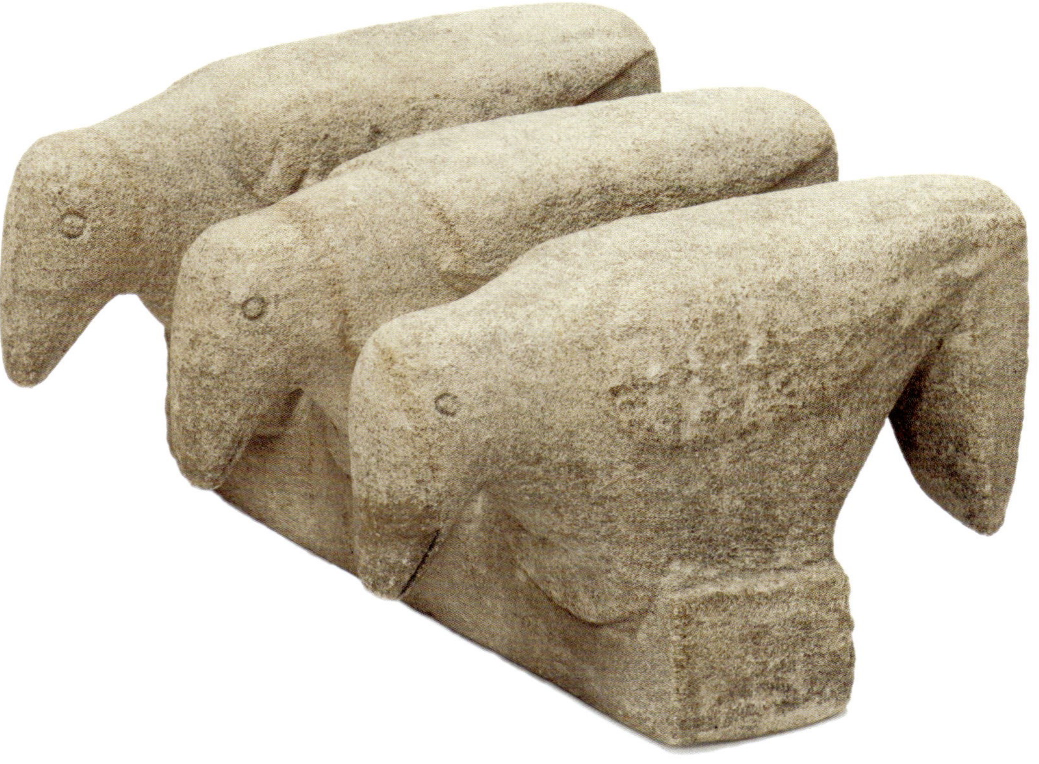

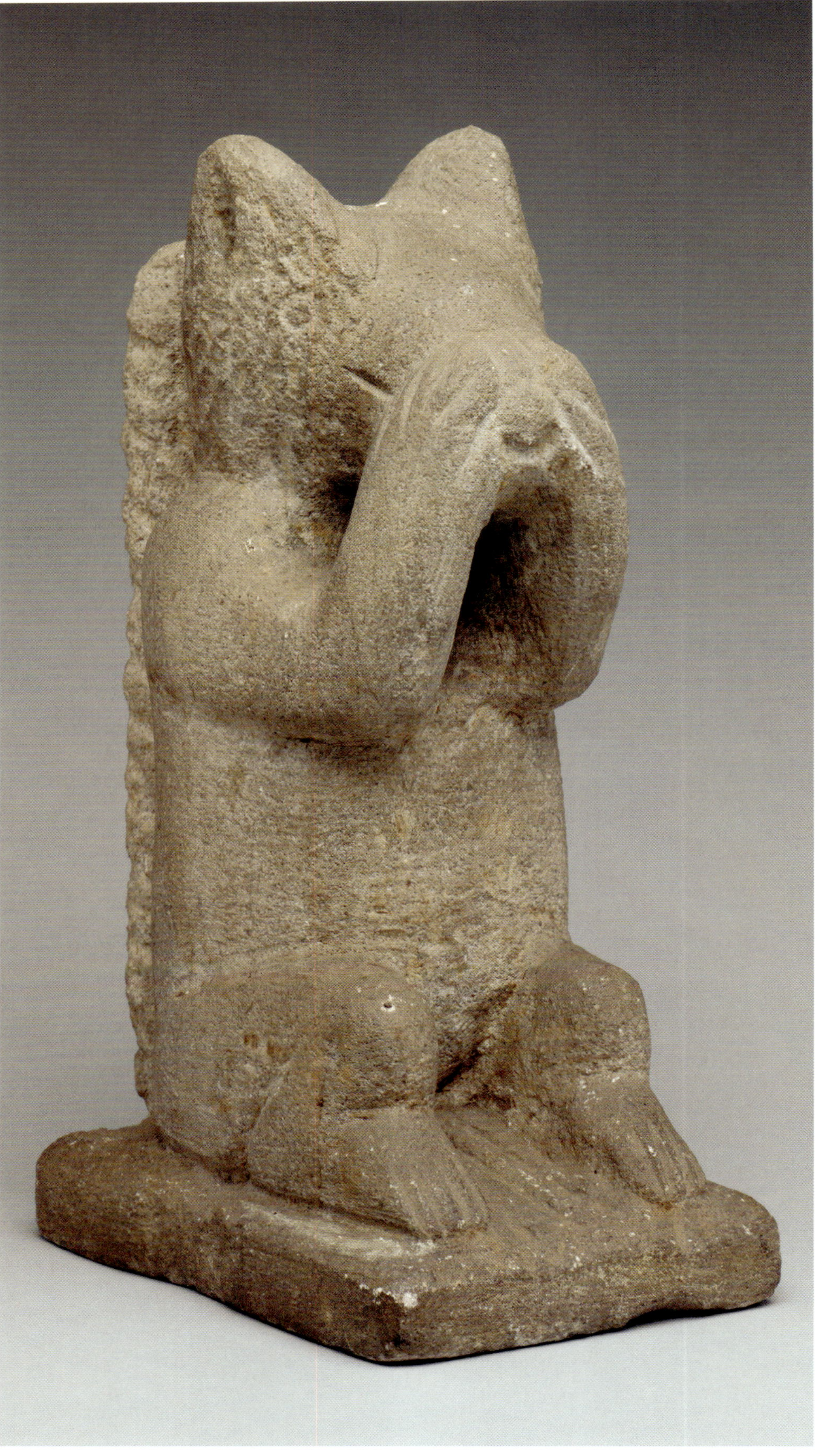

Cat. 48. (Verso) William Edmondson, *Squirrel*, 1940

Cat. 49. (Below) William Edmondson, *Lion*, 1935–40

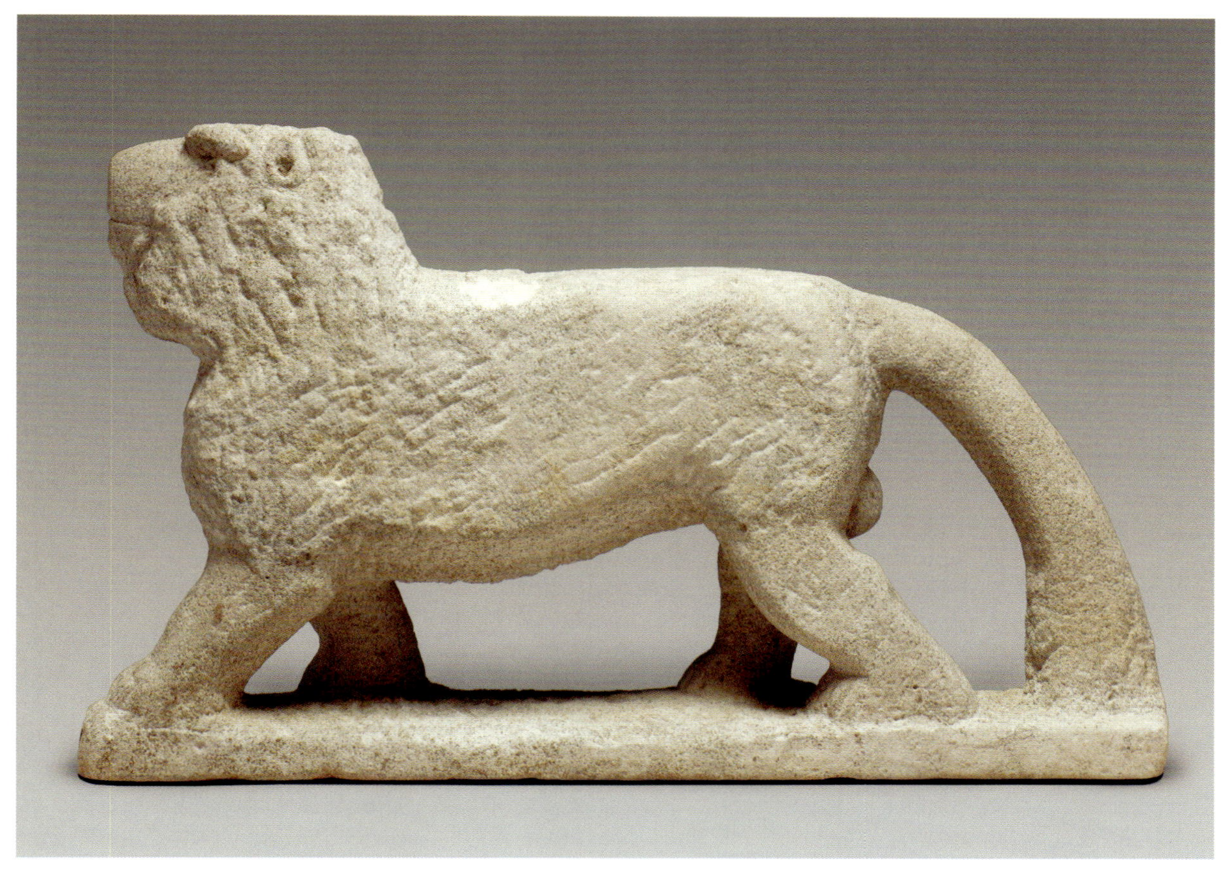

Cat. 50. William Edmondson, *Ram*, 1935–40

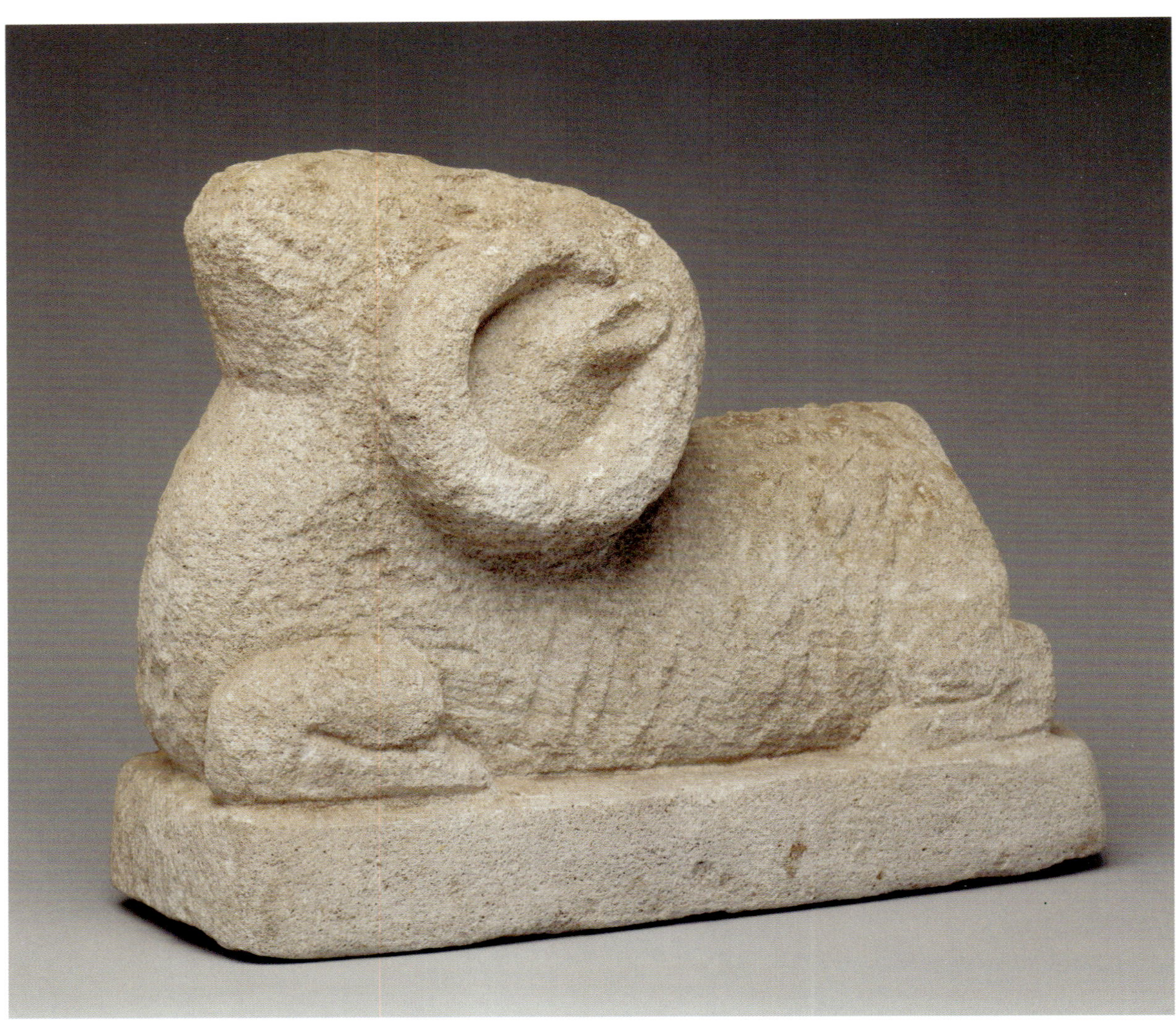

Cat. 51. William Edmondson, *Untitled (Turtle)*, c. 1940

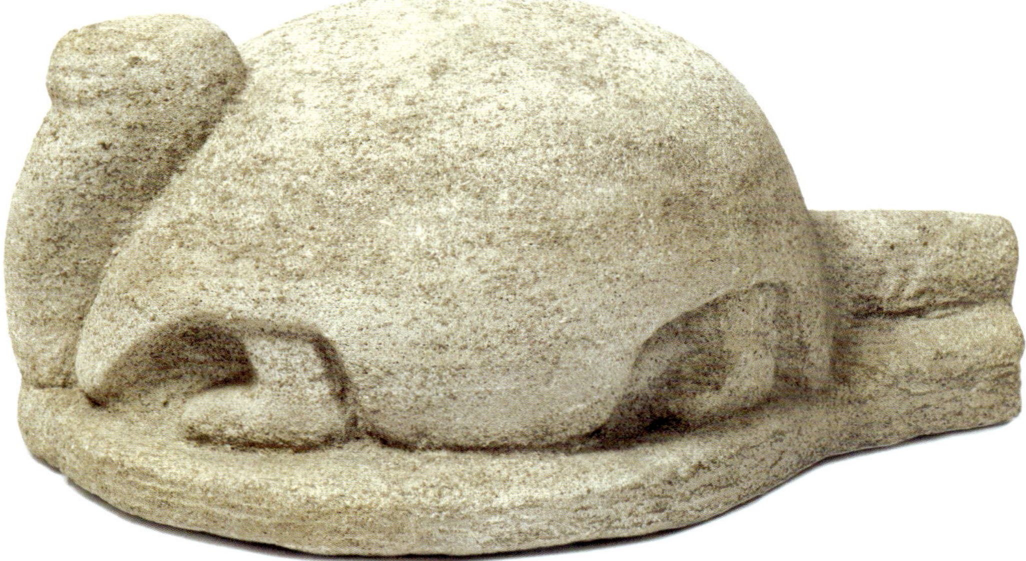

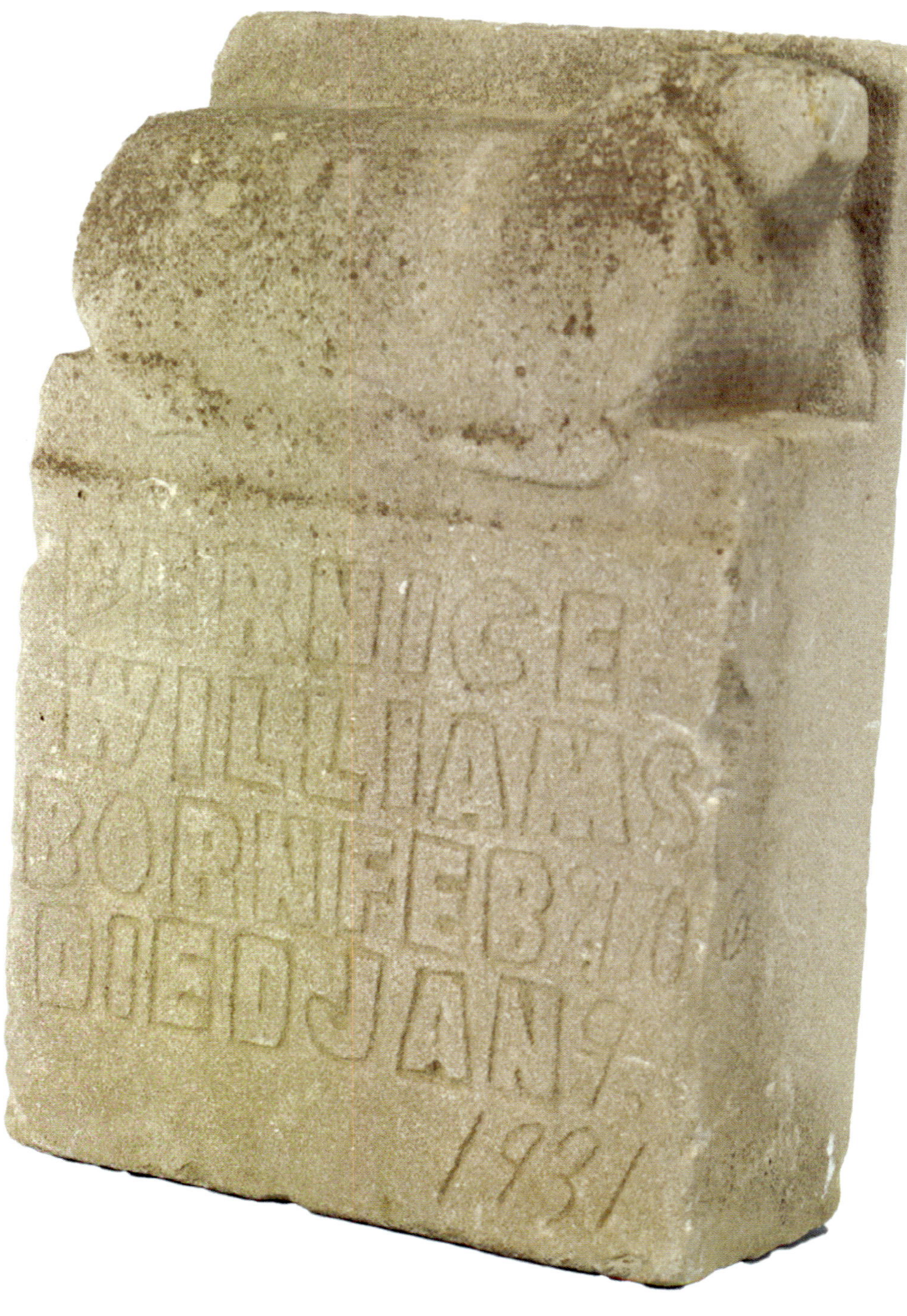

Cat. 52. William Edmondson, *Williams Tombstone*, 1931

Cartography

Anne Monahan

Sculpture tells you, you are here. **Maren Hassinger**, 2020

While William Edmondson was not the subject of sculptor Maren Hassinger's recent observation, it is a salient frame of reference for his carvings nonetheless. By nature, the headstones he made for friends and neighbors are wayfinding devices by which mourners orient themselves in the material landscape of the cemetery and the immaterial one of memory. Likewise, the thickset figures and animals that populated his yard in Nashville and the gardens of some local collectors were tangible affirmations of his presence in and contribution to a city and country that has only grudgingly acknowledged the Black labor that built it.

This dimension of his practice dovetails with geographic conceits often deployed to relate self-taught artists to the broader field of contemporary production. The most famous, "outsider art," conjures a border that separates those with social capital from those without. Coined in 1972 as an English analogue to Jean Dubuffet's *art brut*, the term "outsider art"—like the concept it denotes—has been stubbornly resistant to charges that it romanticizes and codifies the marginalization it purports to redress.[1] Taking another tack, curator Lynne Cooke recently expanded the border into a borderland by proposing "outlier," which, she argues, "sidesteps questions of 'inside' versus 'outside' in favor of distances nearer and farther from an aggregate."[2] Similarly, Leslie Umberger advertised liminality as a defining trope in the title of her exhibition *Between Worlds: The Art of Bill Traylor* (2018).[3] Leaning into that model, I envision a space of "uneven reciprocity" akin to the one that historian James Clifford outlined in "Museums

Epigraph. Maren Hassinger, in "Maren Hassinger and Virginia Overton: Sixtieth Anniversary Virtual Program," Storm King Art Center, Storm King, NY, October 14, 2020. Thanks to Lynne Cooke, Marin Sullivan, and Katharine J. Wright for the conversations that precipitated this essay.

1. Roger Cardinal, *Outsider Art* (London: Studio Vista, 1972).
2. Lynne Cooke, *Outliers and American Vanguard Art* (Washington, DC: National Gallery of Art in association with the University of Chicago Press, 2018), 4, exhibition catalog. Perhaps unsurprisingly, some have taken up "outlier" as a trendy replacement for "outsider," the construct it was devised to correct; see, for example, Sanford Schwartz, "In Their Own Words," *New York Review of Books*, June 7, 2018.
3. Leslie Umberger, *Between Worlds: The Art of Bill Traylor* (Washington, DC, and Princeton: Smithsonian American Art Museum in association with Princeton University Press, 2018), exhibition catalog.

as Contact Zones," in which "a center and a periphery are assumed: the center a point of gathering, the periphery an area of discovery . . . [where] geographically and historically separated groups [here, autodidacts and their modernist supporters] establish ongoing relations. These are not relations of equality, even though processes of *mutual* exploitation and appropriation may be at work."[4]

Whatever their differences, these spatial metaphors—outsider, outlier, contact zone, and so forth—counterpose autodidacts identified by ostensibly fixed conditions of biography and modernists determined by volitional ones of style and taste. As a curatorial practice, such strategic essentialism is hardly unique to the self-taught or even especially novel. That much was evinced during the interwar years in the campaign to market such artists under the label "modern primitive." Devised to do double duty, this designation consolidated disparate practitioners united only by talent, distance from formal art training, and indifference to linear perspective and naturalistic modeling, and positioned them in a genealogy reaching back through the French "primitive" Henri Rousseau (1844–1910)—a patron saint, in the proponents' eyes—to antecedents in, say, the fourteenth century, either painters in Italy or carvers on Rapa Nui (misnamed Easter Island by Europeans).

Sometimes lost in revisionist attention to this interwar episode is the porosity of that period classification in the period itself.[5] Within just a few years of their debuts, several of the most celebrated "modern primitives," painters John Kane (1860–1934), Horace Pippin (1888–1946), and Jacob Lawrence (1917–2000), achieved crossover success as contemporary artists, and Lawrence outlived the label entirely by the late 1940s. Astute critics were also sensitive to the term's limitations, among them the *New York Times*' Edward Alden Jewell, who offered the supplement "neo-primitive" to denote those whose formal sophistication outstripped the homespun simplicity conventionally associated with the self-taught.[6] His suggestion, albeit rhetorical, invites us to locate heterogeneity within and across the interwar cohort on whom he trained his gaze. Ideally, such attention can produce

4. Emphasis in original. James Clifford takes "contact zone" from Mary Louise Pratt; see his essay, "Museums as Contact Zones," in James Clifford, *Routes: Travel and Translation in the Late Twentieth Century* (Cambridge, MA: Harvard University Press, 1997), 193–4.
5. See, for example, MoMA's 2019 reinstallation, which sequesters interwar self-taught artists in *Gallery 521: Masters of Popular Painting* (www.moma.org/calendar/galleries/5142), named for *Masters of Popular Painting: Modern Primitives of Europe and America* (MoMA, April 27–July 4, 1938), even though that show included few artists in the 2019 installation. Likewise, as of fall 2020, the Metropolitan Museum has installed "modern primitives" in the context of "folk" art in the American Wing (Gallery 751, maps.metmuseum.org/galleries/fifth-ave/2/751) and "European primitivism" in the Modern and Contemporary galleries (Gallery 911, maps.metmuseum.org/galleries/fifth-ave/1/911).
6. Edward Alden Jewell, "European and American," *New York Times*, February 20, 1944, X6, reviews Horace Pippin's second solo show in New York.

Fig. 18. John Kane (American, 1860–1934), *Touching Up*, c. 1931–32. Oil on canvas, 20 ¾ × 27 in. Carnegie Museum of Art, Pittsburgh: Gift of Thomas Mellon Evans.

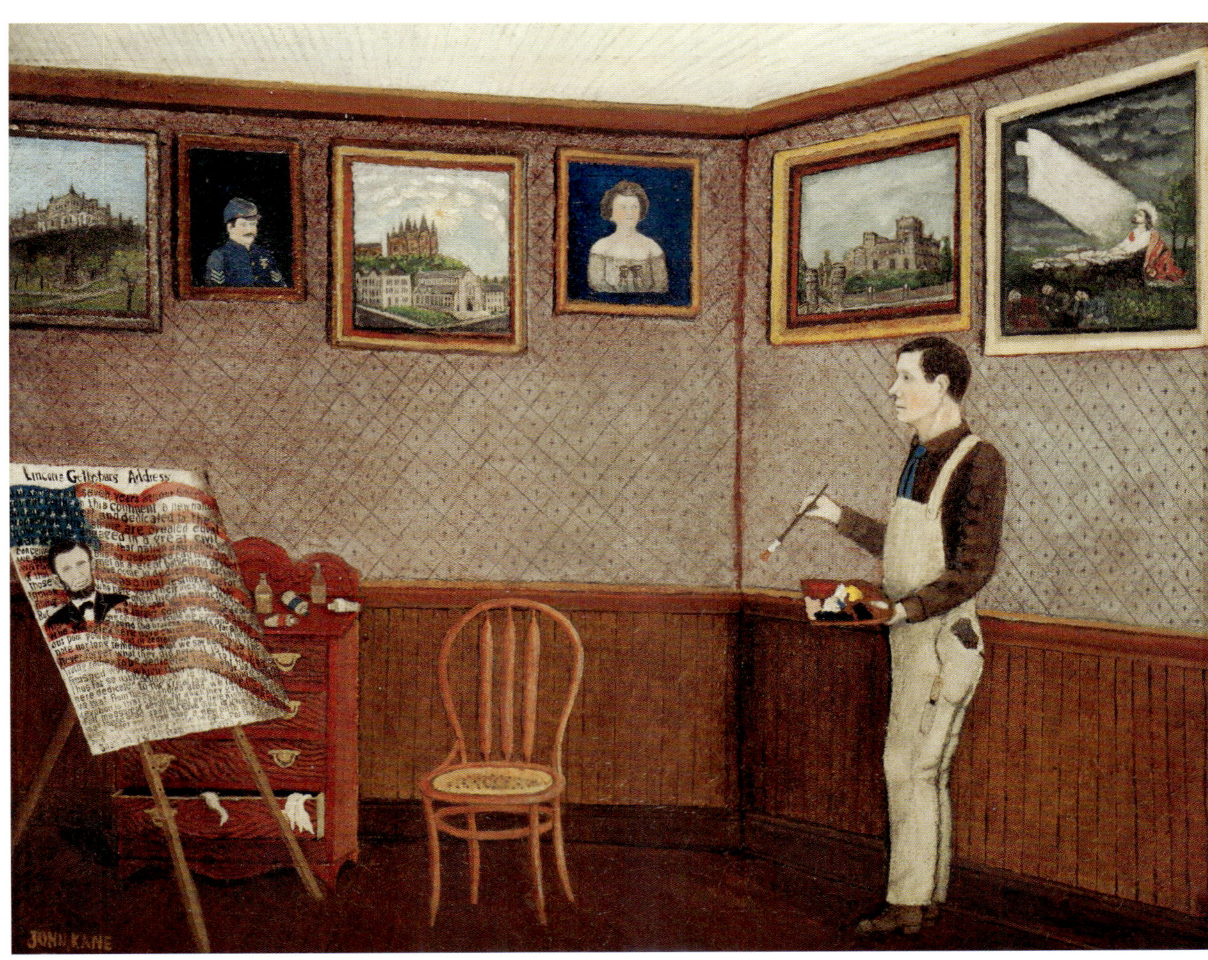

something akin to a topographical map—to deploy another cartographic metaphor—that highlights the field's internal complexities rather than the prevailing topological one focused on its external boundaries. The career of Edmondson, the group's most prominent sculptor, crystallizes the challenges and opportunities that attend such an effort.

As has been well rehearsed, Edmondson helped put "modern primitives" on the map in the 1930s with roles in back-to-back exhibitions organized by the Museum of Modern Art (MoMA). His professional debut, *Sculpture by William Edmondson* (1937), was the museum's first solo show of a Black artist or a self-taught one and a relative rarity for a living US artist of any stripe.[7] On its heels, MoMA used his

7. By 1938, MoMA had mounted solo shows of eight US artists: Charles Burchfield (1930); Maurice Sterne, Edward Hopper, and Walker Evans (1933); Gaston Lachaise (1934, 1935); Edward Steichen and John Marin (1936); and E. McNight Kauffer, who lived and worked in London (1937). Alfred H. Barr Jr., "Painting and Sculpture in the United States," *Trois Siecles d'Art aux États-Unis*, 2nd ed. (Paris: Musee du Jeu de Paume, 1938), 23, exhibition catalog. Edmondson was the only Black artist named in the checklist, which also included unidentified "folk" artists.

Fig. 19. Horace Pippin (American, 1888–1946). *Self-Portrait*, 1941. Oil on canvas board, 14 × 11 in. Collection Albright-Knox Art Gallery, Buffalo, New York; Room of Contemporary Art Fund, 1942 (RCA1942:2).

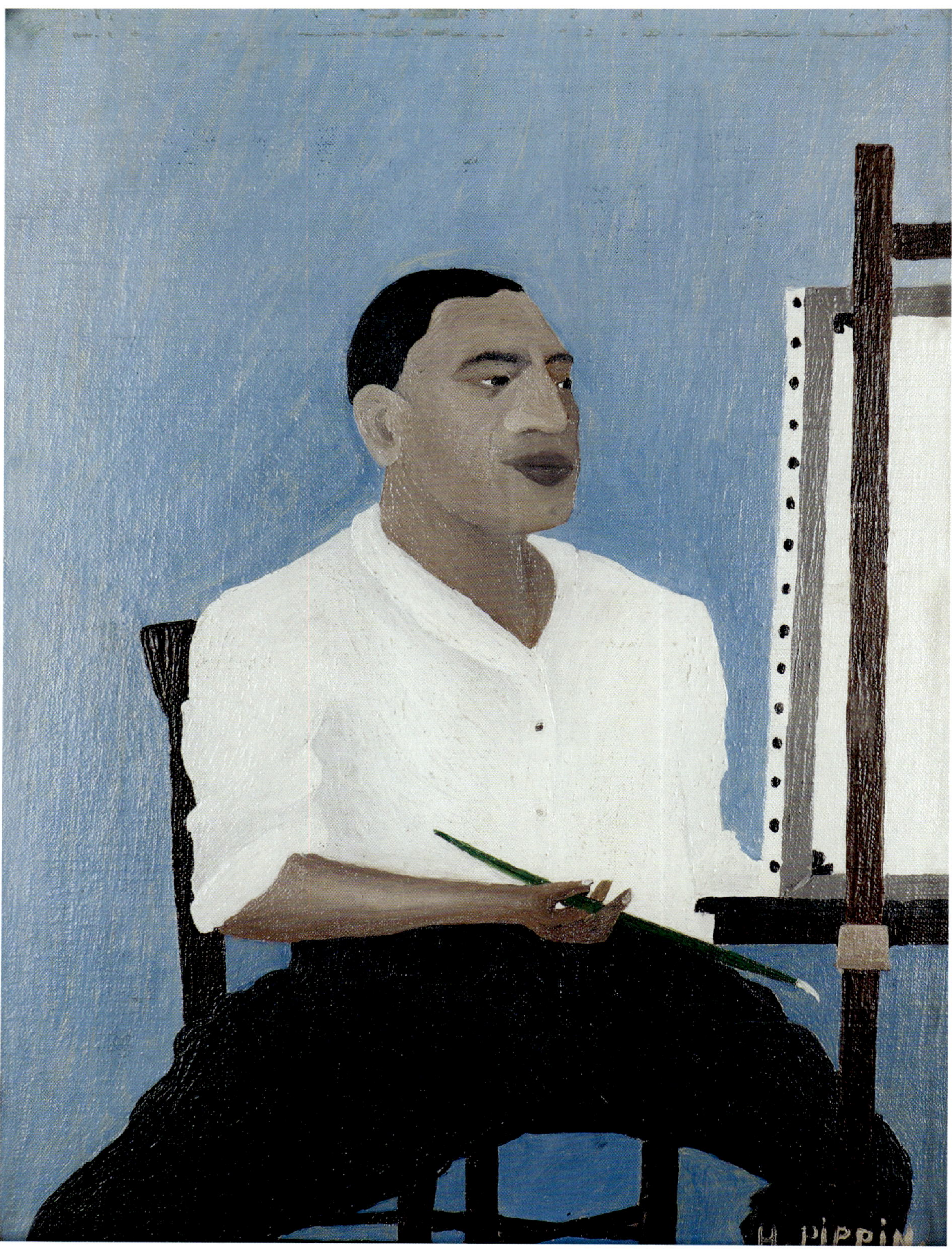

work and Kane's to anchor the "American Folk and Popular Art" section of *Three Centuries of American Art* (1938) at the Jeu de Paume in Paris, a project designed to boost the nation's stock in the epicenter of European modernism.

Edmondson came to the museum's attention via a diffuse network of his collectors and their contacts that reached from Nashville to New York and eventually to Paris. In fact, they—not the carver himself—supplied most of the work in those shows, much of it for sale.[8] As a result, the projects are textbook contact zones in which intermediaries increasingly removed from him, personally and geographically, collaborated to raise his profile and, in so doing, those of contemporary US art, their own institutions, and themselves. Their multiform investments and incentives extended well beyond the commercial.[9] For example, an early local collector recalled her visits to his yard as an individualistic pursuit heavy on modernist aesthetics—"I was just buying what I liked"—and light on progressive politics—"no one that I knew even thought of it that way." And, unlike many in her social set, she displayed his work indoors, along with Mesoamerican and African objects, then also subjects of interest at MoMA.[10]

Edmondson's motives in cooperating with the MoMA projects are opaque. While hardly the cultural isolate his press clippings describe, he stuck close to home in Nashville, neither actively soliciting broader curatorial and critical attention nor making much of an effort to capitalize on what came his way. He was still holding that line in a 1941 interview that disavowed artistic ambition—"I is just doing the Lord's work. I didn't know I was no artist till them folks come tole me I was"—and deflected credit to the "WPA and fine folk spreadin' the Lord's work [i.e., his carvings] around." Yet he offset that modesty in the same conversation with a market sensitivity that easily qualifies as astute: "There ain't many people doing things like this. They's different. Seems like folk would buy more of these antiques," his term for his carvings in a secular context.[11]

Where might we locate Edmondson's ambivalent professional persona in our developing topography? To be sure, it separates him from figures like Kane and Pippin, who saw themselves as artists long before the art world did. Both

8. Thanks to Marin Sullivan for bringing the lender information to my attention. Apparently, Edmondson lent only *The Ark*; photographer Louise Dahl-Wolfe supplied much of the rest of the show. See the lenders' list, Series IV, Exhibitions, *The Art of William Edmondson*, Box 103, Folder 1: General Research, MoMA Archives; and "Master Checklist," *Sculpture by William Edmondson* (October 20–November 4, 1937), MoMAExh_0063c_MasterChecklist, MoMA, available at https://assets.moma.org/documents/moma_master-checklist_333061.pdf.
9. For the social and cultural dynamics animating these incentives, see Pierre Bourdieu, *Distinction: A Social Critique of Judgement and Taste*, trans. Richard Nice (Cambridge, MA: Harvard University Press, 1987).
10. Estelle Friedman, telephone interview with the author, December 2, 1997. She reported that she and her friends visited Edmondson separately, without prior discussion or coordination, and none saw her or his purchases as a racially progressive statement. See MoMA's *American Sources of Modern Art (Aztec, Mayan, Incan)* (1933; https://www.moma.org/calendar/exhibitions/2932) and *African Negro Art* (1935; https://www.moma.org/calendar/exhibitions/2937).
11. William Edmondson, quoted in John Thompson, "Negro Stone Cutter Here Says Gift from the Lord; Work Praised," *Nashville Tennessean*, February 9, 1941.

painters courted curatorial and commercial attention via informal exhibitions and local art shows and, once it arrived, advertised their agency in self-portraits at the easel and artist's statements geared to a national audience. That each recruited help with those autobiographical texts—Kane collaborated with reporter Marie McSwigan on the posthumous *Sky Hooks: The Autobiography of John Kane* (1938), and Pippin started using unidentified amanuenses in the late 1930s—suggests that Edmondson's limited literacy was not the only obstacle to similar exercises in self-fashioning.[12] In lieu of assuming such authorship, he relied on "fine folk"—white collectors, curators, photographers, and reporters—to represent him and his project, often, as Bridget Cooks has detailed, in language and imagery that reinforced the Unite States' racial caste system.[13] Edmondson's self-effacement has usually been taken as an index of his humility, faith, and/or naivety. It might just as easily function as strategic self-protection, given that frank expressions of Black ambition were often met with hostility, especially but not only in the Jim and Jane Crow South. It might likewise telegraph a form of self-actualization inscrutable to his agents, intermediaries, and interlocutors.

If "sculpture tells you, you are here," Edmondson's project was a deliberately hometown—and, arguably as important, an outdoor—affair. Installed in the local landscape, his headstones and carvings were testaments to his calling and invention, perennially accessible to him and to any passersby and thus largely unaffected by the "processes of *mutual* exploitation and appropriation" characteristic of modern primitives' engagement with the art world and mainstream press.[14] That kind of agency and immediate social reinforcement was unavailable to those like Kane and Pippin, whose rising status as contemporary artists meant their works quickly disappeared into private and institutional collections, sometimes not to resurface for decades. In that respect, perhaps the most significant feature of our conceptual topography can be distilled in yet another spatial metaphor: the gap between the radical democracy of Edmondson's ostensibly public project and his contemporaries' interventions in the elite precincts of the museum and gallery.

12. John Kane, *Sky Hooks: The Autobiography of John Kane* (Philadelphia, PA: J. B. Lippincott, 1938). Horace Pippin sent "The Story of Horace Pippin as Told by Himself" and "How I Paint" to MoMA curator Dorothy C. Miller in spring (probably March) 1938; they are printed in full in Anne Monahan, *Horace Pippin, American Modern* (New Haven, CT: Yale University Press, 2020), 208–10.
13. Bridget R. Cooks, *Exhibiting Blackness: African Americans and the American Art Museum* (Amherst: University of Massachusetts Press, 2011), 24–33.
14. Clifford, *Routes*, 194.

Cat. 53. Louise Dahl-Wolfe, *William Edmondson*, 1937

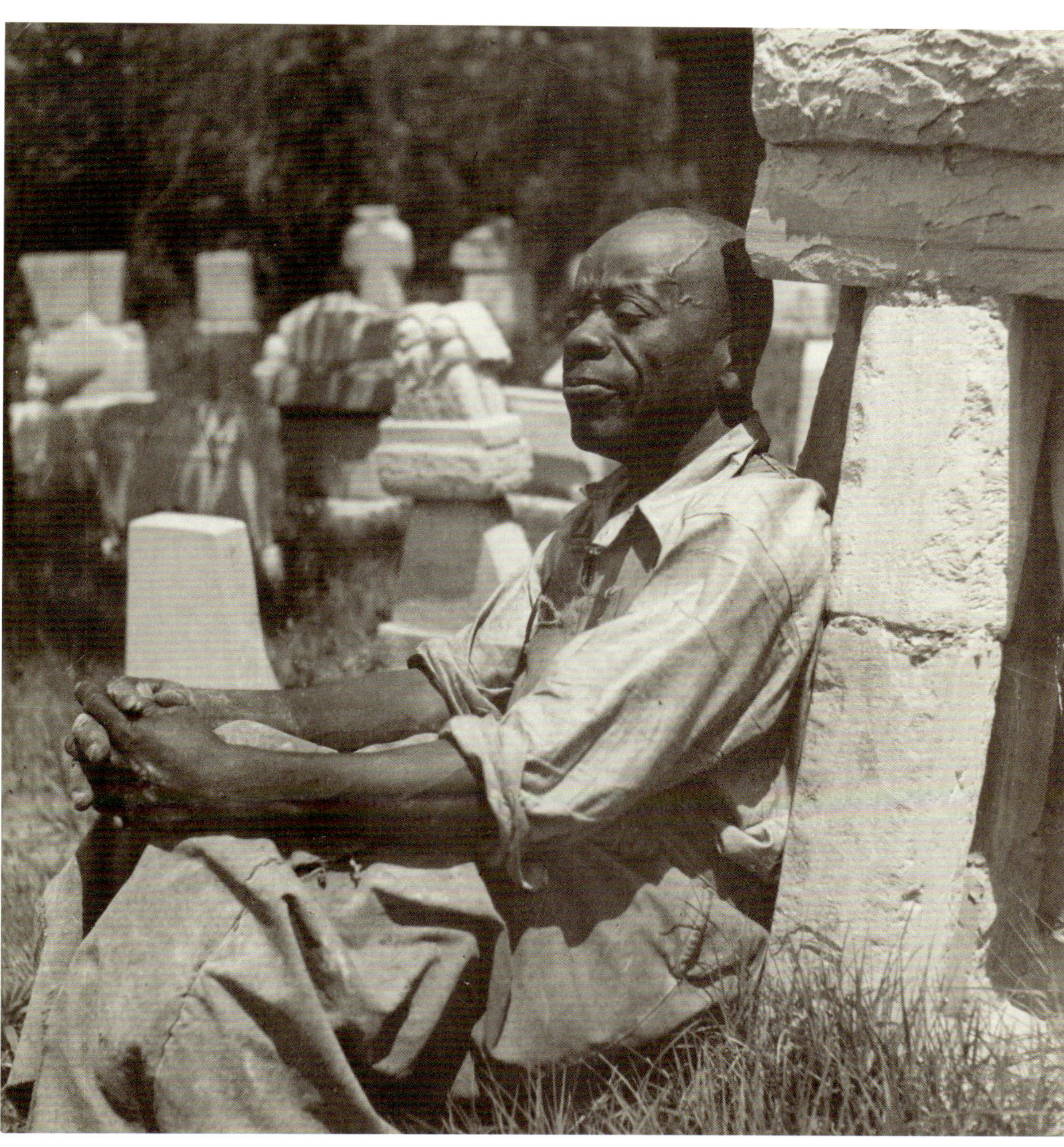

Cat. 54. (Below) William Edmondson, *Seated Nude*, n.d.

Cat. 55. (Recto) William Edmondson, *Seated Nude*, n.d.

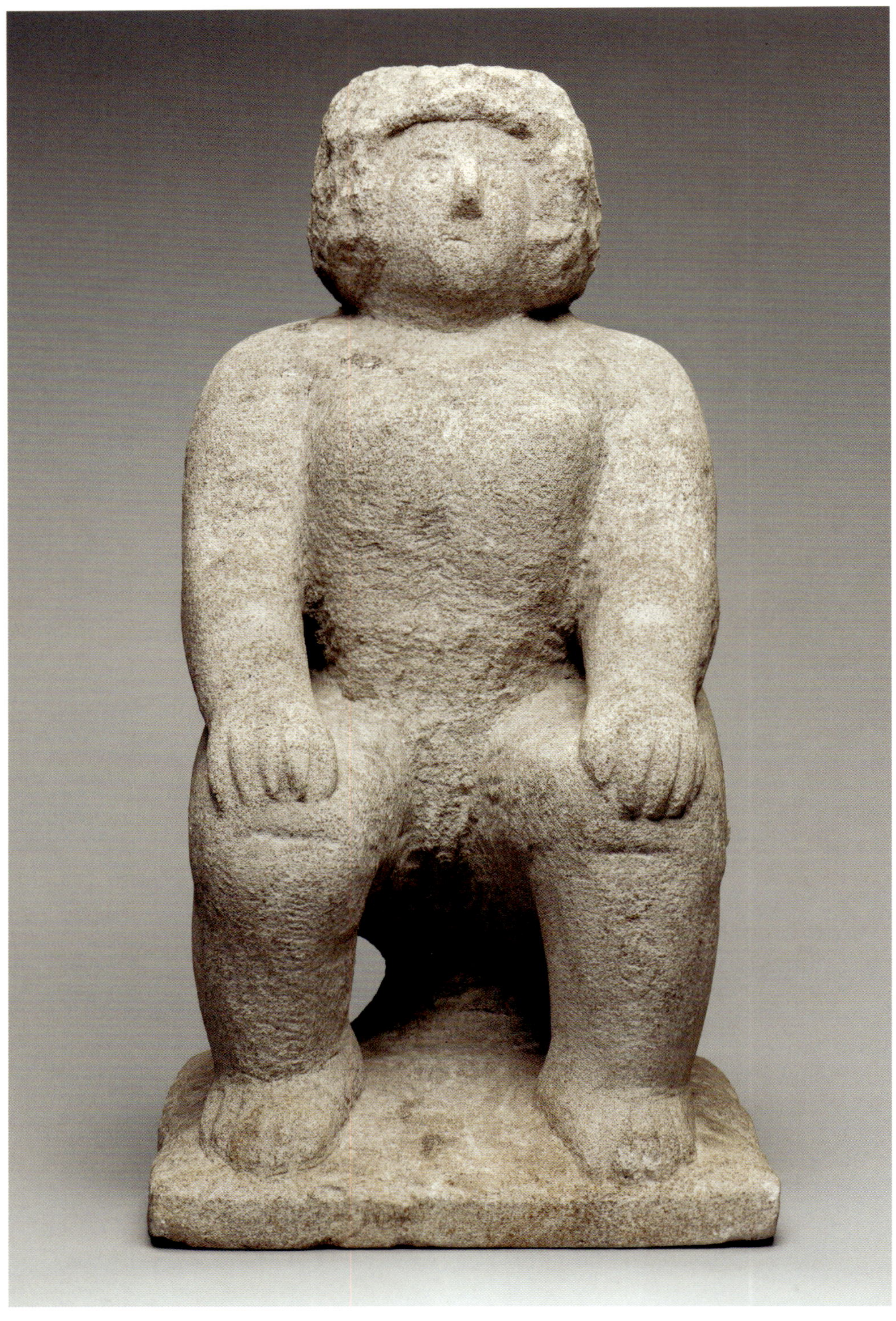

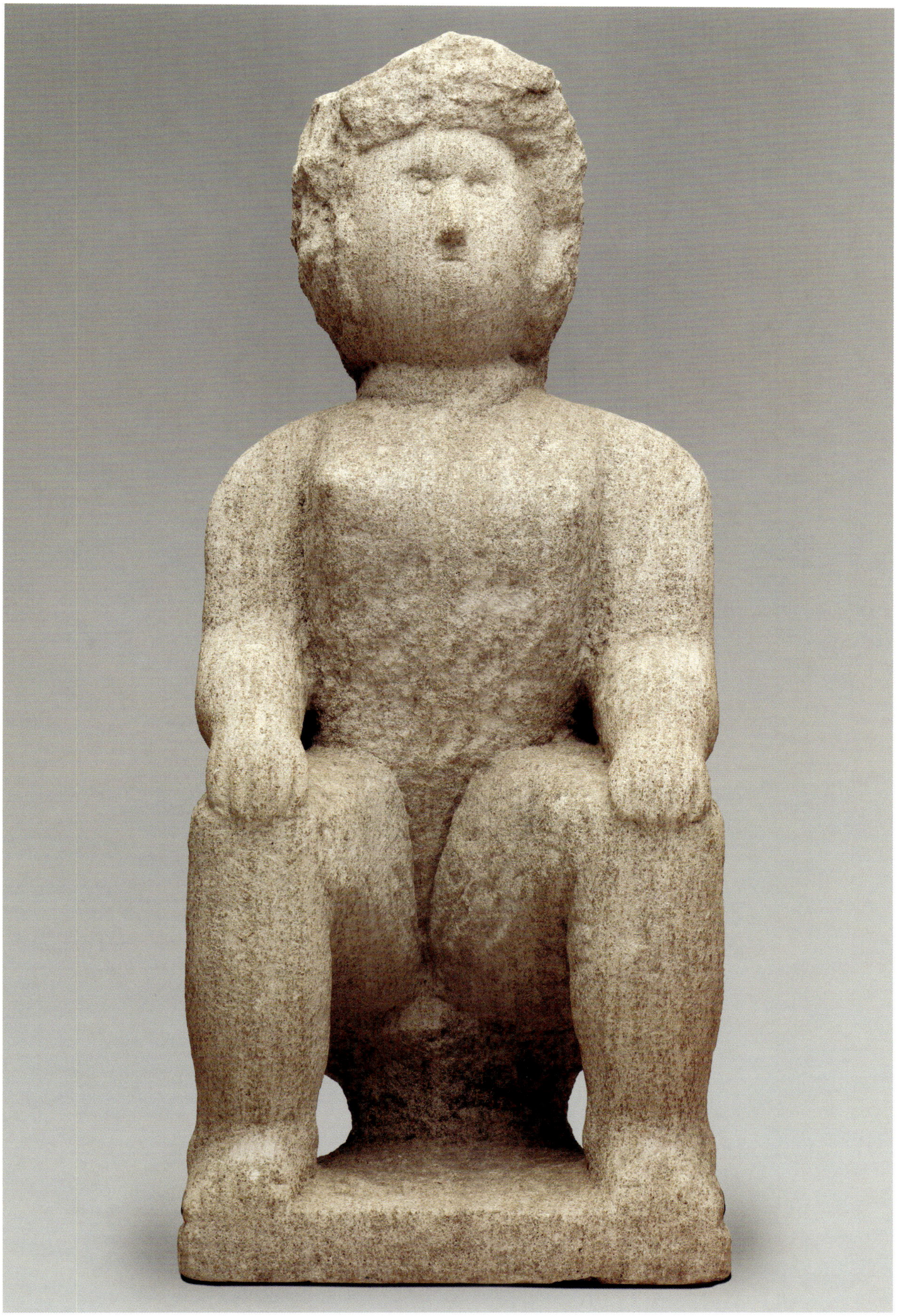

Cat. 56. (Below) William Edmondson, *Crucifix*, n.d.

Cat. 57. (Recto) William Edmondson, *Eve*, 1935

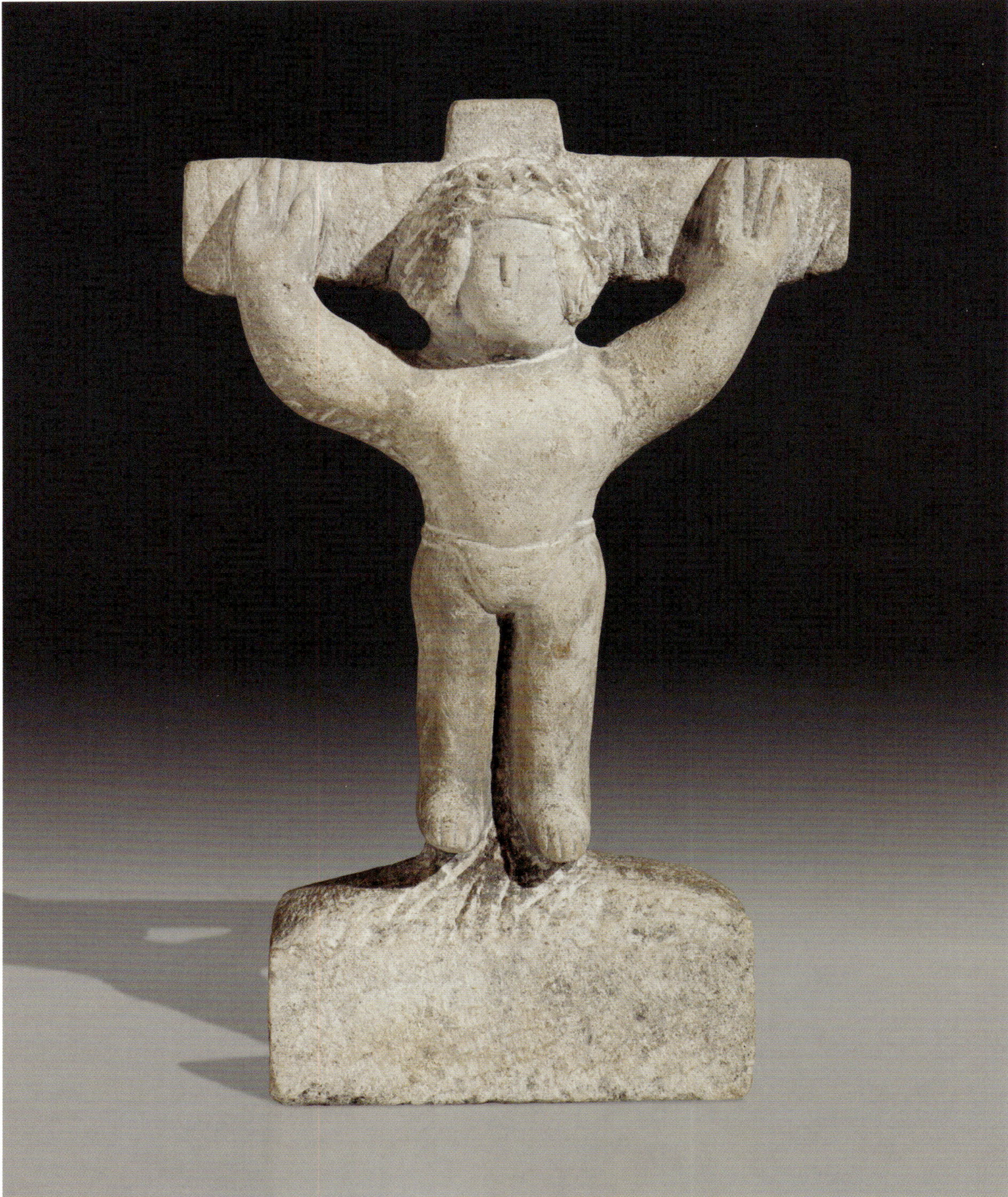

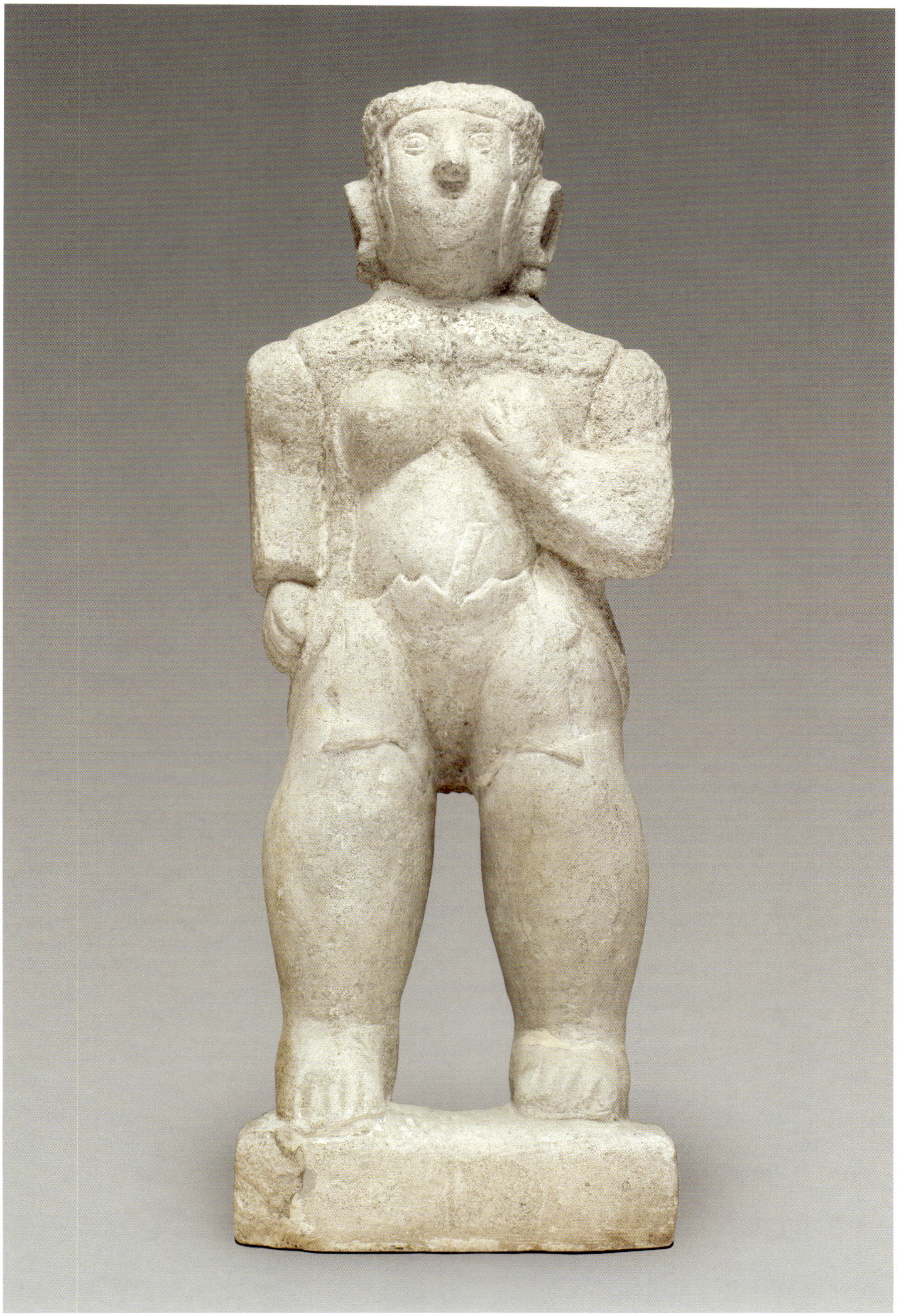

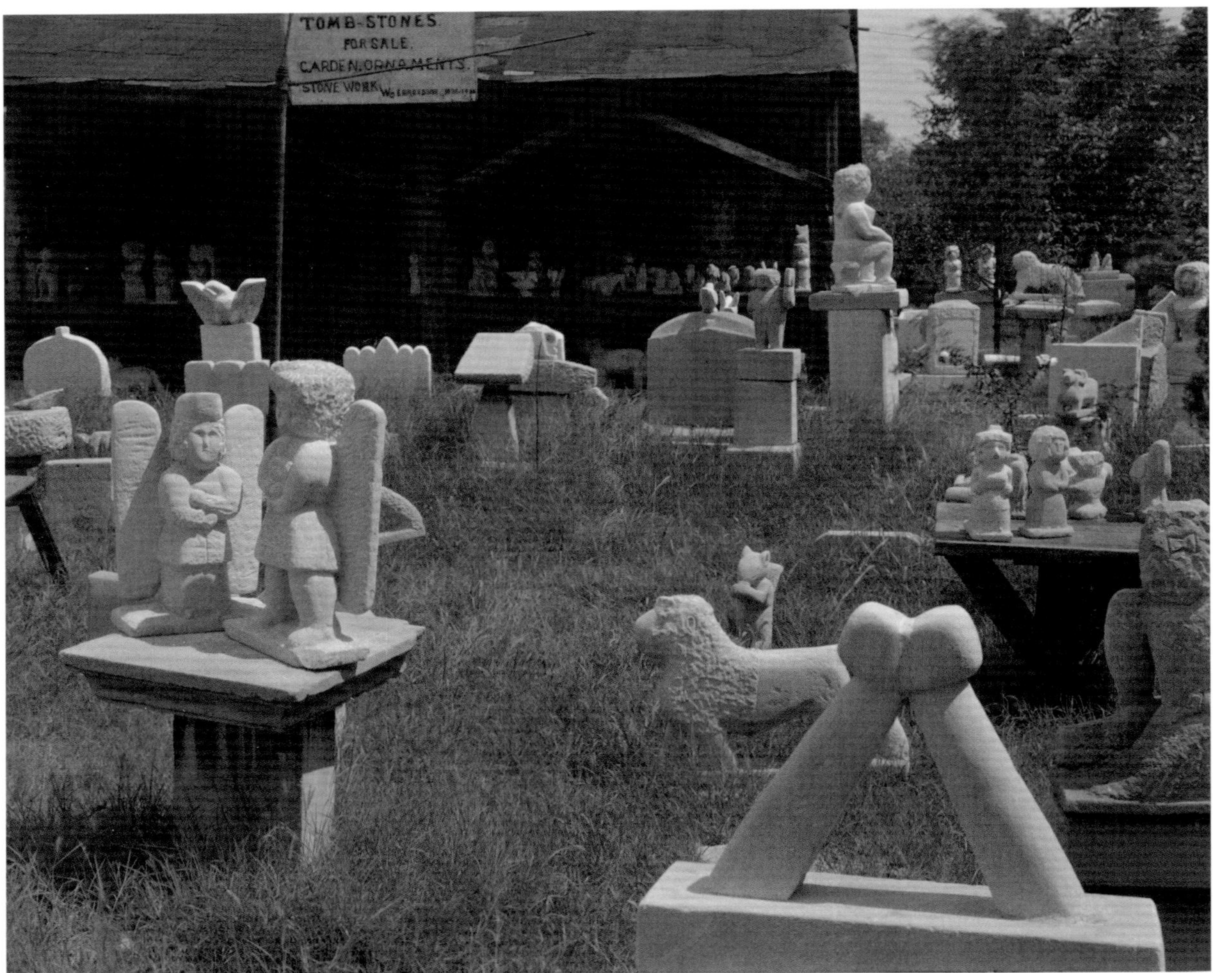

Fig. 20. Edward Weston, *Stone Sculpture, Wm. Edmondson*, 1941. Gelatin silver print, 7 ½ × 9 ½ in. Center for Creative Photography, University of Arizona: Edward Weston Archive.

The Labor of Commercial Collaboration

Photographs of William Edmondson and His Sculpture

Ellen Macfarlane

What would be revealed about American interwar artistic practice if the photographs of William Edmondson and his sculpture were studied through the lens of commercial collaboration? What new ways of understanding photography and sculpture are possible if one were to approach these pictures also as collaborations between media?[1] A photograph by Edward Weston (fig. 20) that depicts the yard of Edmondson's gravestone business begins to offer a response. In Weston's picture, stonework of different sizes and shapes is scattered throughout the yard and storage shed behind it. Edmondson's sculptures crowd the picture's edges, while its center is nearly empty. This negative space magnifies the presence of a stone memorial with two bold diagonal lines in the foreground. These lines guide the viewer's eye toward the congregation of stone on one side of the lawn, through the yard, and up to the sign advertising Edmondson's business

1. Sarah Hamill and Megan Luke address the ways photographs shape sculptural knowledge in their edited volume *Photography and Sculpture: The Art Object in Reproduction* (Los Angeles: Getty Research Institute, 2017).

on the other. The observer traverses a multitude of sculptures that showcase Edmondson's artistic skill and also indicate the wide selection of objects for purchase at his studio. In this sense, the photograph's composition stages the yard not only as a site of artwork, but also of inventory. With this duality in mind, this essay shows how photographs by Louise Dahl-Wolfe, Consuelo Kanaga, and Weston reveal the extent to which they and Edmondson were commercial practitioners, and thus pulls back the curtain on interwar modernist myths of the rarified artist.[2]

That Edmondson was a businessman who in fact performed manual labor undermines established narratives of the sculptor as a naïve, isolated primitive.[3] The idea that art is the product of actual physical labor, rather than intellectual purity, runs against the grain of most modernist narratives. This is especially the case in discussions of Black artists, whom art historian John Ott has demonstrated were often relegated to the status of "laborer" rather than "artist" during the interwar period.[4] However, in the context of Edmondson's business, labor can be re-read as testifying not to his demeaned status as an artist, but to his commercial success.

Dahl-Wolfe's photographs of Edmondson touching his sculpture, such as *William Edmondson, Sculptor, Nashville, Tennessee* (Cat. 58), particularly elucidate this point. On the one hand, art historian Bridget Cooks has argued that photographs, including *William Edmondson, Sculptor*, show Edmondson's carved stones not as precious fine artworks, but as objects that can be touched and handled at one's whim—completely unlike how one would behave in an art museum.[5] On the other, Edmondson scholar Jennifer Jane Marshall has suggested that such photographs emphasize the sculptures' haptic qualities, and empathically ask the viewer to imagine the experience of touching stone.[6] Re-read as photographs that document a commercial enterprise, the images' emphasis on tactility also suggests labor. Signs of Edmondson's labor appear throughout Dahl-Wolfe's image: scuffs and bits of stone clutter the worker's table, while the rough wrinkles of Edmondson's hands harmonize

2. Sybil Gordon Kantor offers an intellectual history of these ideas and their foundation in the origins of the Museum of Modern Art and the leadership of its founding director Alfred Barr in *Alfred H. Barr, Jr. and the Intellectual Origins of the Museum of Modern Art* (Cambridge, MA: MIT Press, 2002).
3. Such narratives are challenged in the following texts: Jennifer Jane Marshall, "'Ever Not Quite': Empathy, Experience, and William Edmondson," in *Experience*, ed. Alexander Nemerov (Chicago: Terra Foundation for American Art, 2017), 102–33; Marshall, "Nashville, New York, Paris, and Nashville: William Edmondson, Mobilized and Unmoved," *American Art* 31, no. 2 (Summer 2017): 69–76; Marshall, "Find-and-Seek: Discovery Narratives, Americanization, and Other Tales of Genius in Modern American Folk Art," in *Outliers and American Vanguard Art* (Washington, DC: National Gallery of Art in association with the University of Chicago Press), 52–63; John Ott, "Labored Stereotypes: Palmer Hayden's *The Janitor Who Paints*," *American Art* 22, no. 1 (Summer 2008): 108; and Lowery Stokes Sims, "The Self-Taught among Us: William Edmondson and the Vanguardist Dilemma," in *The Art of William Edmondson* (Nashville, TN: Cheekwood Museum of Art, 1999), 71–78. Relatedly, Michael Harris addresses the international celebration of Black primitivism by white intellectuals during the interwar era in *Colored Pictures: Race and Visual Representation* (Chapel Hill: University of North Carolina Press, 2003); and, in his chapter "From the Sidewalk to the Marketplace: Traylor, Edmondson, and the Modernist Impulse," Josef Helfenstein investigates Edmondson's short period of reception and inclusion in interwar modernist discourses, particularly in regard to Alfred Barr's presentation of Edmondson's sculpture in the 1937 exhibition *Sculpture by William Edmondson*, in *Bill Traylor, William Edmondson, and the Modernist Impulse*, ed. Josef Helfenstein and Roxanne Stanulis (Urbana, IL: Krannert Art Museum and Kinkead Pavillion, 2004), 45–52.
4. Ott, "Labored Stereotypes," 102–15.
5. Bridget R. Cooks, *Exhibiting Blackness: African Americans and the American Art Museum* (Boston: University of Massachusetts Press, 2011), 28.
6. Marshall, "'Ever Not Quite,'" 106.

Cat. 58. Louise Dahl-Wolfe, *William Edmondson, Sculptor, Nashville, Tennessee*, 1933–37

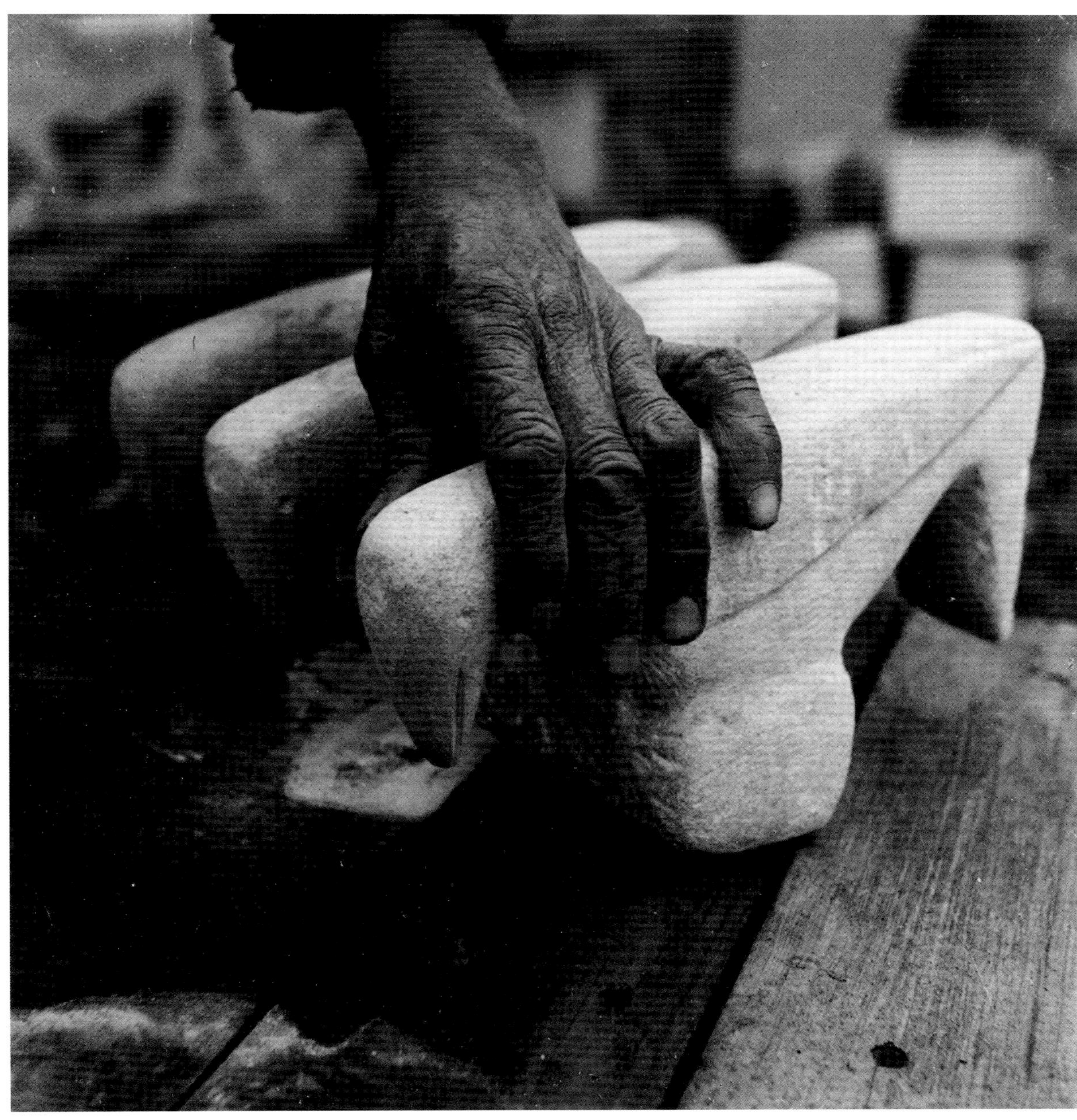

with the carved striations on the dove's stone surface.[7] The trace of the author's hand has been considered a sign of value in artwork for much of the modern era; it has been regarded as a marker of originality and irreproducibility. Read in the context of a commercial business, photographs depicting Edmondson's touch thus capture the artist producing a unique commodity.

7. Judith McWillie, "William Edmondson with Edward Weston and Louise Dahl-Wolfe, 1934–1941," in *The Art of William Edmondson*, 53–55.

Fig. 21. Edward Weston, *Stone Sculpture, Wm. Edmondson*, 1941. Gelatin silver print, 7 ⅝ × 9 ⁹⁄₁₆ in. Center for Creative Photography, University of Arizona: Edward Weston Archive.

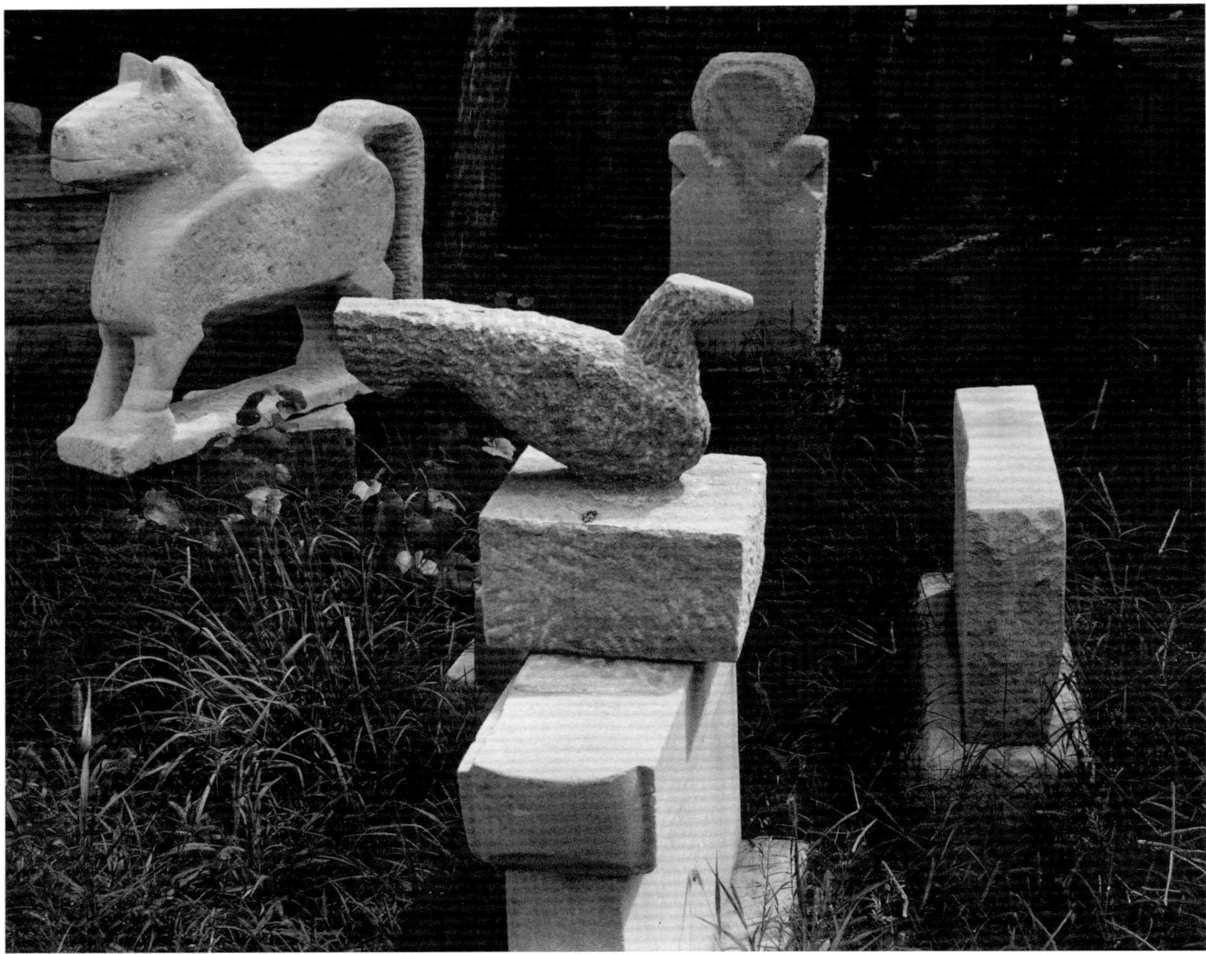

Dahl-Wolfe, Kanaga, and Weston were also commercial workers, skilled in a medium that itself required one to manually operate a machine. In this sense, it is perhaps unsurprising that photographs depicting the hands of artists and workers engaged with their materials were completely conventional during the interwar era.[8] Edmondson's photographers had a deep recognition for the labor of both art making and running a business, as each operated commercial studios while also pursuing their craft as artists. At the time they visited Edmondson in 1934 to 1937, 1941, and 1950, respectively, Dahl-Wolfe was a staff photographer for *Harper's Bazaar*, Weston was on assignment shooting photographs to illustrate a deluxe edition of Walt Whitman's *Leaves of Grass*, and Kanaga made most of her living as a photographer for

8. For example, the De Young Museum curated an exhibition of such work titled *A Showing of Hands* in June 1932 that traveled to Alma Reed's Delphic Studios in New York City in November 1932. *A Showing of Hands* exhibition file, 1932, American Art Study Center, The M. H. de Young Memorial Museum. Interwar photographs of hands are also the subject of Max Fraser's "Hands Off the Machine: Workers' Hands and Revolutionary Symbolism in the Visual Culture of 1930s America," *American Art* 27, no. 2 (2013): 94–117.

Fig. 22. Edward Weston, *William Edmondson, Sculptor, Nashville*, 1941. Gelatin silver print. Center for Creative Photography, University of Arizona: Edward Weston Archive.

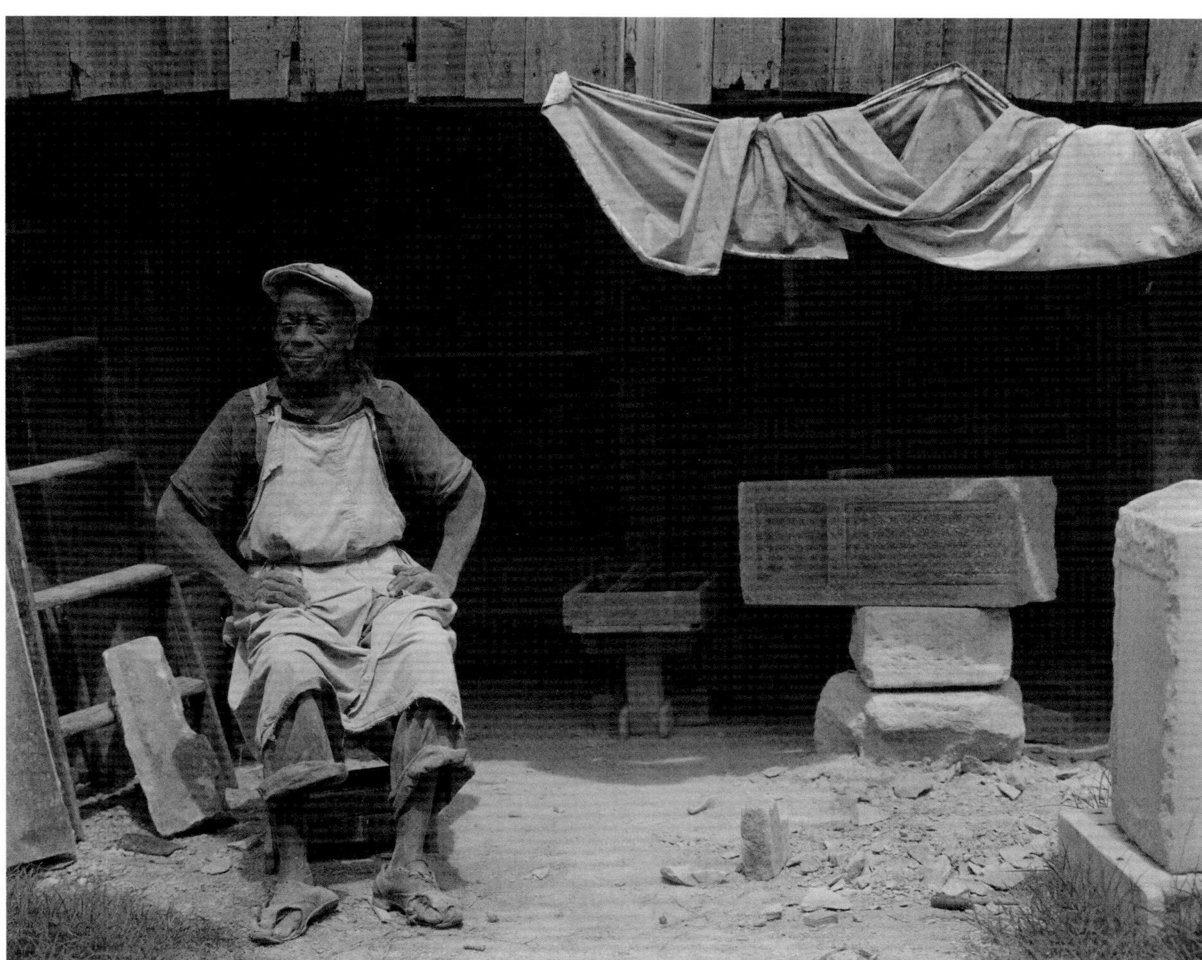

women's magazines, including *Women's Day*.[9] Ultimately, both *Harper's Bazaar* and the editor of the Whitman project, George Macy, declined to print photographs of Edmondson in their publications because he was Black.[10]

In an era of racial segregation, it is tempting to interpret the exchanges that took place between Edmondson and Dahl-Wolfe, Kanaga, and Weston as encounters in which Edmondson acquiesced to the desires of white photographers.[11] Or, that because of his race, only the sculptor's exploitation was possible. However, either of these interpretations denies Edmondson agency. In fact, the photographers had much to gain through an affiliation with Edmondson. In the interwar era, photography still fell far behind other creative media, including sculpture, in terms of artistic hierarchy.[12] By the time Weston

9. Marshall, "'Ever Not Quite,'" 112; Jennifer A. Watts, *Real American Places: Edward Weston and* Leaves of Grass (San Marino, CA: Huntington Library, 2017), 3; Barbara Head Millstein and Sarah M. Howe, *Consuelo Kanaga: An American Photographer* (New York: Brooklyn Museum in assoc. with University of Washington Press, 1992), 42.
10. Marshall, "'Ever Not Quite,'" 131; Watts, *Real American Places*, 7.
11. Cooks, *Exhibiting Blackness*, 28.
12. McWillie, "William Edmondson," 45, 58–59.

photographed Edmondson in 1941, and Kanaga traveled to the sculptor's studio in 1950, Dahl-Wolfe's earlier photographs had already prompted Alfred Barr Jr. to arrange a solo exhibition for Edmondson in 1937 at the Museum of Modern Art, then the ultimate ratifier of modernist legitimacy.

In this sense, Kanaga's and Weston's projects benefitted from the artistic cachet that Edmondson's sculpture appeared to provide. Affirming this recognition is the fact that MoMA later accessioned several of Weston's photographs of Edmondson.[13] Further demonstrating sculpture's advanced standing in relation to photography is the fact that Weston was not given a retrospective at MoMA until 1946, and Kanaga's work was not displayed at the museum until a few prints were included in Edward Steichen's *In and Out of Focus: A Survey of Today's Photography* and *50 Photographs, 50 Photographers* exhibitions in 1948.[14]

Indeed, the success of Weston's and Kanaga's day jobs—their portrait studios and paid assignments—depended in large part on the photographers' credibility as artists. Customers sought out Weston's Carmel studio because of his artistic renown. Kanaga received commissions because she operated within a multi-media network of artists, including Alfred Stieglitz, through which she met patrons.[15] In other words, an association with Edmondson and his sculpture benefitted the photographers' work. It is true that Edmondson was subject to an "outsider" status—he was Black, untrained, isolated, and largely immobile—but he was still a sculptor who had a solo exhibition at MoMA and worked in a medium that was much more on the "inside" than photography was.[16] This idea runs counter to the notion that it is only Black artists who might have something to gain professionally from relationships with white artists or benefactors, and not the other way around.[17]

However, the photographers' portraits of Edmondson suggest an exchange that was more ambivalent. Artist Judith McWillie has addressed this issue, suggesting that Weston's horizontal portraits of Edmondson, such as *William Edmondson, Sculptor, Nashville* (fig. 22), capture the "nobility of American labor," while the photographer's vertical shots, including *William Edmondson, Tennessee* (fig. 6), indicate

13. Cooks, *Exhibiting Blackness*, 29.
14. McWillie, "William Edmondson," 45; Millstein, *Consuelo Kanaga*, 39 and 43.
15. See Millstein, "Consuelo Kanaga, An American Photographer," in *Consuelo Kanaga*, 17–57.
16. Marshall, "Mobilized and Unmoved," 69–76; Marshall, "Find-and-Seek," 52–63.
17. The complicatedness of these relationships has also been addressed in Jeffrey Stewart, "Black Modernism and White Patronage," *International Review of African American Art* 11, no. 3 (1994): 43, and Marshall, "'Ever Not Quite,'" 118.

Fig. 23. Louise Dahl-Wolfe, *Edmondson*, n.d. Gelatin silver print. Center for Creative Photography, University of Arizona: Louise Dahl-Wolfe Archive/Gift of the Louise Dahl-Wolfe Trust.

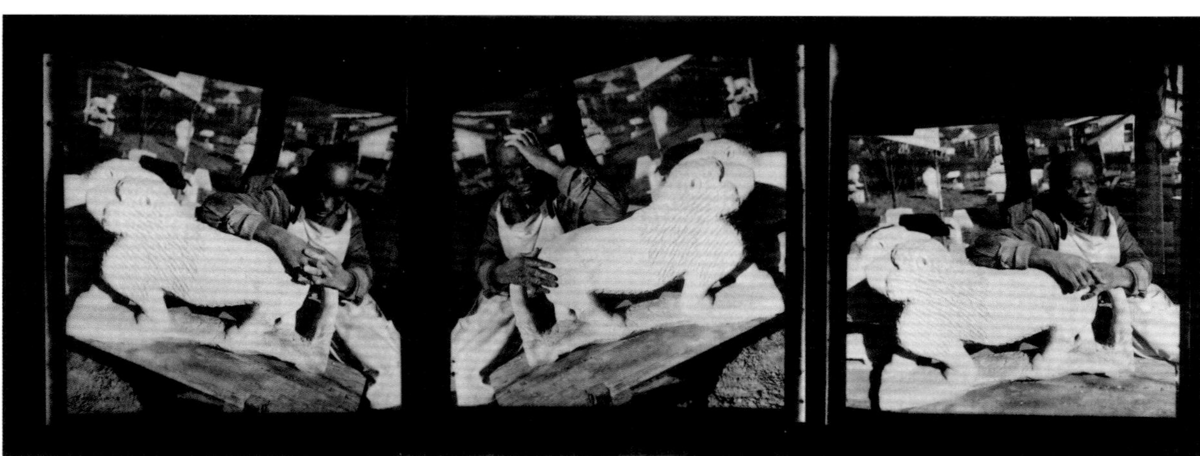

18. McWillie, "William Edmondson," 59.

the sculptor's "insightful shrewdness and confident poise of an artist at the height of his creative power." On the other hand, she writes, Dahl-Wolfe's proofs depicting an exhausted Edmondson (fig. 23) are "stereotypically romantic" and portray Edmondson as a "long-suffering idealist."[18] Each of these pictures shows the artist absorbed with the labor of his commercial trade. Dahl-Wolfe's shots depict Edmondson worn out and leaning over the carved lion and resting his hands on the stone, as though psychically connected to his artwork through touch. Weston's vertical portrait of Edmondson presents the artist covered tip to toe in the trappings of his work: a hat on his head, protective goggles pulled to the side of his face, while a long smock, pants, and boots shield the gravestone cutter from the shards of debris that are cast off his stones. Notably, Edmondson's hands, the agents of his labor, are uncovered and rest prominently across his confidently poised chest. Conversely, Weston's representation of Edmondson seated reads as much less heroic: the neatly laced work boots of the first portrait have been replaced with tattered shoes that unceremoniously expose Edmondson's toes, rhyming with the remnants of cut limestone that litter the ground and the dilapidated wooden planks above Edmondson's head.

Kanaga's portraits of Edmondson, made the year before he passed away, are markedly different. Two shots of Edmondson, each titled *William Edmondson (Tennessee)* (Cat. 59 and 60), portray the artist outdoors and removed from the

Cat. 59. Consuelo Kanaga, *William Edmondson (Tennessee)*, 1950

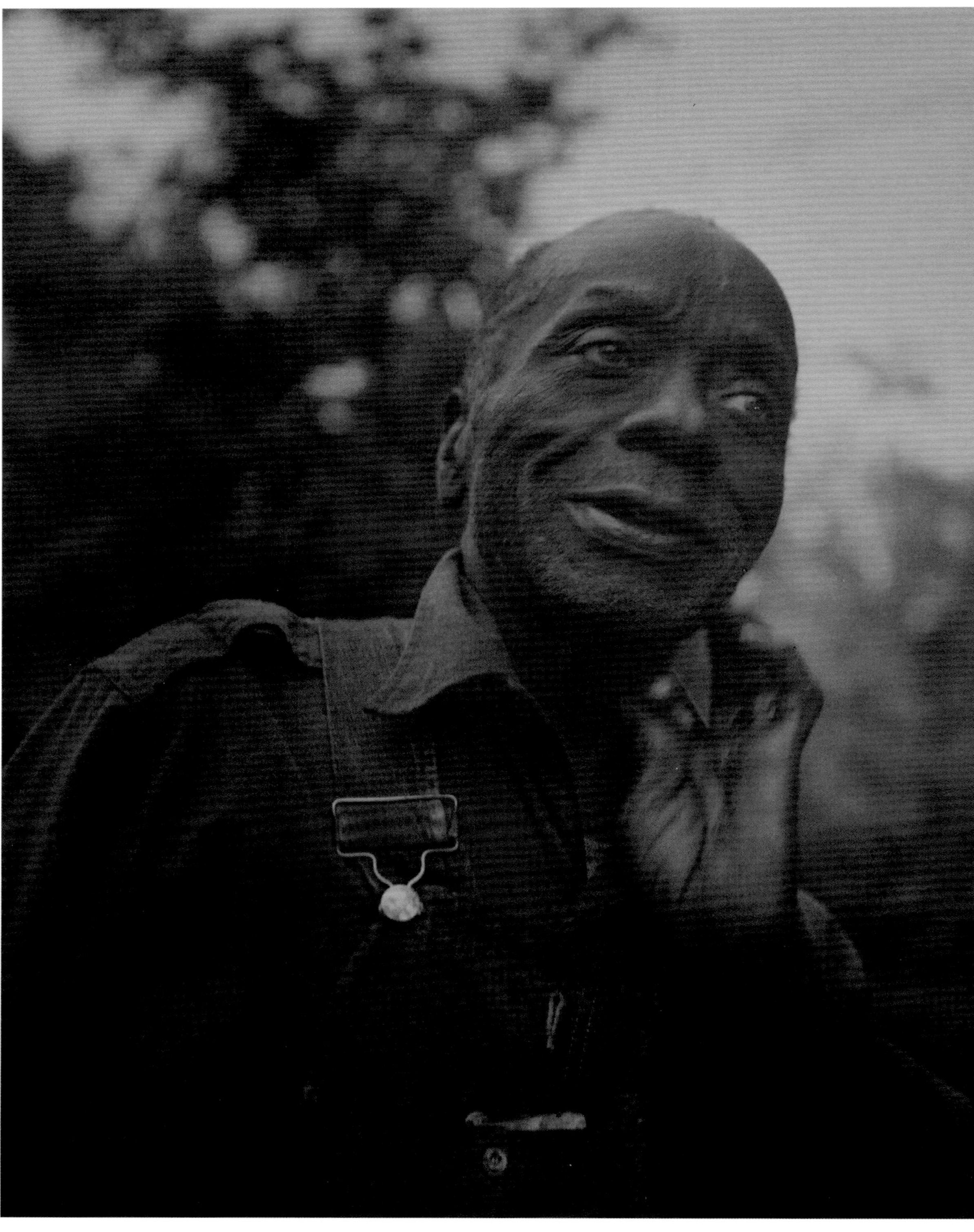

Cat. 60. Consuelo Kanaga, *William Edmondson (Tennessee)*, 1950

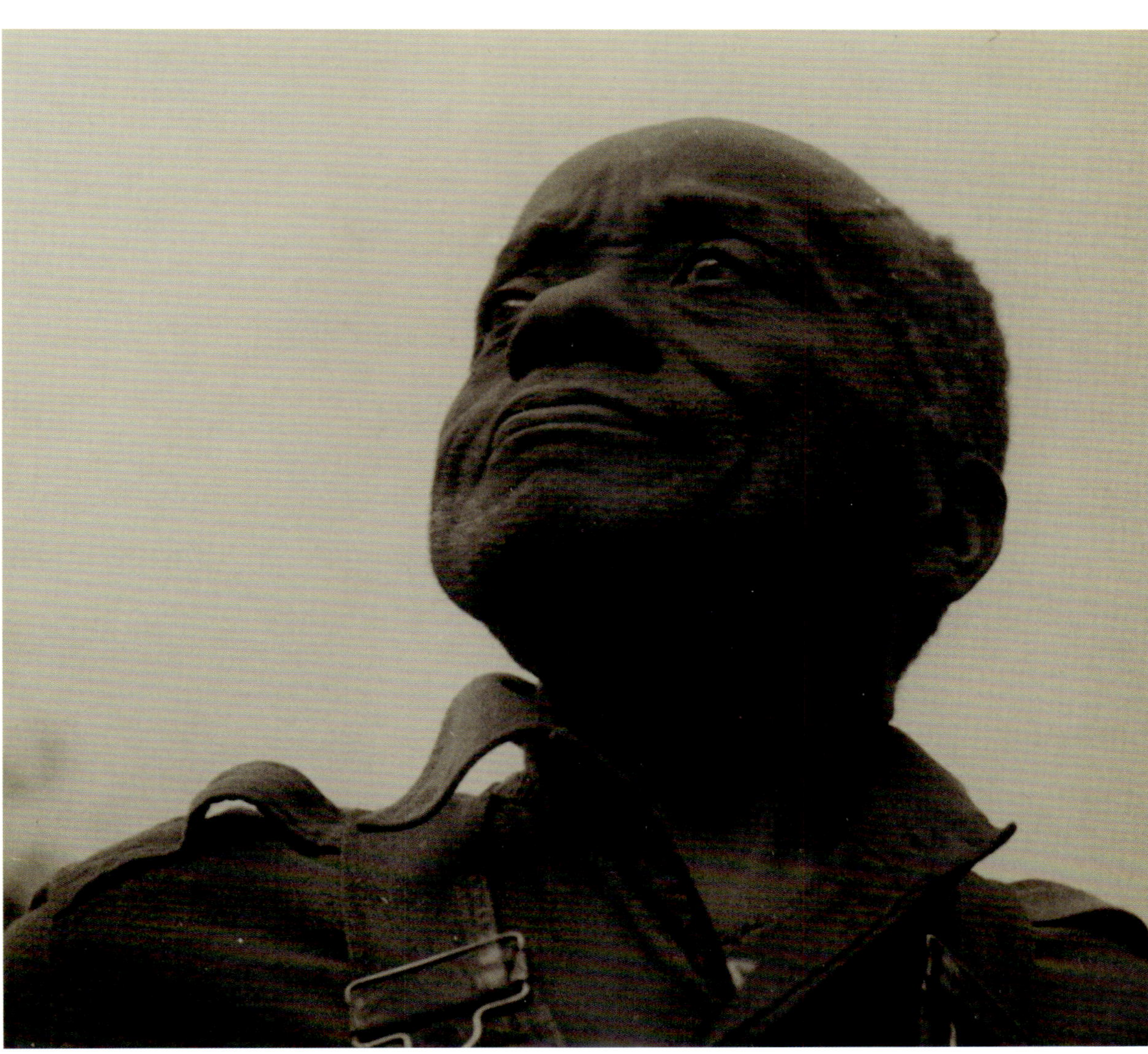

context of his business. As with Kanaga's many other interwar and mid-century portraits of Black sitters, such as her series picturing the bass singer Kenneth Spencer (fig. 24), the photographer is concerned with the expressive potential of the human face and the pathos that oblique camera angles evoke. Kanaga's prints seem less concerned than Dahl-Wolfe's and Weston's with characterizing Edmondson specifically as a fine artist or as an entrepreneur. Instead, Kanaga's images have the aesthetic of candid photographs: one picture captures Edmondson in motion, as suggested in the blur of his hand grazing his face and the diagonal, forward-reaching position of his body in space, while the second marshals proximity to suggest access to Edmondson's inner being, perhaps staging what Marshall has referred to as "an empathic encounter with otherness."[19] Just as Dahl-Wolfe's, Kanaga's, and Weston's work was always already commercial and artistic, Kanaga's prints suspend Edmondson in an appropriately liminal space in which he is neither solely a commercial grave cutter, nor singularly an artist.

19. Marshall, "'Ever Not Quite,'" 109.

Fig. 24. Consuelo Kanaga, *Kenneth Spencer*, 1933. Gelatin silver photograph, 9 ⅜ × 7 ⅛ in. Brooklyn Museum, Gift of Wallace B. Putnam from the Estate of Consuelo Kanaga, 82.65.368.

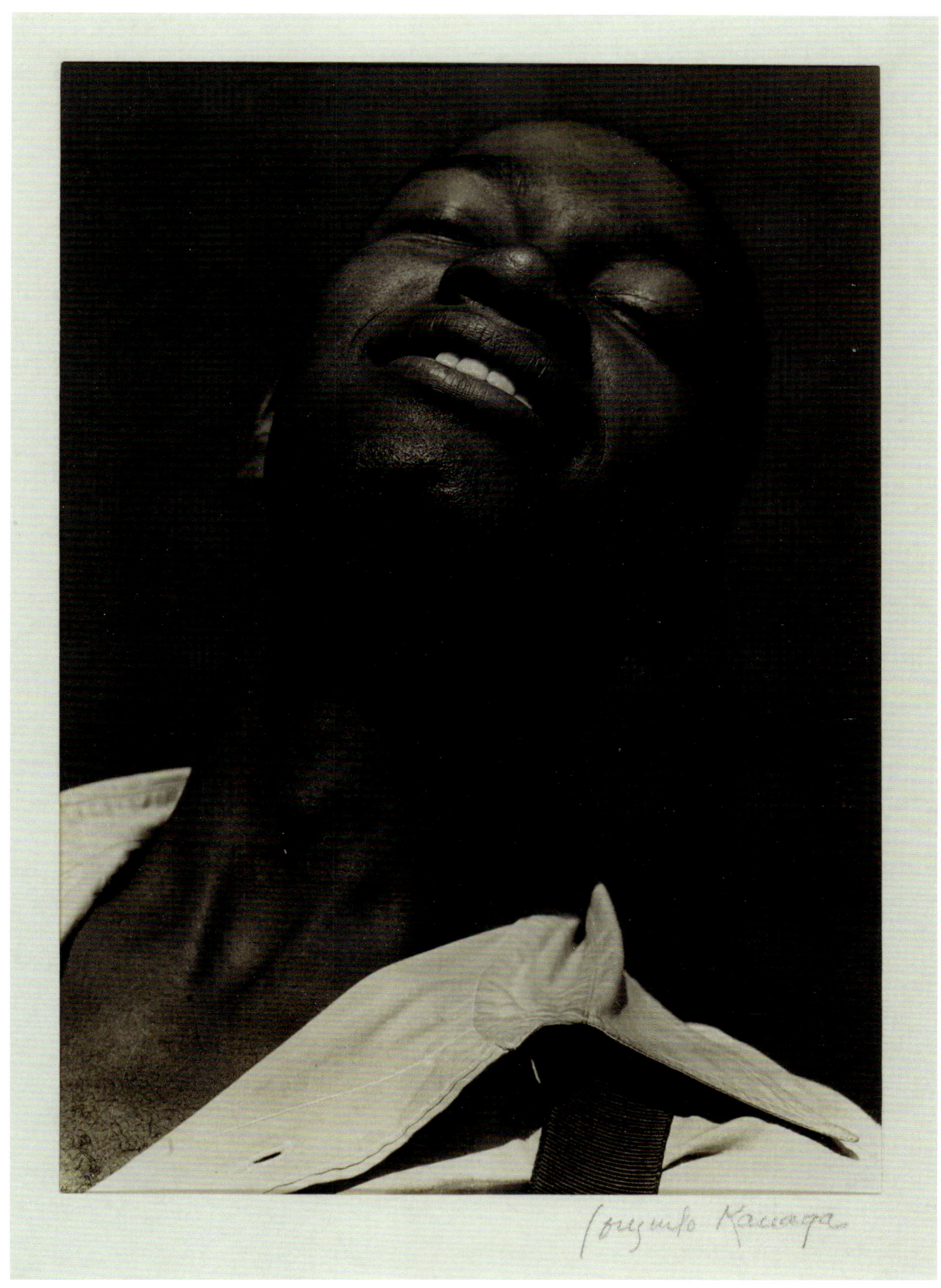

Cat. 61. Louise Dahl-Wolfe, *Sculpture, William Edmondson (Three Doves)*, c. 1933

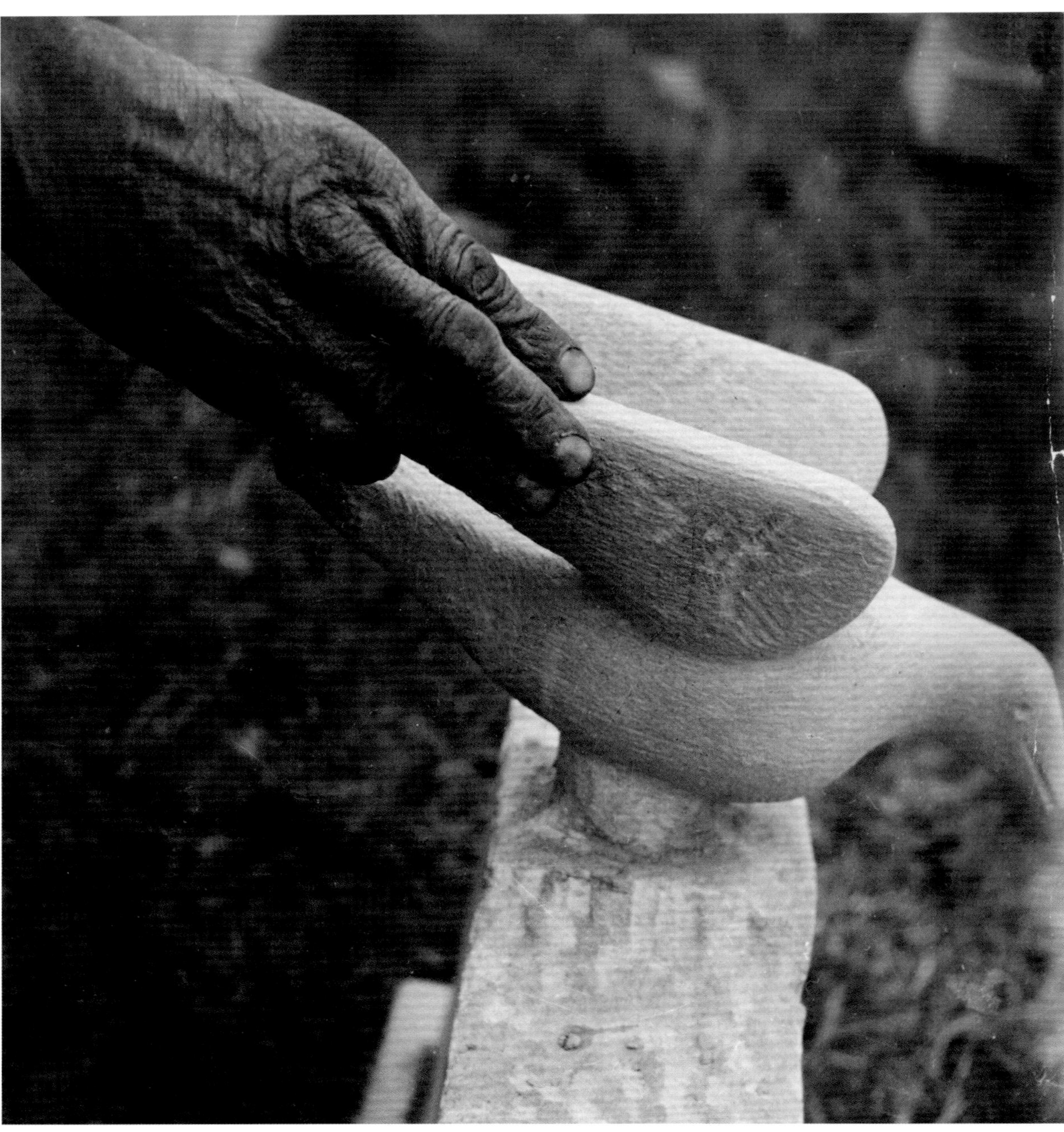

Cat. 62. Louise Dahl-Wolfe, *William Edmondson*, 1937

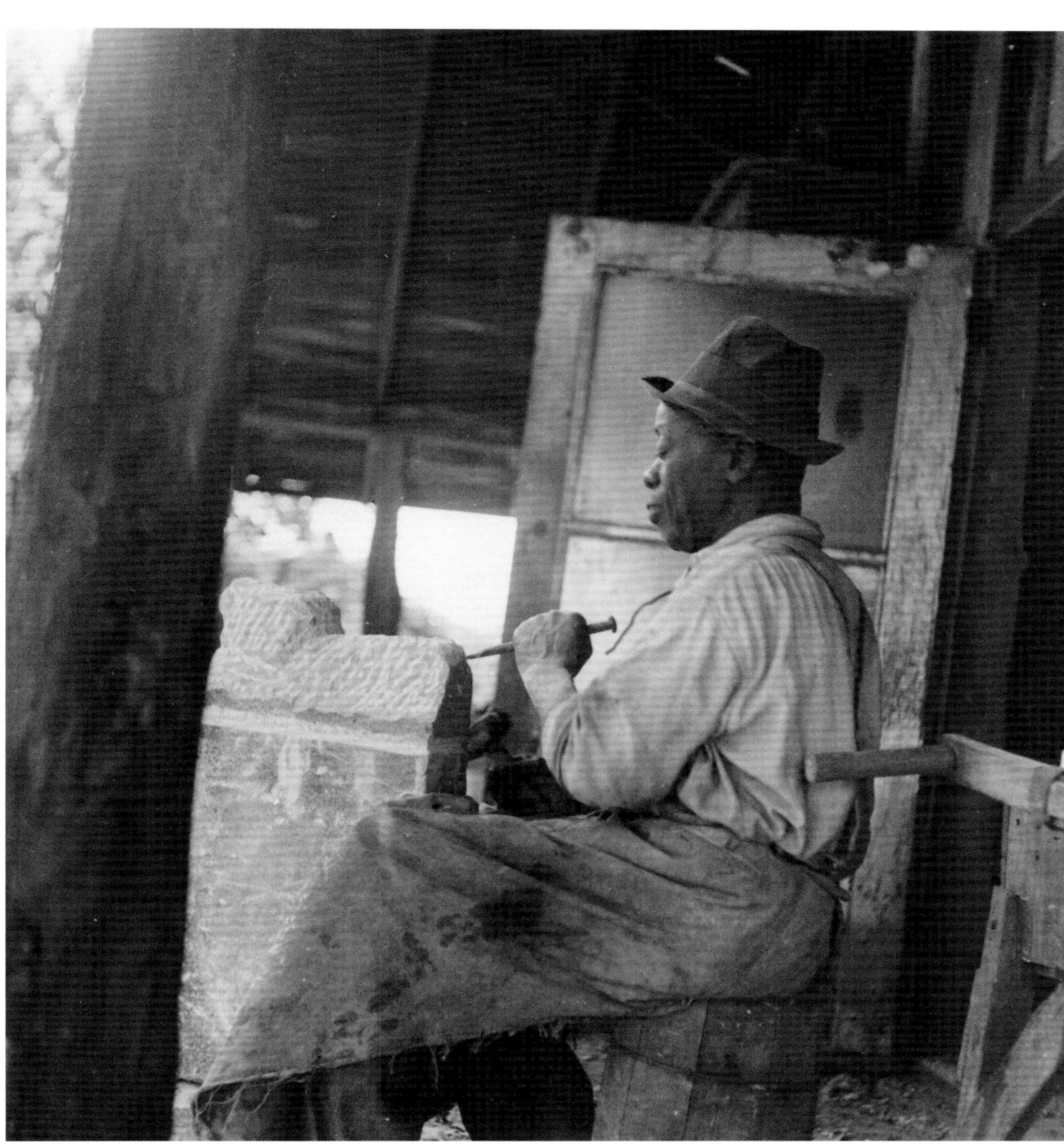

Cat.63. Louise Dahl-Wolfe, *William Edmondson, Sculptor, Nashville, Tennessee*, 1937

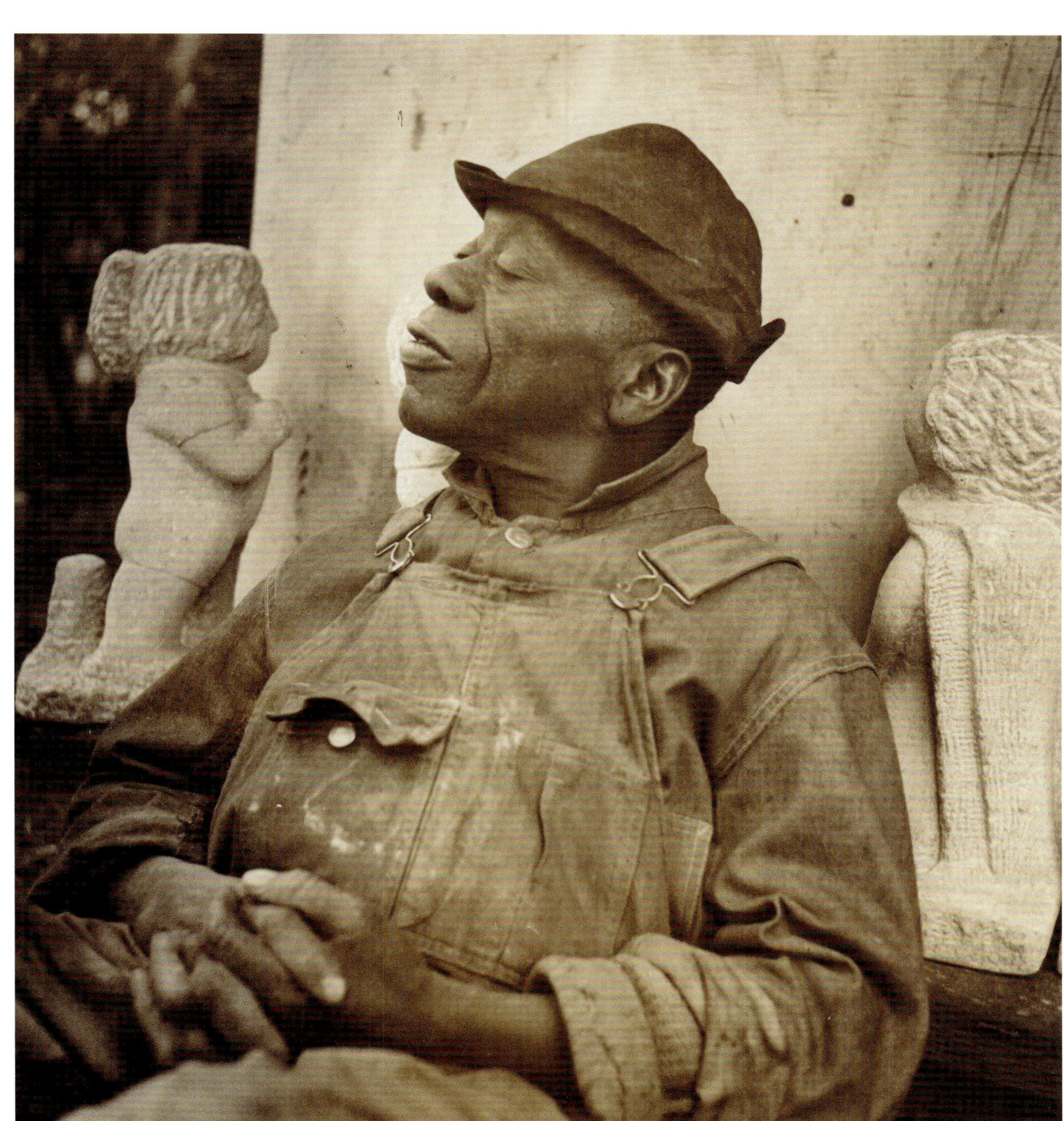

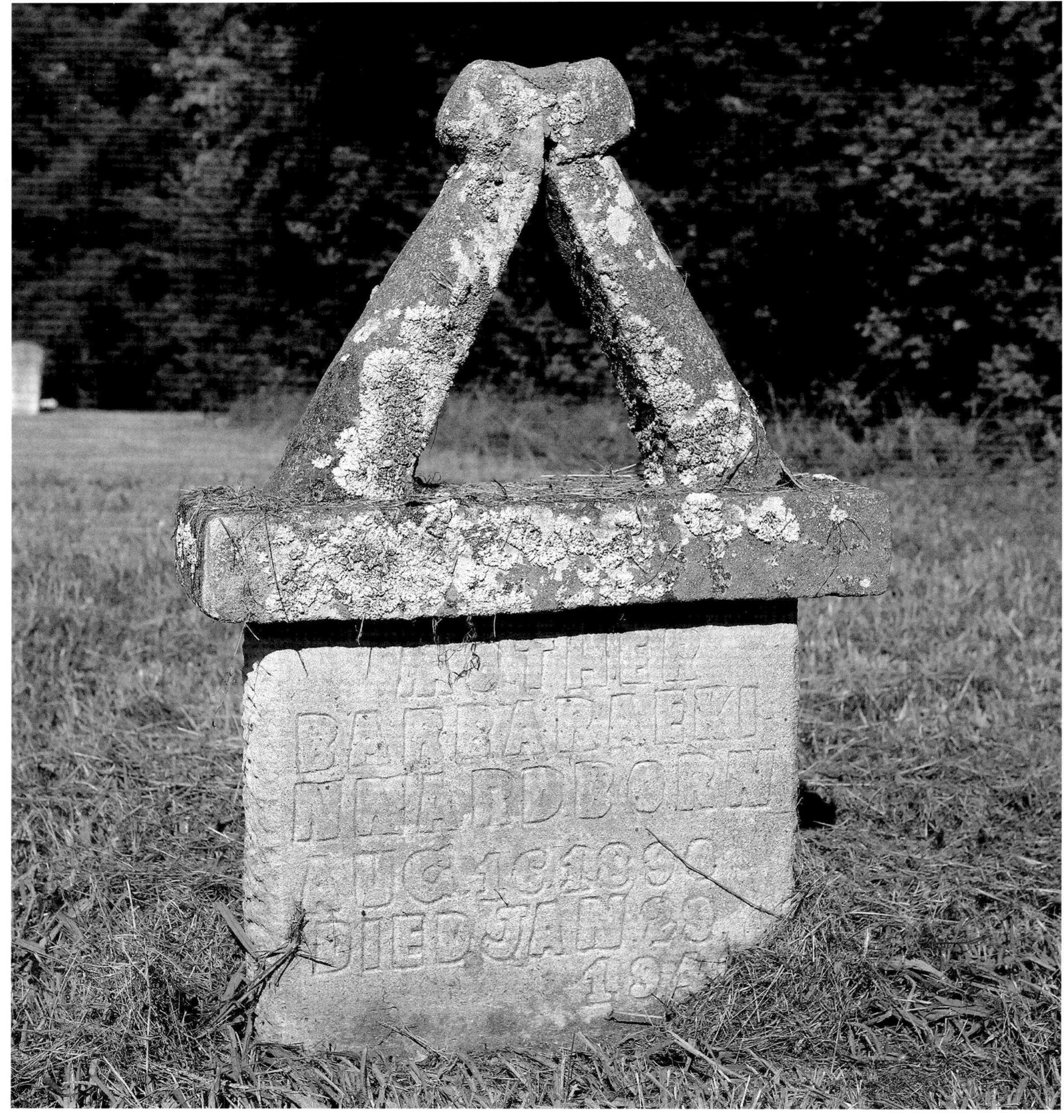

Fig. 25. William Edmondson, *Barbara Kinnard Tombstone*, n.d. Photo courtesy of Marin R. Sullivan

Tombstones by William Edmondson in Nashville Cemeteries

Betsy Phillips

Though we do not know how many grave markers William Edmondson carved, there are fewer than forty such gravestones still left in Middle Tennessee graveyards. Exposed to the elements and to thieves, many of the stones are eroding and many of the sculptures we know were part of the markers are gone. Still, these graveyards remain the most accessible places to see Edmondson works. The Tennessee State Museum, for instance, is free to the public, but it has only three sculptures on permanent display. That is as many as you would find in Toussaint L'Ouverture cemetery in Franklin, Tennessee. Most of the Nashville cemeteries that contain his stones hold many more than that.

Those stones tell us a lot about Edmondson and his relationship to his community. Most of the stones he made were for friends, neighbors, and family members. The Anthony family, for instance—Thomas, Mintha, and their daughter, Hazel Foster—who are buried at the Greater Pleasant View Missionary Baptist Church cemetery just south of where Edmondson's family was enslaved, lived at 1412 Fourteenth Avenue South and 1402 Thirteenth Avenue South.

Edmondson lived at 1434 Fourteenth Avenue South. Lucious William Work and his wife, Myrtle, who share an Edmondson headstone in Greenwood Cemetery, lived around the corner from Edmondson at 916 Horton.

Orange Edmondson was married to Addie Watkins who had a brother named James. James W. Watkins, who is buried in Mount Ararat Cemetery under an Edmondson marker, appears to be the brother of Edmondson's brother's wife. We know that William's cousin, Rev. Albert Whitlow, had a headstone for his wife, Mary Alice Bolyjack Whitlow, carved by Edmondson when she was buried in the Edmondson Cemetery in Lake Providence.[1] This headstone is now in the Cheekwood collection. The Edmondson Cemetery, located south of the intersection of Nolensville Road and Edmondson Pike, no longer has any visible headstones, so we don't know if there was more of Edmondson's work in there or not.

The stones reveal a puzzle in the death dates. Of the forty known death dates, twenty-eight take place between December and March. Surely winter was hard on the laborers, domestics, and hospital workers who made up many of Edmondson's customers, but such a large cluster is peculiar.[2] If we look at a similar sample—Black people who died between 1931 and 1951 who are buried in either the Briarville Cemetery or the nearby Benevolent Society #79 cemetery in Nashville—we find thirty-three deaths from the time period when Edmondson was active, but only fourteen took place in the December through March stretch. By far the hardest month for residents of Briarville was April, which saw twelve deaths. More research needs to be done as to why Edmondson sculpted so many headstones in the winter months.

Though many of the cemeteries where Edmondson headstones are located are now church cemeteries—Mount Pisgah, Greater Pleasant View Missionary Baptist Church, etc.—they were not at the time Edmondson placed his work there. They were almost all benevolent society cemeteries. African American benevolent societies were popular social clubs in the early to mid-1900s in Middle Tennessee. Among other things, dues-paying members were guaranteed burial, usually in a benevolent society cemetery. Greater Pleasant View

1. The Edmondson family the cemetery is named for does not appear to be related to William Edmondson's family.
2. This number is larger than the number of known stones because some stones contain multiple names.

Missionary Baptist Church is the steward of Benevolent Order #151's cemetery. What is now known as the Mount Pisgah United Methodist Church cemetery was the Benevolent Order #10's cemetery. Though Mount Ararat is now owned and operated by Greenwood Cemetery, it was opened by the Sons of Relief #1 and Benevolent Order #1. The Dry Creek Cemetery was dedicated by the Sons of Ham #1.

Though information about the cemetery on Taliaferro Road in Williamson County that contains an Edmondson is limited, the lack of any nearby church and the presence of certain grave decorations suggests it also might be an old benevolent cemetery. The other cemeteries that contain Edmondson headstones—Greenwood and Toussaint L'Ouverture—while not founded by benevolent societies, are full of benevolent society and lodge members.

It seems possible that there may still be unrecognized Edmondson works in other benevolent society cemeteries in Middle Tennessee. There is no comprehensive list of all the benevolent society cemeteries. Often, you have to stumble across them or hope that a church's website will reveal its cemetery's ties to such societies. It also seems very likely that there were Edmondsons in benevolent society cemeteries that have been destroyed. After Mount Ararat, the largest benevolent society cemetery in the area was located along Brick Church Pike in Bordeaux. That cemetery was destroyed in the late 1900s.

There was a benevolent society lodge on Twelfth Avenue South, around the corner from Edmondson's brother's, but it is unknown if Edmondson or his family were members. It is also unclear why Edmondson's headstones are most likely to be in benevolent cemeteries.

The Edmondson headstones that remain in Middle Tennessee cemeteries are rapidly deteriorating. Most of the sculptures that adorned the tops of the markers are gone. Local preservationists are working to find some way to conserve the stones, but that will take coordination between the families who own the headstones, the cemeteries where they're located, and local governments.

Known Tombstones by William Edmondson in Cemeteries

Cemetery	Name	Birth	Death
Dry Creek	Manthy Lamon	December 1888	December 4, 1941
Greater Pleasant View Missionary Baptist	*Mintha Anthony	1874	January 4, 1939
	*Thomas Anthony	October 2, 1866	April 28, 1937
	Rev. I. W. Berry	September 22, 1874	May 16, 1944
	Hazel A. Foster	September 18, 1902	August 13, 1946
	Baby Murrey	—	—
	†Catherine Smith	August 13, 1876	February 24, 1935
	†Richmond Smith	October 27, 1865	August 14, 1940
Greenwood	James Ernest Binkley	September 1, 1870	December 20, 1942
	Cordelia Clay	March 21, 1890	January 22, 1941
	John A. Floyd	March 12, 1873	May 8, 1932
	Isaac Jones	July 9, 1899	February 22, 1938
	‡Cordelia Mitchell	—	—
	‡Fee Mitchell	May 1, 1884	September 8, 1946
	Mary Morris	December 11, 1938	—
	Mamie Rand	May 5, 1884	February 17, 1944
	Mrs. Lizzie Stokes	April 9, 1887	January 20, 1937
	Rosa Wade	1859	November 11, 1931
	Sarah Williams	February 8	March 27, 1937
	Cora Winstead	1869	March 2, 1940
	**L. W. Work Sr.	1872	1940
	L. W. Work Jr.	1898	1933
	**Myrtle Work	—	—
Mount Ararat	Henry Armstrong	June 6, 1914	July 14, 1944
	Mary Barker	1880	February 6, 1940
	Hallie Potter Beaver	June 1904	November 13, 1940
	††C. M. Brown	November 10, 1886	February 25, 1940
	Ellen Brown	—	June [illegible]
	Lou Cockrill	March 15, 1875	January 17, 1947
	Lucinda Edmondson	March 30, 1934	—

Known Tombstones by William Edmondson in Cemeteries

Cemetery	Name	Birth	Death
Mount Ararat (*continued*)	Lizzy O. Reynolds	February 15	July 28, 1947
	Mary Sherrod	June 23, 1892	March 24, 1936
	James W. Watkins	April 7, 1892	February 10, 1941
	Jennie White	May 25, 1885	January 29, 1946
	††G. C. Young	March 5, 1912	March 21, 1935
Mount Pisgah	Barbara Kinnard	August 16, 1890	January 29, 1940
	Gus Owens and Family	February 22, 1942	—
	Harvey Owens	November 23, 1910	June 19, 1938
	‡‡Henrietta Sneed Owens	January 11, 1938	—
	‡‡Lanears Owens	March 30, 1938	—
Taliaferro Road Alt 31 and Hwy 12	T. E. Scales Sr.	August 15, 1884	February 27, 1943
Toussaint L'Ouverture	Susie Buchanan Starnes Beal	September 12, 1879	January 11, 1944
	Florence Berry	October 12, 1885	March 11, 1944
	Nanie Carter	1894	October 2, 1935

Known Tombstones by William Edmondson in Museums

Museum	Name	Birth	Death
Cheekwood Estate and Gardens	Mary Alice Whitlow	November 16, 1883	April 3, 1944
Newark Museum of Art	Mother [topper only]	—	—
Tennessee State Museum	Bernice Williams	February 2, 1906	January 9, 1931

Note: Names accompanied by symbols share a headstone.
Tables prepared by Betsy Phillips

Selected Biographical and Historical Chronology

Compiled by Marin R. Sullivan

This is an updated and revised version of the chronology "Life during William Edmondson's Time," originally compiled by Catherine Kuhnle and Rusty Freeman and published in *The Art of William Edmondson* (Nashville, TN: Cheekwood Museum of Art, 1999), 211–14.

1874 William Edmondson is born in Davidson County, Tennessee, to Jane Brown and Orange Edmondson. He is one of five children: Sarah, born in November 1869; Richard, born in December 1875; Orange Jr., born in September 1879; and James, born in October 1881. Jane Brown had her first child, Ellen Brown, in March 1864, and she was raised as one of Orange's children.

1876 Meharry Medical College, the first medical school for African Americans, is founded as the Medical Department of Central Tennessee College. The school separated and began operating independently in 1915.

1881 One of the earliest Jim Crow laws is passed by the Tennessee legislature, requiring separate but equal accommodations for African Americans in railroad cars.

1889 Orange Edmondson, William's father, dies.

Tennessee General Assembly passes four acts of electoral reform, including the Myers Laws, the Lea Law, the Dortch Law, and a poll tax, that disenfranchise African American voters.

Greenwood Cemetery is established for African Americans in Nashville.

1890 Edmondson, along with his mother and siblings, moves to Nashville; he finds work with the city's sewer works.

1892 Ephraim Grizzard, a Black man accused of the assault of two white women, is dragged through the streets of Nashville and lynched by a mob of six thousand men on the Woodland Street Bridge on April 30.

1897 The Tennessee Centennial Exposition opens in Nashville, including a replica of the Parthenon. The structure was rebuilt in 1920 and included replica sculptures made by George Julian Zolnay, Belle Kinney, and Leopold Scholz. A recreation of the forty-two-foot statue of Athena for the interior by Nashville sculptor Alan LeQuire was completed in 1990.

1900 Edmondson works as a farmhand at the Whitland Farm. Along with his brother James, he begins working for the Nashville, Chattanooga and St. Louis Railway.

1904 First Nashville Bank, One Cent Savings Bank and Trust is founded by African American business leaders for the African American community.

1906 The *Nashville Globe* is founded. The biweekly Black newspaper ceased publication in 1960.

1907 Edmondson ends work with the Nashville, Chattanooga and St. Louis Railway following an accident that injured his leg; he begins work at Nashville's all-white Woman's Hospital at 301 North Spruce Street.

1908 Boxer Jack Johnson (1878–1946) becomes the first African American world heavyweight champion. He defended his title in 1910 in an infamous fight with James J. Jeffries, called the "fight of the century," that triggered racially motivated violence across the United States.

1909 Tennessee Agricultural and Industrial School (now Tennessee State University) is established in Nashville.

1913 Tax records list Edmondson as a property owner at 1434 Fourteenth Street South.

1914 John Crowe Ransom and Walter Clyde Curry, professors of English at Vanderbilt University, along with Sidney Mttron Hirsch, begin meeting to discuss literature. After WWI, the group reconvened and began publishing their work in the literary journal *The Fugitive* in April 1922. Members also included Donald Davidson, Alfred Starr, and Robert Penn Warren.

1922 Jane Brown, Edmondson's mother, dies.

1926 In late December, heavy rains lead to the worst flood in Nashville's history.

1929 The Wall Street crash, known as "The Great Crash," leads to the start of the Great Depression.

The Museum of Modern Art (MoMA) opens in New York.

1931 Edmondson stops working at the Woman's Hospital in Nashville, and soon after begins work as a stonemason's assistant. By 1933, Edmondson begins carving tombstones and other stone objects using discarded and/or donated limestone from building projects and damaged infrastructure from around the city.

1932 Franklin Delano Roosevelt is elected president of the United States.

Curator Holger Cahill organizes *American Folk Art: The Art of the Common Man in America, 1750–1900* at MoMA.

1934 President Franklin D. Roosevelt and First Lady Eleanor Roosevelt visit Nashville.

1934–35 Sidney Hirsch befriends Edmondson and begins bringing friends like Alfred and Elizabeth Starr, Meyer Wolfe, and Louise Dahl-Wolfe to see the sculptor at his home studio/yard.

1936 Franklin D. Roosevelt is reelected president of the United States.

1936–37 Louise Dahl-Wolfe photographs Edmondson at his home.

1937 The solo exhibition *Sculpture by William Edmondson* is held from October 20 to December 1 at MoMA's temporary site at Rockefeller Plaza in New York.

1938 One of Edmondson's works, *Martha and Mary*, is included in the exhibition *Trois Siècles d'Art aux États Unis (Three Centuries of Art in the United States)*, organized by MoMA at the Musée du Jeu de Paume, Paris, France.

1939 Edmondson is first employed by the Works Progress Administration (WPA) between November 20 and July 6, 1940.

1940 Edmondson is employed for a second time by the WPA between November 11 and June 26, 1941.

1940 Franklin D. Roosevelt is reelected for a third term as president of the United States.

1941 Edward Weston visits Nashville to photograph Edmondson.

Edmondson's work is included in the exhibition *American Negro Art: Nineteenth and Twentieth Centuries* organized by Alain Locke and held at the Downtown Gallery in New York. The first solo exhibition of Edmondson's work in Tennessee takes place at the Nashville Art Gallery.

Pearl Harbor is attacked and the United States enters World War II.

1943 Sarah Edmondson, William's sister, dies.

1944 Franklin D. Roosevelt is reelected for a fourth term as president of the United States.

1945 Franklin D. Roosevelt dies, and Vice President Harry Truman succeeds him as president.

WWII ends.

1948 Edmondson's work is featured in an exhibition of Folk Art at Fisk University as part of their annual Spring Arts Festival.

1949 Fisk University receives a portion of the collection of the estate of Alfred Stieglitz, the noted American photographer. The gift was distributed by the artist Georgia O'Keeffe, who had been married to Stieglitz for twenty-two years at the time of his death in 1946 and who selected Fisk University along with the Metropolitan Museum of Art in New York, the Art Institute of Chicago, the National Gallery in Washington, the Philadelphia Museum of Art, and the Library of Congress. The Stieglitz Collection at Fisk University includes 101 works by some of the most notable artists of American and European modernism such as Charles Demuth, Arthur Dove, O'Keeffe, Pablo Picasso, Diego Rivera, and Stieglitz.

1950 Consuelo Kanaga visits Nashville and photographs Edmondson.

1951 Edmondson dies on February 7.

Nashville Artists Guild organizes a solo exhibition of Edmondson's work in Nashville.

1964 A solo exhibition, *Will Edmondson's Mirkels*, opens at the Tennessee Fine Arts Center at Cheekwood in Nashville.

1973 Edmund Fuller, a noted author, literary critic, and collector, publishes *Visions in Stone: The Sculpture of William Edmondson*, which draws on extensive interviews and research undertaken by Fuller. The following year an exhibition of the same title opened at the Montclair Art Museum in New Jersey. *Visions in Stone* closed on January 26, 1975.

1975 Edmondson's work is included in the exhibition *Amistad II: Afro-American Art* at the Van Vechten Gallery at Fisk University.

1976 The Inaugural Exhibition at the Hirshhorn Museum and Sculpture Garden in Washington, DC, features work by Edmondson.

1981 The Tennessee State Museum in Nashville opens its new building, the James J. Polk Center, with the exhibition *William Edmondson: A Retrospective*, which runs from June 18 to October 25.

2000 The most comprehensive exhibition of William Edmondson's work to date opens at Cheekwood Botanical Garden & Museum of Art before traveling to four other venues around the United States through 2001.

Selected Exhibition History

Compiled by Marin R. Sullivan

1937 *Sculpture by William Edmondson*, Museum of Modern Art, New York, New York

1938 *Trois Siècles d'Art aux États-Unis (Three Centuries of Art in the United States)*, Musée du Jeu de Paume, Paris, France

1941 *American Negro Art: Nineteenth and Twentieth Centuries*, Downtown Gallery, New York, New York

Untitled solo exhibition of William Edmondson, Nashville Art Gallery, Nashville, Tennessee

1948 *Stone Carvings by William Edmondson*, Nineteenth Anniversary Spring Festival of Arts, Fisk University, Nashville, Tennessee

1951 Untitled solo exhibition of William Edmondson, Nashville Artists Guild, Nashville, Tennessee

1955 Untitled exhibition, Peabody College for Teachers, Nashville, Tennessee

1964 *William Edmondson's Mirkels*, Tennessee Arts Center at Cheekwood, Nashville, Tennessee

American Folk Arts, Willard Gallery, New York, New York

Painting and Sculpture by Four Tennessee Primitives, Lyzon Galleries, Nashville, Tennessee

1965 *Folk Carvings by Will Edmondson*, Museum of Early American Folk Arts (now Museum of American Folk Art), New York, New York

1967 *The Evolution of Afro-American Artists: 1800–1950*, Great Hall, City College, in cooperation with the Harlem Cultural Council and New York Urban League, New York, New York

1970 *Twentieth Century Folk Art*, Museum of American Folk Art, New York, New York

Dimensions of Black, La Jolla Museum of Contemporary Art, La Jolla, California

1971 Untitled exhibition, Willard Gallery, New York, New York

Black Artists: Two Generations, Newark Museum, Newark, New Jersey

1972 *American Folk Sculpture: The Personal and the Eccentric*, Cranbrook Academy of Art, Bloomfield Hills, Michigan

1974 Inaugural Exhibition, Hirshhorn Museum and Sculpture Garden, Washington, DC

American Folk Sculpture from the Hall Collection, University of Kentucky Art Gallery, Lexington, Kentucky

Visions in Stone: William Edmondson, Montclair Art Museum, Montclair, New Jersey

1975 *Amistad II: Afro-American Art*, Van Vechten Gallery, Fisk University, Nashville, Tennessee

1976 *Folk Sculpture USA*, Brooklyn Museum, Brooklyn, New York; Los Angeles County Museum, Los Angeles, California

Two Centuries of Black American Art, Los Angeles Museum of Art, Los Angeles, California; High Museum of Art, Atlanta, Georgia; Dallas Museum of Fine Arts, Dallas, Texas; Brooklyn Museum, Brooklyn, New York

America Expresses Herself: Eighteenth, Nineteenth, and Twentieth Century Folk Art from the Herbert W. Hemphill Jr. Collection, Children's Museum, Indianapolis, Indiana

American Folk Art from the H. W. Hemphill Jr. Collection, American Information Service, Tokyo and Osaka, Japan

1979 *Black Artists/South*, Huntsville Museum of Art, Huntsville, Alabama

1981 *William Edmondson: A Retrospective*, Tennessee State Museum, Nashville, Tennessee

1981 *Transmitters: The Isolate Artist in America*, Philadelphia College of Art (now University of the Arts), Philadelphia, Pennsylvania

American Folk Art: The Herbert Waide Hemphill Jr. Collection, Milwaukee Art Museum, Milwaukee, Wisconsin

1982 *Black Folk Art in America 1930–1980*, Corcoran Gallery of Art, Washington, DC

1983 *Religious Folk Art in America: Reflections of Faith*, Museum of American Folk Art, New York, New York

Masters of American Folk Art, Janet Fleisher Gallery, Philadelphia, Pennsylvania

1984 *Major Black Artists*, Janet Fleisher Gallery, Philadelphia, Pennsylvania

1984 *Since the Harlem Renaissance: Fifty Years of Afro-American Art*, University Center Gallery, Bucknell University, Lewisburg, Pennsylvania

A Shifting Wind: View of American Folk Art, New York State Historical Association, Cooperstown, New York

1985 *A Time to Reap: Late Blooming Folk Artists*, Museum of American Folk Art, New York; Seton Hall University, South Orange, New Jersey

Masterpieces of Folk Art, Janet Fleisher Gallery, Philadelphia, Pennsylvania

Afro-American Art: Twentieth Century Selections, National Museum of American Art, Washington, DC

1986 *Naivety in Art*, Setagaya Art Museum, Tokyo, Japan; Tochigi Prefectural Museum of Fine Arts, Tokyo, Japan

1987 *Outsider Art*, Carnegie Center, Princeton, New Jersey

1988 *Spirit and Forum: The Sculpture of William Edmondson and Puryear Mims*, Metro Arts Commission Gallery, Nashville, Tennessee

1990 *Black Art Ancestral Legacy: The African Impulse in African-American Art*, Dallas Museum of Art, Dallas, Texas

Visions: Expressions beyond the Mainstream from Chicago Collections, Arts Club of Chicago, Chicago, Illinois

Five Star Folk Art: One Hundred American Masterpieces, Museum of American Folk Art, New York, New York

1992 *Dream Singers, Story Tellers: An African-American Presence*, New Jersey State Museum, Trenton, New Jersey; Fukui Fine Arts Museum, Fukui, Japan; Tokushima Modern Art Museum, Tokushima, Japan; Otani Memorial Art Museum, Nishinomiya, Japan

Selected Works by African-American Folk Artists, Philadelphia Museum of Art, Philadelphia, Pennsylvania

American Self-Taught and Outsider Art, Ricco/Maresca Gallery, New York

1993 *Passionate Visions of the American South: Self-Taught Artists from 1940 to the Present*, New Orleans, Louisiana

Visionaries, Outsiders, and Spiritualists: American Self-Taught Artists, David Winton Bell Gallery, Brown University, Providence, Rhode Island; Sheldon Memorial Art Gallery, University of Nebraska, Lincoln; Heckscher Museum, Huntington, New York

1993	*Common Ground / Uncommon Vision: The Michael & Julie Hall Collection of American Folk Art*, Milwaukee Art Museum, Milwaukee, Wisconsin
1994	*Free within Ourselves: African-American Artists in the Collection of the National Museum of American Art*, National Museum of American Art, Washington, DC
	Community Fabric: African-American Quilts & Folk Art, Philadelphia Museum of Art, Philadelphia, Pennsylvania
	African-American Art: Nineteenth and Twentieth Century Selections, National Museum of American Art, Washington, DC
1995	*A World of Their Own: Twentieth Century American Folk Artists*, Newark Museum, Newark, New Jersey
	Miracles: The Sculptures of William Edmondson, Janet Fleisher Gallery, Philadelphia, Pennsylvania
	The Figure in American Sculpture: A Question of Modernity, Los Angeles County Museum, Los Angeles, California
1996	*African-American Art: Twentieth Century Masterworks III*, Michael Rosenfeld Gallery, New York
1997	*African-American Art: Twentieth Century Masterworks IV*, Michael Rosenfeld Gallery, New York; Fisk University, Nashville, Tennessee
1998	*African-American Art: Twentieth Century Masterworks V*, Michael Rosenfeld Gallery, New York; Newcomb Art Gallery, Tulane University, New Orleans, Louisiana
1999	*This World and the Next: African Art and the Sculpture of William Edmondson*, Albany Museum of Art, Albany, Georgia
2000–2001	*The Art of William Edmondson*, organized by Cheekwood Botanical Garden & Museum of Art, Nashville, Tennessee; Museum of American Folk Art, New York, New York; Memorial Art Gallery at the University of Rochester, Rochester, New York; High Museum of Art, Folk Art and Photography Galleries, Atlanta, Georgia; and The Mennello Museum of American Folk Art, Orlando, Florida
2004–2005	*Bill Traylor, William Edmondson, and the Modernist Impulse*, organized by the Krannert Art Museum, University of Illinois at Urbana-Champaign; Birmingham Museum of Art, Birmingham, Alabama; The Studio

Museum in Harlem, New York, New York; and The Menil Collection, Houston, Texas

2014 *William Edmondson and Friends: Breaking the Mold*, Cheekwood Estate & Gardens, Nashville, Tennessee

2015 *The Shadow of the Avant-Garde: Rousseau and the Forgotten Masters*, Museum Folkwang, Essen, Germany

2017 *Visions from Above: The Enduring Legacy of William Edmondson*, Cheekwood Estate & Gardens, Nashville, Tennessee

2018 *Outliers and American Vanguard Art*, National Gallery of Art, Washington, DC

2019 *Memory Palaces: Inside the Collection of Audrey B. Heckler*, American Folk Art Museum, New York, New York

Selected Bibliography

Aat, Senemeht Sasen. "After Hours: A Craft Nurtured in Limestone: Edmondson at American Folk Art after Sixty-Three Years." *Network Journal* 7, no. 10 (August 31, 2000): 30.

Abrahams, Roger D. *Afro-American Folktales: Stories from Black Traditions in the New World*. New York: Pantheon, 1985.

"Aged Negro Says God Bade Him Sculpt Stones; Now U-T Prizes Them as Art." *Knoxville News-Sentinel*, January 19, 1941.

"American Negro Art." *Design* 43 (February 1942): 27–28.

Ames, Kenneth L., Jeffrey Russell Hayes, and Lucy R. Lippard. *Common Ground / Uncommon Vision: The Michael and Julie Hall Collection of American Folk Art*. Milwaukee, WI: Milwaukee Art Museum, 1993.

Anderson-Green, Paula H. "'The Lord's Work': Southern Folk Belief in Signs, Warnings, and Dream Visions." *Tennessee Folklore Society Bulletin* 43, no. 3 (1977): 113–27.

Arnett, Paul, and William Arnett, eds. *Souls Grow Deep: African American Vernacular Art of the South*. Vol. 1. Atlanta, GA: Tinwood Books in association with Schomburg Center for Research in Black Culture, New York Public Library, 2000.

"Art by Negroes." *Art Digest* 16, no. 2 (October 15, 1941): 11, 23.

"At God's Command." *Art Digest* 12, no. 2 (October 15, 1937): 23.

"At God's Command: William Edmondson Preaches Inspired Sermons in Stone: He Sees Visions in the Sky and Fixes Them in Carvings." *Art Instruction* 2 (1938): 30–31.

The Art of William Edmondson. Nashville, TN: Cheekwood Museum of Art, 1999.

Barr, Alfred, Jr. *Trois Siècles d'Art aux États-Unis*. Paris and New York: Musée du Jeu de Paume and Museum of Modern Art, 1938.

Bearden, Romare, and Harry Henderson. *A History of African-American Artists: From 1792 to the Present*. New York: Pantheon, 1993.

Beardsley, John, and Jane Livingston. *Black Folk Art in America, 1930–1980*. Jackson: University Press of Mississippi, 1982.

Beasley, Kay. "Sculpture 'Miracles I Can Do.'" *Nashville Banner*, September 9, 1987, A7.

Black Art Ancestral Legacy: The African Impulse in African-American Art. Dallas, TX: Dallas Museum of Art, 1989.

Bostick, Alan. "Chiseled in Stone: Nashville Sculptor William Edmondson Gains New Attention from Art World." *Nashville Tennessean*, July 26, 1988.

Cahill, Holger. *American Folk Art: The Art of the Common Man in America, 1750–1900*. New York: Museum of Modern Art, 1932.

"Colored Sculptor Wins Wide Fame." *Cleveland Press*, October 9, 1937.

Conger, Amy. *Edward Weston: Photographs from the Collection of the Center for Creative Photography*. Tucson: Arizona Board of Regents, 1992.

Conwill, Kinshasha. "In Search of an 'Authentic' Vision: Decoding of the Appeal of the Self-Taught African-American Artist." *American Art* 5, no. 4 (Fall 1991): 2–9.

Cooke, Lynne, with Douglas Crimp, Darby English, Suzanne Hudson, Thomas J. Lax, Jennifer Jane Marshall, Richard Meyer, and Jenni Sorkin. *Outliers and American Vanguard Art*. Washington, DC: National Gallery of Art in association with the University of Chicago Press, 2018.

Cotter, Holland. "Untrained but Inspired, Hands Dreamed in Stone." *New York Times*, June 9, 2000.

Dewhurst, C. Kurt, Betty MacDowell, and Marsha MacDowell. *Religious Folk Art in America: Reflections of Faith*. New York: E.P. Dutton in association with the Museum of American Folk Art, 1983.

Driskell, David. *Two Centuries of Black American Art*. New York: Alfred A. Knopf, 1976.

Ebony, D. "William Edmondson." *Art in America* 89, no. 3 (March 2001): 136–37.

"Edmondson's Angels." *Nashville Banner*, October 22, 1937.

"Edmundson Sculpture." *Bennington Banner* (Vermont), May 21, 1940.

English, Darby, and Charlotte Barat. *Among Others: Blackness at MoMA*. New York: Museum of Modern Art, 2019.

"'Errand Boy' Wins High Recognition in World of Art." *Danville Bee* (Vermont), October 11, 1937.

Farrington, Lisa E. *African-American Art: A Visual and Cultural History*. New York: Oxford University Press, 2017.

Fletcher, Georganne, and Jym Knight, eds. *William Edmondson: A Retrospective*. Nashville: Tennessee Arts Commission, 1981.

Fort, Ilene Susan. *The Figure in American Sculpture: A Question of Modernity*. Los Angeles: Los Angeles Museum of Art, 1995.

Frankel, Robert S. "Sculpture in the Modern Tradition by a Tombstone Carver." *Art News* 23 (October 1937): 13.

Fuller, Edmund L. *Visions in Stone: The Sculpture of William Edmondson*. Pittsburgh, PA: University of Pittsburgh Press, 1973.

Gardner, Henry. "Myron Lyzon King: Art Impresario." *Nashville Magazine*, April 1967, 26–28.

Goldstein, Rosalie, ed. *American Folk Art: The Herbert Waide Hemphill Jr. Collection*. Milwaukee, WI: Milwaukee Art Museum, 1981.

"Gravestone Cutter Honored as Sculptor." *Indianapolis Times*, October 9, 1937.

Halasz, Piri. "Montclair Shows 'Vision in Stone.'" *New York Times*, December 1, 1974.

Hamilton, William. "Outsider Art: In from the Edge and under the Gavel." *New York Times*, January 23, 2003.

Helfenstein, Josef, and Roxanne M. Stanulis. *Bill Traylor, William Edmondson and the Modernist Impulse*. Urbana, IL: Krannert Art Museum, 2004. Distributed by University of Washington Press.

Hieronymus, Clara. "Edmondson's Sculptures a 'Command of the Lord.'" *Nashville Tennessean*, February 8, 1981, 6E.

"Honor to Negro." *Kansas City Journal-Post*, October 9, 1937.

Hudson, Ralph M. *Black Artists / South*. Huntsville, AL: Huntsville Museum of Art, 1979.

"Inspired, Self-Taught Artist, William Edmondson, Dies." *Nashville Tennessean*, February 9, 1951, 1, 6.

James, Milton M. "Art." *Negro History Bulletin*, November 22, 1958, 41.

Jentleson, Katherine. *Gatecrashers: The Rise of the Self-Taught Artist in America*. Berkeley: University of California Press, 2020.

Jewell, Edward Alden. "Tennessee Negro Shows Sculpture." *New York Times*, October 20, 1937, 20.

Johnston, Jill. "Reviews and Previews: New Names This Month—Four Tennessee Primitives. *Art News* 62, no. 10 (February 1964): 18–19.

King-Hammond, Leslie. *African-American Art: Twentieth Century Masterworks, V*. New York: Michael Rosenfeld Gallery, 1998.

König, Kasper, and Falk Wolf. *The Shadow of the Avant-Garde: Rousseau and the Forgotten Masters*. Ostfildern: Hatje/Cantz, 2015.

LeQuire, Louise. "Edmondson's Art Reflects His Faith Strong and Pure." *Smithsonian* 12, no. 5 (August 1981): 50–55.

_______. "Wisdom, Humor, and Primitive Vision." *Motive*, February 1957, 16–21.

Lindsey, Jack. *Miracles: The Sculpture of William Edmondson*. Philadelphia, PA: Janet Fleisher Gallery, 1994.

_______. "William Edmondson." *Folk Art* 20, no. 1 (Spring 1995): 43–47.

Locke, Alain. "The Negro's Contributions in Art to American Culture." *Proceedings of the National Conference of Social Work*, nos. 15-16 (May 1932): 315–22.

_______, ed. *The Negro in Art: A Pictorial Record of the Negro Artist and of the Negro Theme in Art*. Washington, DC: Associates in Negro Folk Education, 1940.

Logan, Walt. "Fame Leaves Him Unmoved: God Planted Him in Nashville, Says Negro Sculptor." *Nashville Tennessean Magazine*, October 31, 1937, 3, 5.

Longhauser, Elsa Weiner, and Harald Szeemann, eds. *Self-Taught Artists of the Twentieth Century: An American Anthology*. New York: Museum of American Folk Art, 1998.

Lovett, Bobby L. *From Winter to Winter: The Afro-American History of Nashville, Tennessee, 1870–1930*. Nashville: Tennessee State University, 1981.

Lovett, Bobby L., and Linda T. Wynn. *Profiles of African Americans in Tennessee*. Nashville, TN: Annual Afro-American Culture and History Conference, 1996.

Maresca, Frank, and Roger Ricco. *American Primitive: Discoveries in Folk Sculpture*. New York: Alfred A. Knopf, 1988.

Marshall, Jennifer Jane. "Nashville, New York, Paris, and Nashville: William Edmondson, Mobilized and Unmoved. *American Art* 31, no. 2 (Summer 2017): 69–76.

_______. "'Ever Not Quite': Empathy, Experience, and William Edmondson." In *Experience*, edited by Alexander Nemerov, 102–33. Chicago: University of Chicago Press, 2017.

Metcalf, Eugene W. “Black Art, Folk Art, and Social Control.” *Winterthur Portfolio* 18, no. 4 (1983): 271–89.

“Mirkels.” *Time*, November 1, 1937, 52.

“Modern Art Museum and Simple Faith Bring Fame to a Sculptor.” *Newsweek*, October 24, 1937, 22.

“Modern Museum to Show Negro Art.” *New York Times*, October 9, 1937.

“Modern Art Museum Shows William Edmondson’s Work.” *Washington Post*, November 7, 1937.

Monahan, Anne. *Horace Pippin: American Modern*. New Haven, CT: Yale University Press, 2020.

“Negro Primitive.” *Art Digest*, November 1, 1937, 18.

“Negro Sculptor with God-Given Genius to Have Work Displayed in New York.” *Nashville Banner*, October 9, 1937, 2.

“Negro Who Turned Sculptor at God’s Command Gets Manhattan Exhibition.” *Life*, November 1, 1937, 79.

“A New Sculptor.” *Washington Weekly Afro-American*, November 6, 1937.

“Odd-Job Man’s Sculpture Displayed at Art Museum.” *St. Louis Post-Dispatch*, October 31, 1937.

Paintings and Sculpture by Four Tennessee Primitives. Nashville, TN: Lyzon Galleries, 1964.

Percy, Ann. *Great and Mighty Things: Outsider Art from the Jill and Sheldon Bonovitz Collection*. New Haven, CT: Yale University Press, 2013.

Perry, Regina A. *Free within Ourselves: African American Artists in the Collection of the National Museum of American Art*. Washington, DC: National Museum of American Art, Smithsonian Institution, 1992.

Porter, James A. *Modern Negro Art*. New York: Dryden Press, 1943.

Powell, Richard J. “Art History and Black Memory: Toward a ‘Blues Aesthetic.’” In *History and Memory in African American Culture*, edited by Genevieve Fabre and Robert O’Meally, 228–43. New York: Oxford University Press, 1994.

_______. *Black Art and Culture in the Twentieth Century*. London: Thames and Hudson, 1997.

Puchner, Edward M. "'A Tried Stone': Community, Conversion, and Christ in the Sculpture of William Edmondson." In *Beholding Christ and Christianity in African American Art*, edited by James Romaine and Phoebe Wolfskill. University Park: Pennsylvania State University Press, 2017.

Richard, Paul. "The Folk Masters: The Eerie, Leaping Beauty of the Corcoran's Show of Black Artists." *Washington Post*, January 15, 1982, C1.

Ridley, Greg. *Visions of My People: African-American Art in Tennessee*. Nashville: Tennessee State Museum, 1997.

Rogerson, Ann S. *William Edmondson: Visions in Stone*. Montclair, NJ: Montclair Art Museum, 1975.

Rosenak, Chuck, and Jan Rosenak. *Museum of American Folk Art Encyclopedia of Twentieth-Century American Folk Art and Artists*. New York: Abbeville Press, 1991.

"Sculptor in the Rough." *Dallas News*, October 13, 1937.

Spires, Elizabeth. *I Heard God Talking to Me: William Edmondson and His Stone Carvings*. New York: Farrar, Straus and Giroux, 2008.

"Tennessee Tombstone Cutter Exhibits Sculpture." *New York Herald Tribune*, October 20, 1937.

Thomas, Don. "William Edmondson: Self-Taught African American Sculptor of the Twentieth Century." *New York Beacon*, May 31, 2000, 31.

Thompson, John. "Negro Stone Cutter Here Says Gift from Lord; Work Praised." *Nashville Tennessean*, February 9, 1941, 11A.

"Tombstone Cutter and His Arresting 'Sermons in Stone': How a Negro Worker in Nashville, Tennessee, Who Never Had an Art Lesson, Won National Recognition as a 'Modern Primitive.'" *St. Louis Post-Dispatch*, November 12, 1937.

Trotter, F. Thomas. "Artist William Edmondson Was 'Just Doing Lord's Work.'" *Nashville Banner*, March 23, 1986, A19.

Vlach, John Michael. *By the Work of Their Hands: Studies in Afro-American Folklife*. Charlottesville: University Press of Virginia, 1991.

"Vogue Covers the Town: Town Gossip . . . 'Modern Primitive' Is the Aesthetic Term with Which the Work in Sculpture of an Untrained Negro, William Edmondson, Has Been Tentatively Tagged." *Vogue*, November 15, 1937, 53.

Wallis, Brian. “William Edmondson at Janet Fleisher.” *Art in America*, January 1996, 108.

“William Edmondson, a Primitive Sculptor.” *New York Times*, February 10, 1951, 13.

“William Edmondson Dies.” *Art Digest* 25, no. 11 (March 1, 1951): 31.

Woolsey, F. William. “Edmondson’s Vision in Stone.” *Look*, October 21, 1952, 61–63.

_______. “Persistent Primitive.” *Nashville Tennessean Magazine*, December 14, 1947, 6–7.

Wynn, Linda T. “‘I’se Just Doin’ the Lord’s Work’—William Edmondson: Inspired Sculptor.” *Courier* (Tennessee Historical Commission) 20, no. 1-2 (1981–82): 4–5.

Yelen, Alice Rae. *Passionate Visions of the American South: Self-Taught Artists from 1940 to the Present*. New Orleans, LA: New Orleans Museum of Art, 1993.

Zibart, Mrs. Carl [Grace], Harry Lowe, and Walter Sharp. *Will Edmondson’s Mirkels*. Nashville: Tennessee Fine Arts Center at Cheekwood, 1964.

Zohn, Kristen Miller. *This World and the Next: African Art and the Sculpture of William Edmondson*. Albany, GA: Albany Museum of Art, 2000.

William Edmondson (American, 1874–1951)

Cat. 1 *Birdbath*, 1938
Limestone
31½ × 20 ½ × 16 ½ in.
Cheekwood, Nashville. Gift of Sophia Ezzell Dobson (1994.20a-d)

Cat. 3 *Martha and Mary*, c. 1930–39
Limestone
14 × 16 ⅞ × 6 ⅞ in.
Hirshhorn Museum and Sculpture Garden, Smithsonian Institution, Washington, DC. Gift of Joseph H. Hirshhorn, 1972 (72.107)

Cat. 5 *Eleanor Roosevelt*, n.d.
Limestone
12 ¼ × 7 × 3 ¼ in.
Tennessee State Museum, Nashville (1997.128)

Cat. 6 *Bess and Joe*, c. 1930–40
Limestone
17 ¼ × 20 ¼ × 10 ½ in.
Cheekwood, Nashville. Gift of Salvatore Formosa Sr.; Mrs. Pete Formosa Sr.; Angelo M. Formosa Jr.; and Mrs. Rose Formosa Bromley in memory of Angelo Formosa, Sr., wife Mrs. Katherine St. Charles Formosa; and Pete A. Formosa Sr. and Museum Purchase through the bequest of Anita Bevill McMichael Stallworth (1993.2.3)

Cat. 7 *Martha and Mary*, c. 1930s
Limestone
10 ½ × 13 ½ × 6 ½ in.
Cheekwood, Nashville. Gift of Hester Moore Brooks in memory of her parents Merrill Moore and Ann Leslie Nichol Moore (2018.01)

Cat. 8 *Tombstone with Bird*, 1934–41
Limestone
6 ⅝ × 18 ¾ × 5 ¼ in.
Newark Museum of Art, Newark. Bequest of Edmund L. Fuller Jr., 1985 (85.27)

Cat. 9 *Bowl*, 1935–40
Limestone
7 × 22 × 17 in.
Cheekwood, Nashville. Gift in memory of Gertrude G. and John S. Fletcher by their children Bee, John, and Whit (1999.11.6)

Cat. 10 *Garden Ornament*, n.d.
Limestone
7 × 21 × 18 in.
Tennessee State Museum, Nashville (1985.121)

Cat. 14 *Whitlow Tombstone*, 1944
Limestone
30 ¾ × 27 ¼ × 8 in.
Cheekwood, Nashville. Gift of Mr. and Mrs. Duiel (Sadie) Overton, Lucy Whitlow Burney, and Richard Whitlow in memory of Rev. Alfred and Mrs. Alfred (Mary Alice) Whitlow (1998.2)

Cat. 15 *Reclining Man (Sidney Hirsch)*, n.d.
Limestone
6 ¾ × 25 ½ × 7 ½ in.
Cheekwood, Nashville. Gift of Michael LeBeck in memory of Sidney Mttron Hirsch (1973.4.8)

Cat. 21 *Untitled (Schoolteacher)*, c. 1930–40
Limestone
16 ½ × 6 ½ × 9 ½ in.
Collection of Jaime Frankfurt, New York

Cat. 22 *Lady with Two Pocketbooks*, n.d.
Limestone
12 × 3 ½ × 7½ in.
Austin Peay State University, Clarksville, Tennessee, Trahem Family Collection

Cat. 24 *Schoolteacher*, c. 1937
Limestone
14 ½ × 6 × 7 ¾ in.
Cheekwood, Nashville. Gift of John Thompson Jr. (1960.1)

Cat. 25 *Angel*, 1937–39
Limestone
17 ¾ × 13 ¼ × 7 in.
Collection of Robert A. Roth, Chicago

Cat. 26 *Seated Girl with Folded Legs*, 1934–41
Limestone
21 ½ × 16 ¾ × 10 ½ in.
Newark Museum of Art, Newark. Bequest of Edmund L. Fuller Jr., 1985 (85.32)

Cat. 27 *Untitled (Seated Girl)*, c. 1940
Limestone
19 ½ × 6 ½ × 9 ½ in.
Collection of KAWS, New York

Cat. 28 *Girl with a Cape*, n.d.
Limestone
26 ½ × 14 ½ × 7 ¼ in.
Cheekwood, Nashville. Gift from the Estate of Elizabeth Lyle Starr (1982.8.1a-b)

Cat. 30 *Lady with Cape*, c. 1935–40
Limestone
18 × 9 × 7.5 in.
Collection of KAWS, New York

Cat. 31 *Lady with Muff*, c. 1940
Limestone
15 ½ × 6 ½ × 6 ¾ in.
American Folk Art Museum, New York. Gift of Ralph Esmerian (20131.54)

Cat. 32 *Miss Amy*, c. 1935
Limestone
14 ½ × 4 ¾ × 7 ⅜ in.
Collection of Jaime Frankfurt, New York

Cat. 33 *Untitled*, n.d.
Limestone
Collection of KAWS, New York

Cat. 34 *Bride*, n.d.
Limestone
18 ½ × 7 × 10 in.
Cheekwood, Nashville.

Cat. 35 *Bride*, n.d.
Limestone
19 × 6 ¾ × 14 in.
McClung Museum of Natural History and Culture, University of Tennessee, Knoxville. Acquired through US Works Progress Administration (WPA), Federal Arts Project, 1941 (1993.9.2)

Cat. 39 *The Preacher*, 1934–41
Limestone
17 ½ × 5 ½ × 4 ½ in.
Newark Museum of Art, Newark. Bequest of Edmund L. Fuller Jr., 1985 (85.16)

Cat. 40 *Preacher*, n.d.
Limestone
17 ⅞ × 7 ⁹⁄₁₀ × 8 ½ in.
McClung Museum of Natural History and Culture, University of Tennessee, Knoxville. Acquired through US Works Progress Administration (WPA), Federal Arts Project, 1941 (1993.9.1)

Cat. 41 *Critter*, c. 1935
Limestone
20 ½ × 21 ½ × 5 ¼ in.
Cheekwood, Nashville. Gift of the 1993 Collectors Group with Matching Funds through the bequest of Anita Bevill McMichael Stallworth (1993.22)

Cat. 42 *Critter*, n.d.
Limestone
12 ½ × 21 ½ × 5¼ in.
Austin Peay State University, Clarksville, Tennessee, Trahem Family Collection

Cat. 44 *Horse*, c. 1930–40
Limestone
26 ¾ × 33 × 7 in.
Cheekwood, Nashville. Gift of Salvatore Formosa Sr.; Mrs. Pete Formosa Sr.; Angelo M. Formosa Jr.; and Mrs. Rose Formosa Bromley in memory of Angelo Formosa Sr., wife Mrs. Katherine St. Charles Formosa; and Pete A. Formosa Sr. and Museum Purchase through the bequest of Anita Bevill McMichael Stallworth (1993.2.2)

Cat. 45 *Eagle*, c. 1930–40
Limestone
25 ¼ × 14 ½ × 7 in.
Cheekwood, Nashville. Gift of Salvatore Formosa Sr.; Mrs. Pete Formosa Sr.; Angelo M. Formosa Jr.; and Mrs. Rose Formosa Bromley in memory of Angelo Formosa Sr., wife Mrs. Katherine St. Charles Formosa; and Pete A. Formosa Sr. and Museum Purchase through the bequest of Anita Bevill McMichael Stallworth (1993.2.1)

Cat. 46 *Eagle*, n.d.
Limestone
25 ½ × 17 × 6 ½ in.
Austin Peay State University, Clarksville, Tennessee, Trahem Family Collection

Cat. 47 *Untitled (Three Doves)*, c. 1930–40
Limestone
10 × 5 × 9 in.
Collection of KAWS, New York

Cat. 48 *Squirrel*, 1940
Limestone
11½ × 4 ½ × 7 in.
Cheekwood, Nashville. Gift in memory of Gertrude G. and John S. Fletcher by their children Bee, John, and Whit (1999.11.3)

Cat. 49 *Lion*, 1935–40
Limestone
19 ½ × 33 × 6 ½ in.
Cheekwood, Nashville. Gift in memory of Gertrude G. and John S. Fletcher by their children Bee, John Jr., and Whit (1999.11.1)

Cat. 50 *Ram*, 1935–40
Limestone
10 ¼ × 14 ¾ × 5 ¾ in.
Cheekwood, Nashville. Gift in memory of Gertrude G. and John S. Fletcher by their children Bee, John Jr., and Whit (1999.11.2)

Cat. 51 *Untitled (Turtle)*, c. 1940
Limestone
6 ½ × 15 × 13 in.
Collection of KAWS, New York

Cat. 52 *Williams Tombstone*, 1931
Limestone
17¼ × 11¾ × 5½ in.
Tennessee State Museum, Nashville (1984.44)

Cat. 54 *Seated Nude*, n.d.
Limestone
28 ¼ × 12 ¼ × 11 ¾ in.
Cheekwood, Nashville. Gift of Mr. John Thompson and his sister, Mrs. Con Thompson Ball, Nashville, Tennessee (1969.5)

Cat. 55 *Seated Nude*, n.d.
Limestone
21 ½ × 11 ¼ × 11 ¾ in.
Cheekwood, Nashville. Gift of Mrs. Alfred Starr (1965.11.9)

Cat. 56 *Crucifix*, n.d.
Limestone
26 × 12 × 5 in.
Abby Aldrich Rockefeller Folk Art Center / The Colonial Williamsburg Foundation, Williamsburg, Virginia. Museum Purchase (1971.907.1)

Cat. 57 *Eve*, 1935
Limestone
33 ¼ × 12 ¼ × 7 in.
Cheekwood, Nashville. Gift of Mrs. Alfred Starr (1964.10)

Louise Dahl-Wolfe (American, 1895–1989)

Cat. 2 *William Edmondson*, 1937
Gelatin silver print
10 ⅝ × 10 $\frac{3}{16}$ in.
Cheekwood, Nashville. Gift of the Artist (1964.3.13)

Cat. 4 *William Edmondson, Sculptor, Nashville, Tennessee*, 1933–37
Gelatin silver print
10 $\frac{13}{16}$ × 10 ¼ in.
Cheekwood, Nashville. Gift of the Artist (1964.3.11)

Cat. 12 *Sculpture, William Edmondson (Birdbath)*, 1937
Gelatin silver print
7 × 7 in.
Cheekwood, Nashville. Gift of the Artist (1964.3.19)

Cat. 13 *William Edmondson*, 1937
Gelatin silver print
9 ⅛ × 8 in.
Cheekwood, Nashville. Gift of the Artist (1964.3.4)

Cat. 16 *William Edmondson*, 1937
Gelatin silver print
10 $\frac{11}{16}$ × 10 $\frac{3}{16}$ in.
Cheekwood, Nashville. Gift of the Artist (1964.3.7)

Cat. 17 *Sculpture, William Edmondson (Eleanor Roosevelt; Crucifix)*, 1933–37
Gelatin silver print
8 $\frac{1}{16}$ × 7 ½ in.
Cheekwood, Nashville. Gift of the Artist (1964.3.26)

Cat. 18 *William Edmondson, Sculptor, Nashville, Tennessee*, 1937
Gelatin silver print
9 ⅛ × 7 ⅞ in.
Cheekwood, Nashville. Gift of the Artist (1964.3.5)

Cat. 23 *William Edmondson, Sculptor, Nashville, Tennessee*, 1937
Gelatin silver print
20 ¼ × 16 ¼ in.
Cheekwood, Nashville. Gift of the Artist (1964.3.1)

Cat. 29 *Sculpture, William Edmondson (Girl with a Cape)*, 1937
Gelatin silver print
9 5⁄16 × 6 ⅞ in.
Cheekwood, Nashville. Gift of the Artist (1964.3.21)

Cat. 36 *Sculpture, William Edmondson (Bride)*, 1933–37
Gelatin silver print
7 × 7 in.
Cheekwood, Nashville. Gift of the Artist (1964.3.24)

Cat. 37 *Sculpture, William Edmondson (Lady with Uplifted Skirts)*, 1937
Gelatin silver print
9 13⁄16 x 7 3⁄16 in.
Cheekwood, Nashville. Gift of the Artist (1964.3.22)

Cat. 38 *Sculpture, William Edmondson (Miss Lucy)*, 1937
Gelatin silver print
9 ¾ × 6 ½ in.
Cheekwood, Nashville. Gift of the Artist (1964.3.28)

Cat. 43 *Critter*, 1933–37
Gelatin silver print
20 ¼ × 16 ¼ in.
Cheekwood, Nashville. Gift of the Artist (1964.3.34)

Cat. 53 *William Edmondson*, 1937
Gelatin silver print
10 13⁄16 × 10 7⁄16 in.
Cheekwood, Nashville. Gift of the Artist (1964.3.14)

Cat. 58 *William Edmondson, Sculptor, Nashville, Tennessee*, c. 1933
Gelatin silver print
11 ⅜ × 11 in.
Cheekwood, Nashville. Gift of the Artist (1964.3.35)

Cat. 61 *Sculpture, William Edmondson (Three Doves)*, 1933–37
Gelatin silver print
10 ⅜ × 10 3/16 in.
Cheekwood, Nashville. Gift of the Artist (1964.3.15)

Cat. 62 *William Edmondson*, 1937
Gelatin silver print
10 13/16 × 10 ⅜ in.
Cheekwood, Nashville. Gift of the Artist (1964.3.10)

Cat. 63 *William Edmondson, Sculptor, Nashville, Tennessee*, 1937
Gelatin silver print
8 × 7 9/16 in.
Cheekwood, Nashville. Gift of the Artist (1964.3.3)

Consuelo Kanaga (American, 1894–1978)

Cat. 59 *William Edmondson (Tennessee)*, 1950
Gelatin silver print
9 ⅝ × 7 ⅞ in.
Brooklyn Museum, Brooklyn. Gift of Wallace B. Putnam from the Estate of Consuelo Kanaga, 82.65.370

Cat. 60 *William Edmondson (Tennessee)*, 1950
Gelatin silver print
3 ¼ × 3 ¾ in. (Mat, 19 ¼ × 14 ¼ in.)
Brooklyn Museum, Brooklyn. Gift of Wallace B. Putnam from the Estate of Consuelo Kanaga, 82.65.2118.2

Meyer Wolfe (American, 1897–1985)

Cat. 19 *Vanderbilt Clinic*, 1939
Lithograph on paper
11 ¾ × 15 ¼ in.
Cheekwood, Nashville. Gift of Mr. Meyer Wolfe (1980.8.63)

Cat. 20 *Brother Matthew Preaching*, 1941
Lithograph on paper
13 ⅞ × 11 11/16 in.
Cheekwood, Nashville. Gift of Mr. Meyer Wolfe (1980.8.65)

Puryear Mims (American, 1906–1975)

Cat. 11 *Bust of William Edmondson*, n.d.
Bronze
15 × 9 × 9 in.
Cheekwood, Nashville. Gift of the Estate of Elizabeth Lyle Starr (1982.8.2)

Photography Credits

All photographs of works from the Cheekwood collection: © Eric Wheeler, 2021

All photographs by Louise Dahl-Wolfe: © 2021 Center for Creative Photography, Arizona Board of Regents / Artists Rights Society (ARS), New York, Center for Creative Photography, University of Arizona: Louis-Dahl-Wolfe, Archive/ Gift of the Louise Dahl-Wolfe Trust

All photographs by Edward Weston: © 2021 Center for Creative Photography, Arizona Board of Regents / Artists Rights Society (ARS), New York

---

Cat. 3	Mysti Scott. Hirshhorn and Sculpture Garden
Cat. 5	Tennessee State Museum
Cat. 10	Tennessee State Museum
Cat. 22	© APSU
Cat. 25	Photo by August Bandai, Courtesy Ricco/ Maresca Gallery, New York
Cat. 27	Bill Jacobson Studio, courtesy KAWS Inc.
Cat. 30	Bill Jacobson Studio, courtesy KAWS Inc.
Cat. 31	American Folk Art Museum / Art Resource, NY
Cat. 33	Bill Jacobson Studio, courtesy KAWS Inc.
Cat. 42	© APSU
Cat. 45	© APSU
Cat. 47	Bill Jacobson Studio, courtesy KAWS Inc.
Cat. 51	Bill Jacobson Studio, courtesy KAWS Inc.
Cat. 52	Tennessee State Museum
Cat. 56	The Colonial Williamsburg Foundation
Fig. 2	Courtesy of Special Collections Library, Vanderbilt University
Fig. 3	Courtesy of Special Collections Library, Vanderbilt University
Fig. 5	Digital Image © The Museum of Modern Art / Licensed by SCALA / Art Resource, NY
Fig. 7	Fisk University, John Hope and Aurelia E. Franklin Library,

Special Collections and Archives

Fig. 8 Fisk University, John Hope and Aurelia E. Franklin Library, Special Collections and Archives

Fig. 9 Vanderbilt University Photographic Archives

Fig. 11 Courtesy National Gallery of Art, Washington

Fig. 12 Art Institute of Chicago/ Licensed by SCALA/ Art Resource, NY

Fig. 13 © High Museum of Art, Atlanta

Fig. 14 © 2021 Museum of Fine Arts, Boston

Fig. 18 © Carnegie Museum of Art, Pittsburgh

Fig. 19 © 1941 Estate of Horace Pippin

Contributors

Renée Ater holds a BA from Oberlin College, and an MA and PhD in art history from the University of Maryland. A public scholar who works at the intersection of art and history, Dr. Ater's research focuses on monuments, race, national identity, and public space. She is the author of *Keith Morrison*, volume 5 of the David C. Driskell Series of African American Art (2005) and *Remaking Race and History: The Sculpture of Meta Warrick Fuller* (2011). She has written on a wide range of public monuments including the Unsung Founders Memorial at the University of North Carolina; the African American Civil War Memorial in Washington, DC; the Martin Luther King Jr. Memorial in Rocky Mount, North Carolina; the Tuskegee Airmen National Historic Site in Alabama; and the Crispus Attucks Memorial in Boston. Currently, Dr. Ater is engaged in an open-source digital project entitled *Contemporary Monuments to the Slave Past: Race, Memorialization, Public Space, and Civic Engagement*, which has been funded through the National Endowment for the Humanities–Mellon Foundation, the Getty Research Institute, and the Smithsonian Office of Fellowships.

Kéla B. Jackson is a PhD student in the department of History of Art and Architecture at Harvard University. Her research and writing interests include modern and contemporary art of the African diaspora, spatial and aesthetic articulations of selfhood and citizenship, and notions of memory and archives among Black women and queer artists. Jackson has held various positions at the Samuel P. Harn Museum of Art at the University of Florida, High Museum of Art, Spelman College Museum of Fine Art, and the Radcliffe Institute for Advanced Study at Harvard University. She received her BA in art with a concentration in art history and a minor in African diaspora studies from Spelman College.

Ellen Macfarlane is a lecturer in the Art History Department at the University of Southern California. Her research focuses on the history of photography, American art, and vernacular visual culture in the twentieth century. She received her PhD in art and archaeology from Princeton University. Her current book project examines the early 1930s California art photography collective Group f.64 and analyzes the group's engagement with Depression-era debates regarding the relationship of aesthetics and politics in light of its strong stance against photographic manipulation. Macfarlane's writing has appeared in *American Art*, *Southern California Quarterly*, and *caa.reviews*. She has held fellowships from the Smithsonian American Art Museum, the ACLS/Luce Foundation, the Center for Creative Photography, and the Huntington Library.

Anne Monahan is an art historian based in New York and focused on modern and contemporary art. She is the author of *Horace Pippin, American Modern* (2020); *Faith Ringgold: Die* (2018); articles in *Art Journal, Metropolitan Museum Journal*, and *Nka: The Journal of Contemporary African Art*, among others; and contributions to various museum catalogues.

Betsy Phillips is the marketing manager at Vanderbilt University Press. Her writing has appeared in the *Nashville Scene* and the *Washington Post*. She is the author of *Dynamite Nashville: Unmasking the KKK, the FBI, and the Bombers beyond Their Control* (forthcoming), and contributed an essay, "Perverse Incentives," to *Greetings from New Nashville: How a Sleepy Southern Town Became "It" City* (2020). She writes for the *Nashville Scene*.

Marin R. Sullivan holds a PhD from the University of Michigan. She is a Chicago-based art historian, consultant, and curator. She is the curator-at-large at Cheekwood Estate & Gardens in Nashville, where she focuses on outdoor and contemporary sculpture initiatives. Sullivan also serves as the director of the Harry Bertoia Catalogue Raisonné and is a member of the board of trustees for the International Sculpture Center. She specializes in the histories of modern and contemporary sculpture, especially its interdisciplinary, intermedial dialogues with design and the built environment. Sullivan is the author of *Sculptural Materiality in the Age of Conceptualism* (2017) and *Alloys: American Sculpture and Architecture at Midcentury* (forthcoming) as well as numerous essays and articles in publications including *American Art, Art History, History of Photography*, and *Sculpture Journal*. Her research has been supported by fellowships from the Smithsonian American Art Museum and the Crystal Bridges Museum of American Art.

Learotha Williams Jr. is an associate professor of African American and Public History and coordinator of the North Nashville Heritage Project at Tennessee State University. Dr. Williams teaches courses that explore enslavement and emancipation in Tennessee, African American history, and public memory. He is also a member of the Tennessee State Review Board for the National Register of Historic Places, serves on the boards of the Metro Historical Zoning Commission, Historic Nashville, Inc., and Promise Land Heritage Association, and is a member of the board of the Friends of Fort Negley. Since his arrival at Tennessee State University, he and his students have worked closely with African American heritage societies and organizations throughout Middle Tennessee, where they have focused on African American history in rural spaces. He is the co-editor with Amie Thurber of *I'll Take You There: Nashville's Social Justice Sites* (2021), and he is currently writing "A Song in a Strange Land: Black Nashville in History and Public Memory." This work will explore the role African Americans have played in Nashville's history and how we study and celebrate it in public spaces. Dr. Williams is a native of Tallahassee, Florida, where earned his PhD from Florida State University in 2003.